Townlands of Leinster

Townlands of Leinster
and the people who lived there

FLANN Ó RIAIN

from the *Irish Times* column
Where's That?

OPEN AIR

OPEN AIR
is an imprint of
FOUR COURTS PRESS LTD
Fumbally Court, Fumbally Lane, Dublin 8, Ireland
e-mail: info@four-courts-press.ie
and in North America for
FOUR COURTS PRESS
c/o ISBS, 5804 N.E. Hassalo Street, Portland, OR 97213.

A catalogue record for this title is available from the British Library.

ISBN 1-85182-465-0

Set in 10.5pt on 12.5pt Bembo by
Carrigboy Typesetting Services
Printed in Ireland by
ColourBooks Ltd, Dublin

Contents

Preface

My Laois mother and my Tipperary father, after they left home to work, spent the remainder of their lives as 'exiles' in Cos. Dublin, Galway, Kerry and Kildare. Was it nostalgia that had them betimes talking by the fireside about their native places? My father talked about Foillaclug, Reagoulane, Glennough, Glennaneigh, and my mother about Tinnalintin, Attanagh, Durrow. For me these names sang euphoniously – containing poetry and a hint of mystery – far away but intimate places. They talked of 'the Dwyers of the Metal Bridge', and 'the Grahams of Tollerton' – 'titles' that might to adults have suggested 'landed' families, but to a 'traveller' child there was a comforting 'belongingness'.

When I went to my first job in Cappamore, Co. Limerick, I had the privilege of working with Tipperaryman Séamus Ó hIcí, principal teacher in the local national school, who apart from his enthusiastic promotion of the Irish language, infected all by his fascination in, and knowledge of, Irish placenames. Later still I was graciously presented by my late mother-in-law, Mary Collins, Timoleague, Co. Cork, with her three volumes of Joyce's *Irish Names of Places*.

And perhaps I shared with my fellow Irishpersons the love of the names of places. 'Toem, Doon and Carnahallia/Foillacleara and Renavanna', rhymed the Tipperary people. And in the song *An tÚll* we find a Co. Cork list: *Do shiúlaois Cléire agus Carraig Aonair/Cuanta Béarra a bhí romham sa tslí/Poinnte na nGréige agus na nDosaí Maola/An Fhia is an Lao taobh amuigh de Bhaoi.*

My thanks to Jim Downey, who, as deputy-editor of the *Irish Times*, invited me some fifteen years ago to do the 'Where's That?' column for that paper. This appears weekly, and this book is composed of a Leinster selection therefrom.

Carlow

'This name is famous in Irish history, not always happily,' says Edward MacLysaght, writing about the surname MacMurrough, *MacMurchadha* (now *MacMurchú*) in his *Surnames of Ireland*. 'It is now rare,' he adds, but we find six of the name in the Dublin telephone directory, with one MacMurphy and three MacMurchú, two of which are in the Ring Gaeltacht of Co. Waterford. This sept was subdivided and became Kavanagh, Kinsella, Hendrick and Mernagh. The unhappy memory relating to this name is of Diarmaid MacMurrough seeking the assistance of the English in 1169, resulting in his being known ever after as Diarmaid na nGall, 'Diarmaid of the foreigners'. His son was Dónal Caomhánach, the ancestor of the Kavanaghs, also anglicised as Cavanagh. Of this surname MacLysaght writes: 'Kavanagh, Caomhánach. A branch of the MacMurroughs. The name is said to have been adopted from the first Kavanagh having been fostered by a successor of St Caomhan. The use of the prefix O with it is wrong.' The Census of 1659 lists them among the principal Irish names in Cos. Kildare and Wexford, and in Co. Carlow in the barony of Forth, wherein one Charles was a titulado. However, they were most numerous in the baronies of Idrone and St Mullins in that county, numbering 39 among the principal Irish names, against Byrne 64, Murphy 61, Doyle 40 and Ryan 31. Here also are two tituladoes, Tirlagh and Symon. The Kavanagh residence at Borris was garrisoned by the Parliamentarians in 1642 and besieged by the Irish, and twice again in the insurrection of 1798, being repelled by Capt. Kavanagh's yeomanry corps. Taylor and Skinner's *Maps* (1778) show Kananagh esq., near Borris but does not name the house; it is Borris-I-Drone in the 1814 *Directory*, being occupied by Wat. Kavanagh esq. Borris House was rebuilt in the first part of the 19th century, being designed by William Vitruvius Morrison, of whom Maurice Craig in *The Architecture of Ireland* says that 'he practised a hybridised classical style seen at its best, perhaps, in Borris, Co. Carlow'. Lewis' *Topographical Dictionary* (1837) says that 'the seat of the late T. Kavanagh Esq., is situated in an extensive and richly wooded demesne ...' Our current map shows Borris House, with 'Golf Course' nearby.

The offical Irish for Borris is An Bhuiríos, presumably from 'borough/
bourg/burg', defined as 'a town possessing a municipal corporation and special
privileges confered by royal charter. Also a town which sends representatives to
parliament.' Lewis informs us that preserved at Boris House was the 'Figeen, a
curious ornament of silver and tin, found on the demense; and a casket called
the Liath-mersicith. Ua Duinnin's *Foclóir Gaelige agus Béarla* gives *fígín* as 'a little
rush or straw; a mark, tag or target'. In 1876 Arthur McMurrough Kavanagh
had 16,051 acres at Borris House.

DUCKETT'S GROVE

Abraham Shackelton, a member of the Society of Friends, came to Ireland from
Bingly in Yorkshire and opened a boarding school at Ballitore in the Co. Kildare
parish of Timolin in 1726. This placename derives from Béal Átha an Tuair, the
ford-mouth of the bleaching-field, according to Joyce's *Names of Places*. On 3
March 1726 the first pupils arrrived, three Braddocks and a Fuller. The next day
two Watsons arrived; the third day two more pupils came, and on the forth day
another Watson and five Ducketts – John Thomas, John William, John John,
John Abraham, and the scantily-named Jonas. In later years five other Ducketts
were to attend this mainly Quaker school. It finally closed in 1826, the last of
the Ducketts being William Jonas in 1772, and Richard in 1775. Not to be
found in MacLysaght's *Surnames*, this name is the diminutive of Marmaduke,
according to the *Penguin Dictionary of Surnames*.

The lands of Urlan More in the Co. Clare parish of Kilmaleery, having been
confiscated from John Delahide, Daniel Clanchy and Conor Oge Clanchy after
the rebellion of 1641, were granted to John Drury, Sir Henry Ingoldsby and
Lord Clare. The Census of 1659 lists Captain William Duckett, gent., as a
titulado in Urlan More. This name derives from Urlan Mór, the big forecourt/
frontyard/lawn. *Lodge's Peerage* states that Judith, daughter of Pierse Power,
grandson of John, Lord le Poer, married Mr Ducket around 1660. The Ducketts
are listed in Hart's *Irish Pedigrees* as being among the post-12th century 'New
Settlers' of Ormond and Decies (Tipperary and Waterford). Taylor and Skinner's
Maps (1778) locates Ducket, Esq. at Whitestown in the Co. Waterford parish of
Rossmire, and the 1814 *Directory* shows D. Ducket, Esq., at Stone-house in the
Co. Waterford parish of Kilmeadan. The same source shows J. Parsons Ducket,
Esq., at Redmondstown in the Co. Tipperary parish of Kilgrant, with John D.
Ducket, Esq., at Duckett's Grove, Co. Carlow. Though this latter names neither
a parish nor a townland, it features clearly on the ½" = 1 mile Ordinance
Survey map. The 1876 *Owners of Land* lists the following Duckett landowners in

Co. Carlow: Stewart, Russelstown Park, Co. Carlow, with 1,232 acres; Joseph F., Kingstown, with 217 acres; Charles F., Knockarda in the parish of Urglin with 339 acres, and William, Duckett's Grove, with 3,441 acres. Other landowners at that time in the townland of Knockarda were two Hickeys, Patrick Nolan, and two O Neills. Also there on three acres was William Hade. MacLysaght states that the origin of this surname, also spelt Haide and Hayde, is uncertain, suggesting that it might be an abbreviated form of Hayden, or possibly a Palatine name in Co. Carlow. In *More Irish Families* this authority considers, though not enthusiastically, another source which gives it as an abbreviation of Ó hEidhin, usually anglicised (O) Heyne. Mentioning Ballyhade in the Co. Kildare parish of Castledermot, he adds that the name Hade is not numerous.

We have found four Duckett entries in the Southern telephone directories – one in Dublin, two in Co. Carlow, and one in Co. Limerick. There are 25 Haydes in the same directories, and 22 Hades. Seven of these are in Co. Carlow.

PAINESTOWN

One wonders if the once popular saying in Co. Carlow, 'The B's of Carlow carry a sting!', is ever heard nowadays and, if so, whether it is understood. Halls' *Ireland* (1841), the chronicle of Mrs and Mr Hall's trip in this country, records this saying, along with 'Beware the B's!' as being references to the number of the landed gentry in that county whose names began with the letter B. These were the Bests, Browns, Bruens, Butlers, Bagenals, Bunburys and Burtons. The Bests were no longer there in 1876, and the only reminder of their once sojourn there is in the townland name Bestfield, an alias of Dunganstown, a name that predates 1640. The Bruens were still there in 1876 in the person of Col. Henry Bruen, residing at Oakpark, north of the town of Carlow, with a tidy estate of 16,477 acres. William Makepeace Thackeray's tour of Ireland, recorded in his *Irish Sketch Book* (1842), relates that 'There are some old towers of a castle here, looking finely from the river; and near the town is a grand modern residence belonging to Colonel Bruen, with an oak park on one side of the road, and a deer-park on the other. These retainers of the Colonel's lay, in their rushy enclosures, in great numbers and seemingly in flourishing condition.' The oak-park appears to be a throwback to the royal order of 1654 creating a regular forestry service in Cos. Carlow and Kildare, with the employment of a head wood-reeve, four assistants and a clerk in 1661 and it is interesting that our current $1/2'' = 1$ mile Ordnance Survey map showing Oakpark House with 'Agricultural Institute' alongside it. The surname Bruen, according to MacLysaght's *Surnames*, is a variant of Breen in Co. Roscommon, the homeland

of one of the Ó Braoin septs. The main family were erenaghs of St Coman at
Roscommon. It was coincidental, however, that an English Cromwellian, James
Bruen, settled in Abbeyboyle, Co. Roscommon in the 17th century. This family
did not long remain there, as in the next century they moved to Co. Carlow,
where they acquired extensive family property. The above colonel also had
6,932 acres in Co. Wexford. The Bagenals were still in this county before the
turn of the century, with Beauchamp F. Bagenall, Bennekerry, on 1,309 acres;
Elizabeth G., 155 acres; Georgina, 250 acres; Philip H., 199, and Sarah C. with
110 acres. This family gave its name to Bagnalstown, now officially Muine
Bheag, 'the small thicket'. Reps. of Colonel Kane Bunbury, Moyle, Co. Carlow
had 3,098 acres, and Thomas K.M.C. Bunbury, Lisnevaght, 4,960 acres. Here also
were four Bunburrys with smaller holdings. There were four members of the
Browne family, with Robert C. Browne, Brown's Hill, having 4,410 acres. Sir
Charles Burton, Pollacton, had 381 acres and William F., Burton Hall, had 4,422
acres. There were four Butlers, with Sir Thomas P. Butler, Bart., Ballintemple,
Tullow, having 6,455 acres. The *Index of Townlands* (1851) gives Painestown,
which is to be found on Petty's map of 1685, as an alias of Oakpark. The Irish
for Painestown is Baile na Phaghanaigh.

COOLNAKISHA

While many of the native Irish had, some would say, sensibly, undergone
religious conversions of convenience, others, no doubt, had genuine conversions
of conviction. One might reasonably conclude that such a troublesome lot as
the (O)Byrnes would never have managed to acquire land and respectability in
the counties of the Pale; nevertheless 22 members of that clan are listed in
Owners of Land (1876) as landowners in their native Co. Kildare, ranging from
one acre to a modest estate of 289 acres. Co. Wexford had twelve Byrnes, again
from the single acre to 920 acres; Co. Wicklow had eleven, ranging from one to
the respectable 3,202 of Reps. of William Byrne, Cronybyrne, Rathdrum, in that
county; there were nineteen Byrnes in Co. Carlow, the largest being the property
of E.A. Byrne of Rosemount, New Ross, Co. Wexford, wherein he had 920
acres. The 'O' had been dropped by the majority, but there was one O Byrne
(Catherine) with 13 acres in Co. Carlow; one with land in Co. Dublin, and one
with a topping 2,363 acres in Co. Wicklow, this being William R. O'Byrne. The
original Irish name was Ó Broin (*bran*, raven). 'The ancient territory of the
O Byrnes was in Co. Kildare but as the Anglo-Normans extended the Pale they
were displaced and found a new home in the hills of southern Co. Wicklow
with the sept centre at Ballinacor in the barony of Ballinacor South; Dublin and

Co. Wicklow account for the largest number of Byrnes and O Byrnes today, and there is still a substantial representation of the name in Ballinacor South barony, in and around Aughrim and Tinahely' (Brian de Breffny, *Irish Family Names*). One member of this family who, to his great disadvantage and discomfort, did not convert, was an Owen Byrne: '4th January 1655, there was paid to Captain Thomas Shepherd the sum of five pounds, pursuant to the declaration of 6th May 1653, for a party of his company that on 27th November last took a priest, with his appurtances, in the house of one Owen Byrne, of Cool-ne-Kiskin, near Old Leighlin, in the county of Catherlogh, which said priest, together with Birne, the man of the house, were brought prisoners to Dublin'. (John P. Prendergast, 1865, *The Cromwellian Settlement*). Coolnakisha in the parish of Tullowcreen, appears to be Cúil na Cise, 'the corner of the wicker road'. We know not what became of the above pair: it is likely they were sent to the Barbados. In that same year, after Admiral William Penn had added Jamaica to the empire of England, and colonists being wanted, Oliver Cromwell, the lord Protector, applied to his son Lord Henry Cromwell, then major-general of the forces in Ireland, to engage 1,500 of the soldiers of the army in Ireland to go thither as planters, and to secure a thousand young Irish girls (usually from 12 years to 45, 'women not past breeding'). Henry replied that there would be no problem, but that force must be used in taking them. 'We could well spare them', he adds, 'and they might be of use to you; and who knows but it might be a means to make them Englishmen – I mean Christians'. Eventually 1,000 girls, and 1,000 boys were shipped out from Galway in October 1655, 'the boys as bondmen, probably, and the girls to be bound by other ties to these English soldiers in Jamaica'.

BALLON

The Irish were to be called 'barbarous' for not having punishments like those of the 'just and honourable law of England' for the crime of high treason, according to Sir John Davies (1569–1626), Attorney-general for Ireland, in his *Discoverie of the true causes why Ireland was never entirely subdued until the beginning of his Majestie's happie raigne.* The guilty person was to be drawn on a hurdle to the place of execution, 'and there to be hanged, and let down alive, and thy privie parts cut off, and thy entrails taken out and burned in thy sight; then thy head to be cut offe, and thy body devided in foure parts, and to be disposed of at Her Majestie's pleasure'. Things had changed for the better by 1921, when four Republican prisoners, convicted of 'high treason by levying war', were hanged on 14 March of that year. Two others, Patrick Moran of Boyle and

Thomas Whelan, Galwayman, accused of complicity in the assassination of British officers, were hanged on 21 November, despite evidence of alibi. Over fifty years earlier another Thomas Whelan, a member of the Fenian Brotherhood, was hanged in Canada. Early on the morning of 7 April 1868, Thomas D'Arcy McGee, poet, historian and orator, and one of the leaders of the Young Irelanders, and at the time of his death a member of the Ministry of the newly-formed Dominion of Canada, was walking to his home in Ottawa, when he was shot by Whelan. McGee was opposed to the Fenian Brotherhood, but his killing had never been ordered or sanctioned by the Fenians. The surname Ó Faoláin (*faol*, a wolf, also wild, untamed), anglicised as Whelan and Phelan, was among the principal Irish names in the Census of 1659 in Cos. Wexford, Waterford and Tipperary, and with the spelling Phelan it was very widespread in Co. Kilkenny. In 1778, Taylor and Skinner's *Maps* shows 'Whelan esq.' residing at Newstonehouse (now Newstown in the Co. Carlow parish of Ardoyne), south of Tullow. This was the property of Robert Eustace, Esq., in 1814. Eustaces were shown on these *Maps* as residing in nearby Castlemore. And while the list of *Owners of Land* (1876) gives only those who actually owned land, we presume it to be a fairly accurate representation of the numbers of any particular surname in that county, and here are the Whelans and Phelans therein at that time: Carlow, 6 Whelans; Dublin, 4; Kildare, 2; Kilkenny, 1, and 3 Phelans; Offaly, 1; Longford, 1; Meath, 1; Laois, 1; Wicklow, 1; Wexford, 3; Clare, 3; Cork, 2, and 3 Phelans; Tipperary, 3, and 2 Phelans; and Waterford with three of each. Thomas Whelan of Rathglass, Tullow, had the largest holding in Co. Carlow with 253 acres; Sir Thomas Whelan, Carlow, the most eminent, with a modest 5 acres, and Rose Whelan, Ballon in the same county, with 1 acre 1 rood and perch. *Gasitéar na hÉireann/Gazetteer of Ireland* gives the offical Irish for Ballon as Balana.

There are 1,895 Whelans, and 1,048 Phelans in Southern telephone directories, predominantly in Dublin and South Leinster.

NOLANSTOWN

In 1564 Maurice ne Dower O'Nolan of Killenbryde, together with twenty other Co. Wicklow men, was pardoned for some earlier misdemeanour, in consequence of his assistance in the capture and detention of George Harvey and Henry Davells, gentlemen. Among the others pardoned were Leasagh, Thady and Feagh m'Willlam O'Nolan. (We leave it to yourself to fathom out 'ne Dower'.) This fiant of 1564 was but one of 54 in which O'Nolans were 'pardoned' between 1559 and 1603. But that, as the man said, was only the half of it! More than 30 more were listed without the 'O', variously spelled Noland, Nolane, Noulan and Nowlan.

Giolla na naomh Ó hUidhrín, in his portion of *Topographical Poems* at the beginning of the 15th century, wrote: 'Ó Nualláin, laoch gan lochta,/airrdi fialghlan Fothorta'. In early times O Nolan held hereditary office under the kings of Leinster, the chief of the sept being known as prince of Leinster, established in the barony of Forth in Co. Carlow (not the better known one in Co. Wexford).

MacLysaght in his *Surnames* is not positive that Ó Nualláin comes from *nuall/uaill*, meaning 'a loud noise, moan, howl, whine, lamentation'. (Older persons who learned songs in Irish in school will remember 'Chuala an uaill á casadh' from Seán Ó Duibhir an Ghleanna: 'I heard the lamentation being chanted').

The (O) Nolans feature widely in the *Transplantation to Connaught 1654–58*, having in some cases quite large holdings in Cos. Galway and Mayo. The *Census* of 1659 lists the Nolan/Nowland/Nolane/ Nollane/Noland/Knolan/Knowlan /Knowland among the principal Irish names in seven Co. Kildare baronies; in four Co. Carlow baronies together with the borough of Carlow; in four Co. Kilkenny baronies and the city of Kilkenny, and in one barony each in Cos. Wexford, Longford, Westmeath and Tipperary. Edmond Noland, gent., was titulado of Aghelare (? Aghade) in the Co. Carlow barony of Forth.

By 1876, the year of publication of *Owners of Land*, members of this family were even more widespread, having land in eighteen of the thirty-two counties – three in Connaught, three in Munster, four in Ulster, and in eight of Leinster's twelve counties. Co. Carlow had the greatest number of Nolan holdings, though the largest was the 204 acres (the only one in three digits) of Mary Nolan, Kilballyhue. They were at Ballintrain, Bennekerry, Cunaberry, Urglin, Ballinrush, Bagnalstown and Boghouse. There were nine Nolan holdings in Co. Galway, among which were the three largest in the country – the 6,866 acres of John P. Nolan, Ballinderry, Co. Galway; the 1,852 acres, property of Walter H. Nolan, Army and Navy Club, London; and one of 1,186 acres at Ballinderry, Cummer.

There is a Ballynowlan in Co. Laois, and Ballynolan names townlands in Cos. Limerick, Kilkenny, and Carlow. That of Limerick is Baile Uí Nialláin, 'the town of Uí Nialláin'; that of Kilkenny is Baile Uí Nualláin, and we assume that that of Co. Carlow is the same.

FENNISCOURT

In his *The Ancient Forts of Ireland* (1902), T.J. Westropp writing of Fenniscourt, a townland in the Co. Carlow parish of Wells, renders it 'Finnerscourt', and on the reasonable presumption that the first element in this placename is a surname, we hared off to MacLysaght's *Surnames*: 'Fenner. A toponymic: Fenner and its variant Finure are placenames found in many parts of Ireland, mainly Leinster.' As a surname it is on record since the 14th century in Cos. Dublin and Kilkenny: in the latter Fennerscourt indicates the location and there was also a place called Fennerstown there in the 16th century. Fenners is a variant of the surname. It is called Fionúir in Irish i.e. a modern spelling of Fionnabhair (the place). Fennerscourt is listed neither as a townland name nor that of a parish, nor is it to be found in Owen O Kelly's *Place-names of County Kilkenny* (1969; 1988). Fenniscourt, so spelled on Sir William Petty's 1685 map of Co. Carlow, is Pheniscourt in the Census of 1659. Along with Killinene, Cloughcoyle, Faraneferny and Tinegarney (now Tinnagarney) it had Ambrose Elton Esq., as titulado. The surname Fenner is not to be found in any of our sources, although there are eight in the current Dublin telephone directory. And while the surname (O) Feeney, Ó Fiannaidhe (soldier), earlier form Ó Feinneadha, is a Galway sept, and a branch of the Co. Sligo sept, Fenniscourt does look like it might be Feeney's Court. In the above book Westropp, writing of 'Long Entrenchments', refers to the 'remarkable works' found in Longford under the name of 'Duncladh': in Armagh and Down under the name of the 'Dane's Cast'; in Cavan as the 'Worm Ditch'; in Waterford and Limerick as the 'Rian Ro Patrick' and the 'Cladh dubh', which ran from Waterford into Cork at right angles to the 'Rian Ro'; in Kerry the 'Cladh ruadh' which ran into Limerick; and the 'Rataduff' on the borders of Kilkenny and Carlow. Patrick Power's 'The Rian Bó Phádraig' (the ancient highway of the Decies) in the *Journal of the Royal Society of Antiquaries of Ireland* (1905), gives this as representing the ancient mainroad from Cashel in Co. Tipperary to Lismore in Co. Waterford. Mercator (1512–94), the well-known Flemish geographer and cartographer, on his large-scale map of the Carlow barony of Idrone west, shows 'Raduffe trenche', running west of Duninga in the Co. Kilkenny parish of Grangesilvia, and Finnerscourt and east of Shankill church (in the Co. Kilkenny parish of Shankill), and forming the bounds of Gowran (Kilkenny) and Idrone down to the Barrow, opposite Kilcrot in the Co. Carlow parish of Lorum, now spelled Kilcruit. O'Donovan and O'Curry, in 1839, found slight traces at Kellymount Commons which an old man aged eighty remembered as distinct and half a mile long. Other traditions, at other places, said it had existed there a century before (1739). It was locally known as 'the gripe(ditch) of the Black Pig'. Owen O'Kelly (*The Place-names of County Kilkenny*) writes of 'Raduffe Trench, an ancient landmark [that] runs between Duninga and Ballytarsna'. Owen O'Kelly gives these two placenames as Dún Einge, 'fort of the territory', and Baile Tarsna, 'a cross-wise place'.

The Irish for Fenniscourt is Cúirt Fhionúir. The second element is the English surname Fenner.

MOUNTPLEASANT

Sometime in the late 1950s Dublin Corporation resolved that henceforth the name plaques on all new roads and streets of that city would bear an Irish name only. A number of residents in a new housing estate in Clontarf objected to this, and at their own expense erected new nameplates bearing an English version, side-by-side with the Irish ones. The explanation for this action was that postmen/fire-brigades etc., would not be able to locate these places – resulting in God's knows what! But the 'liberal' attitude to the Irish language which led to that was but in the 'halfpenny place' compared to what was to be visited by property developers on the landscape – particularly Dublin's – since then. New building developments currently on the market bear the names Riverwood, Harbour Bay, Hazel Meadow, Beach Court and Elliott's Mews (Sorry, that last one is in England – but how can one tell?). But amidst the lot we were chuffed to find a new estate unashamedly named 'Cnoc Aoibhinn'!

Was 'Cnoc Aoibhin', we wondered, an original Co. Dublin placename, possibly anglicized Knockeevan? There is but one in Ireland and that is in Co. Tipperary. Maybe Mountpleasant? There are eight townlands so-named – in Cos. Mayo, Roscommon, Galway, Limerick, Wexford, Wicklow, Offaly, Carlow – but none in Co. Dublin. But *fad saol agus aoibhneas* to those who will come to live there.

Co. Carlow's Mountpleasant is in the parish of Fennagh and is listed in the 1814 *Directory* as the residence of James Garret, Esquire. Taylor and Skinner's 1778 *Maps* shows 'Garret Esq.' at Kilgarron, east of Leighlinbridge, also in the parish of Fennagh, having the alias Janeville. Was Kilgarron, Mountpleasant and Janeville the same place? Two Garretts of Janeville subscribed to Lewis' *Topographical Dictionary* (1837), and *Owners of Land* (1876) listed the Revd William Garrett (no address) with 340 Co. Carlow acres, and in the same county the Revd James P. Garrett, Kellistown, with 874 acres. Then there was the 54 Co. Mayo acres the property of the Revd George Garrett, Dublin; a single Garrett acre in Belfast; 93 acres of Samuel of Summerseat, Clonee, Co. Meath, and the six acres of Joseph, Merrion, Dublin.

Of the surname Garrett, MacLysaght's *Surnames* says that this is mainly of English origin in Ireland, but has also been used as a synonym of Fitzgerald

(Mac Gearailt). Gerrard, we learn, is also used as a synonym. De Bhulbh's *Sloinnte na hÉireann/ Surnames of Ireland*, published in 1996, says that Gearóid is the Irish for both Garrett and Gerrard. Telephone directories list 100 Garretts north of the Border, and almost 340 to its south, scattered throughout the provinces.

In the Lusk area of Co. Dublin in 1474 John Gerrot was listed as a debtor; three years later Patrick Gerrot, smith, is listed as owing 2*s*.; the following year Richard Gerrot of Dublin City is mentioned, and in 1478 we read of William Gerrot: 'In the name of God, Amen. In these writings we excommunicate William Gerrote, of Leixlip, on account of his contumacy incurred before us, at the instance of Janico Dartas, and we have decreed execution.' Was this execution of the decree or William Gerrote? If the latter, one could imagine 'contumacy' rapidly going out of fashion!

The Irish Fiants of the Tudor Sovereigns (1521–1603) lists persons so-named from 1570 up to 1602, in Cos. Kilkenny, Kildare, Dublin, Cork, Waterford, Limerick (Ballylanders), and possibly Tipperary. As was the custom, wives retained their own names, and herein are listed 'ny Garret', and in Co. Cork in 1602 Margaret nyne Gerrot, indicating that these bore an Irish surname in the Irish form (*ní* and *iníon uí*). Mac Garrett was among the principal Irish surnames in the Co. Limerick barony of Kenry in the 1659 Census.

Garrettstown names townlands in Cos. Cork and Meath, and in the Co. Carlow parish of Rahill.

Dublin

CARPENTERSTOWN

Johannes de Castrocnoc Carpentarius, 'John of Castleknock, carpenter', listed in *The Dublin Guild Merchants Roll* (*c.*1190–1265), might have been given the surname John Castleknock, or he might have become John Carpenter. He was listed among tradesmen of the year 1228, a list which contained a number of others of the same trade – Ada Carpentarius de Pembroc, Keivinus de Wykinglo Carpentarius, Thomas Carpentarius de Novo Castro (Thomas carpenter of Newcastle) – to name but a few. The first of the 26 carpenters listed is Willelmus Carpentarius – in 1190 or shortly after.

The Irish Fiants of the Tudor Sovereigns informs of the granting of English liberty to 'Simon Gawill alias Cawill alias Simon Carpenter', a chaplain in Dublin in 1547. This man is mentioned again in 1552 in connection with the site of the monastery of the Hogges by the city of Dublin. The *Calendar of Inquisitions: Co. Dublin* informs further of this man. In 1562 he was one of three chaplains who received grants of land in the city; at Clareston (Claristown), Co. Meath, and at 'Ragarthe alias Ragathe', Co. Dublin. In 1484 John Carpenter was granted 'the dignity of treasurer of the Cathedral of the Holy Trinity'; Philip Carpenter of Claungibon was among the 'pardoned' of 1600, and in 1602 John oge Carpenter, Cloghleige (? Cloghleagh in the Co. Kerry parish of Kiltallagh) was among the then pardoned.

The Census of 1659 has Thomas and William Carpenter, Esquire and Gent. respectively, as tituladoes in Ballyea, Co. Limerick; John Carpenter, titulado in Kilpeacon, also in Co. Limerick; Phillip Carpenter in Sigginstown, and John Carpenter at Quinnagh (now Quinagh) in the borough of Catherlagh. Taylor and Skinner's *Maps* (1778) shows Carpenter Esq. at Newgarden, some few miles north of the town of Carlow, on the Laois bank of the River Barrow. (There is a townland named Newgarden in the Co. Carlow parish of Painestown)

Owners of Land (1876) notes small Carpenter holdings in Cos. Louth, Meath, Cork, Armagh and Carlow. In this latter county Patrick Carpenter, Moanduff had 14 acres, and there were three holdings at Raheen in the same parish of Oldleighlin. One of the latter was the 483 acres of Mary Carpenter – the largest Carpenter holding in Ireland.

Hart's *Irish Pedigrees* enumerates Carpenter among 'The Modern Nobility in Tirconnell'. The title earl of Tyrconnell was granted to O'Donnell in 1543 (though it was not conferred until 1603): in 1685 Richard Talbot was created earl of Tyrconnell, and in May 1761 John Delavel Carpenter was created earl of Tyrconnell, Viscount Carlingford, Baron Carpenter. He was of Keplin Park, Yorkshire.

MacLysaght's *Surnames* says that the surname Carpenter in Ireland is usually for Mac an tSaoir, most usually anglicized MacAteer, with Ballymacateer, Co. Armagh, being their homeland. *Saor* means 'artificer, craftsman; mason', and *saor adhmaid*, a carpenter. Carpenter was additionally 'englished' Mason, and Freeman (*saor* also means 'free'). However, the name in Ireland is sometimes of English origin.

There are only eight entries of this surname in the Northern Ireland *Phone Book*, mainly in Co. Down, and of the 91 the Southern telephone directories, 47 are in the Dublin area. Of the remainder 42 are in the province of Leinster.

Carpenterstown (Baile an Chairpinteírigh) names townlands in Cos. Dublin and Westmeath.

BOLTON STREET

The strangely-named Turn Again Lane no longer exists, and was gone by the time of the publication of the 1836 *Directory*. It is, however, to be found on John Roque's 1756 map of the city of Dublin. Travelling north from Capel Street into Bolton street, the first street on the right hand was Cross Lane, and the second on that same side was Turn Again Lane. These two lanes were linked halfway down their length by Cherry Lane, and again at their bottoms by Loftus Lane. Cherry Lane is also gone, but Loftus is still commemorated in a lane of that name. Bolton Street was named after Charles Powlett, second duke of Bolton, who was sworn in as lord lieutenant of Ireland in 1717, continuing in that office until 1721. About that time there was a growing tendency for the nobility and gentry to spend more time in Dublin than they had in the 17th century, and the duke of Ormond, the duke of Bolton, the duke of Grafton and the duke of Dorset, viceroys from 1703 to 1721, remain commemorated in street names. Bolton Street and Dorset Street were names given to parts of the old country road from the north.

In Bolton Street in 1836 there resided gunmakers, provision dealers, drapers, tailors, confectioners, shoemakers, painters, dressmakers, chandlers, cutlers, booksellers, bakers, haberdashers, cabinetmakers and upholsterers, attorneys, saddlers and coachmakers. Nos. 1 and 2 constituted Walshe's Hotel; Sylvester

Moore had an hotel at No. 3; Mrs Williams had the Londonderry Hotel at No. 5, and a tavern at No. 7, and at No. 64, the last house on the street, was the Enniskillen Hotel, the property of William Dunbar.

The duke of Bolton in opening Parliament in 1719, had urged very strongly the desirableness of more union among the Protestants in the presence of the increasing strength of the papists, and of their notorious inclination to the Pretender. There was a growing number of prelates, friars, and unregistered priests, and as prosecutions appeared to be unsuccessful, 'a more effectual remedy' would have to be found to prevent them coming into 'the kingdom'. One of the heads of a bill drawn up by a committee of the House of Commons was a proposal that every unregistered priest found remaining in the kingdom after 1 May 1720 should be branded with an hot iron on the cheek, as a mark by which he could be immediately recognised. This was rejected, not on the grounds of any humanity, but because of its failure in dealing with the Raparees. The Raparees, it was said, made it a common practice to brand innocent people with the same mark, to destroy the distinction it was intended for. The five or six noble lords, thereupon, recommended as a subsitiute for the iron, a penalty which was reported, rightly or wrongly, to have been used in Sweden with effect against the Jesuits. They accepted Lord Midleton's proposal that all unregistered priests and friars coming in from abroad should be liable to castration. And while J.A. Froud might not always be regarded as being fair in his treatment of the Irish question, he comments in a footnote on the above in his *The English in Ireland*: 'Not certainly as implying a charge of immorality. Amidst the multitude of accusations which I have seen brought against the Irish priests of the last century I have never, save in a single instance, encountered a charge of unchastity. Rather the exceptional and signal purity of Irish Catholic women of the lower order, unparalelled in the civilized world … must be attributed wholly and entirely to the influence of the Catholic clergy.'

DODSBOROUGH

Mrs Anastasia Moore, 12 Aungier Street, Dublin, mother of the poet Thomas Moore, strove to fit her boy for a higher walk of life than that to which he had been born. To that end she sent Tom to one Miss Dodd, 'an elderly maiden lady', in whom, as far as Mrs Moore was concerned, was manifested 'high society'. From her Tom was to learn 'polite usage'. Some fifteen years before Tom's birth in 1779, a Mrs Mabell Dodd, of Aungier Street, was listed in the Convert Rolls, as having conformed on 11 March 1764, and it is possible that she was the mother of Miss Dodd. In the list of priests who 'converted' at that time was the Revd Roger Dodd, who conformed 15 February 1775.

The South Dublin Union received an offer from the Children's Entertainment Committee to supply the children of the workhouse with jam and toys on the day of Queen Victoria's arrival in Dublin in 1900. Many objected to what they saw as 'political souperism'. Mr Donnelly, a member of the Union, said at a meeting that discussed the matter, that he would like to know who constituted the committee, and Mr Nolan added that there was a request that the children should sing 'God Save the Oueen' in return for the donation of the jam. Mrs Browne responded that it was a political action, for 'otherwise they would not surely have been guilty of such inhumanity as to refuse a little jam to the poor children of the workhouse', and Mr Ryan added that the majority of the board were Irish Nationalists. One of those who voted for acceptance was Mrs Dodd. A member of the Dodd family who, not only did not become Protestant, but would have been totally of a different political view to Mrs Dodd, was Mother Patricia Dodd, who said in 1921 that those who were executed by the British 'were strong in the conviction that the fight for country was a fight for Faith'. It was she that Volunteer Paddy Moran invited to stay with him in his cell the night before his execution.

Around 1530 Thomas Dod and his wife Agnes Petit made a gift of a house to the vicars of St Patrick's; in 1598 Dod of Connell was one of the constables of Co. Kildare, and in 1608 Dode Esquire was a Justice of the Peace for Co. Wexford; tituladoes listed in the 1659 *Census* included John Dodd for Rathinsky, Co. Laois, and William Dodd for Ballinderry, Co. Westmeath. The only Dodd in Taylor & Skinner's *Maps* (1783) was the Revd Mr Dodd, Drumahaire, Co. Leitrim. There was only one Dodd in the 1814 *Directory*, a Mrs Dodd, Stapolin, Co. Dublin, though the Dodds were largely to be found in Dublin. In the 1836 Directory there were ten listed – a vintner, a grocer, a wholesale linen merchant, the owner of dress warerooms, a hay and corn factor, an auctioneer, and a few with no listed occupation.

Various meanings have been suggested for the English surname Dodd – 'fat/dowdy/dishonest/close-cropped', a family of which settled in Co. Sligo in the late 16th century. The name is now scattered, according to Mac Lysaght but is mainly found in Cos. Armagh and Down. He adds that it is occasionally used as a corrupt synonym of Dowd in Ulster. In Co. Dublin *Owners of Land* (1876) lists a Dodd in Lusk on 145 acres, and another in Finglas on 102 acres. In Co. Armagh there were two in Keady, on 10 and 15 acres, and one in Brootally on 22 acres, while Wm Henry Dodd, Killorglin, had 1,000 Co. Kerry acres. Today's telephone directories list 16 in Northern Ireland in the south, and 60 in the Dublin area. Doddsborough is Baile na Dodaigh in Irish and is in the Co. Dublin parish of Lucan.

BELVIDERE

Some 270 estates of Catholic landowners in Ireland, comprising something under one million acres, were confiscated after the Williamite victory in 1690. About one third was returned to the old owners, but the remaining estates were put up for sale to Protestants only, yielding £724,501. In Kilkenny the estates of fourteen Catholic landowners, totalling 32,308 acres were conveyed to new Protestant owners in 1702–3. Among those Protestants was Dr Marmaduke Coghill, the purchaser of 140 acres. The Coghills, however, were in Co. Kilkenny before Marmaduke's arrival, as Coghill was listed among the principal Irish names in the 1659 *Census* for the Co. Kilkenny baronies of Gowran and Crannagh. Mac Lysaght in his *Surnames* says that this Yorkshire name came to Ireland in the second half of the 17th century, being mainly associated with Co. Kilkenny. If such be the case, they must have come in large numbers or propagated with rare speed, to be in such numbers and to have degenerated to being listed as 'Irish' by 1659.

From 1730 onwards the destruction of the medieval city of Dublin was in full swing; old streets were considered too narrow, and projecting cagework houses oldfashioned and uncomfortable. 'The city walls with their towers continued to fall, and gates had become anachronisms, impeding traffic, as Thomas Pooley and Marmaduke Coghill stressed in their appeal in 1699 for the removal of Dame's gate which had guarded Dublin's eastern approaches for so long'. Among the street names which indicate the outline of Restoration Dublin was Coghill Court (it still exists, off Dame Street). Dating from the same period was the residence that Coghill built for himself in Drumcondra, naming it Belvidere. This was the address of Marmaduke Coghill in 1717 when he was one of the commitee supporting Madam Steevens for the founding of a general hospital.

Sir Josiah Coghill, Belvidere House, Drumcondra, was among the magistrates of Co. Kilkenny, as listed the *Alamanack, Registry & Directory* of 1836, and in 1876 the *Owners of Land* shows Sir John Jocelyn Coghill, as possessing 4,564 acres in Co. Kilkenny, while the Misses Coghill had a modest 172 acres there. With Glenbarrahane, Castletownsend, Skibbereen, Co. Cork as address, Sir Jocelyn is listed as owning 472 acres in Co. Dublin, and 1,269 acres in Co. Meath.

Belvidere names townlands in Cos. Cork and Westmeath, the latter replacing the old name of Rahin. This change was imposed by Robert Rochfort, who was created earl of Belvidere in 1757, and died in 1772. Paul Walsh in his *Place-names of Westmeath* remarks in a footnote that it was a pity that the people of Westmeath, 'by retaining the name 'Lake Belvidere', have helped to perpetuate the name of a nobleman whose wickedness and inhuman cruelty to his wife does not bear recital'. Apart from the apparent 'Belvidere' connection, it is interesting that the 18th-century bachelor judge, Sir Marmaduke Coghill, advised husbands whose marriages were endangered to beat their wives 'but in moderation, and with a stick of no greater thickness than their thumb'.

The *Phone Book* of Northern Ireland records one of the name Coghill, while south of the Border the small handful of this surname are in Co. Westmeath.

ARBOUR HILL

We cannot say how long the word 'smog' has been in existence; it is not to be found in the *Shorter Oxford Dictionary* (1986), though it is in the 1950 *Funk & Wagnell*. The residents of the city of Dublin had, until recently, good cause to complain about this unpleasant and dangerous condition; it may have been as bad, if not worse, at the start of the 18th century, especially coupled with the sewerage and sanitary arrangements, and the piling up of litter in the streets. It was customary at that time for people who could afford it, to lodge out of the city for the benefit of the air. On 16 May 1705 a petition to the duke of Ormond from the inhabitants of Arbour Hill and places adjacent to the Phoenix Park sheweth; 'that most of the Petitioners do pay great rents for their several holdings, great part where of they did hope to raise by accommodating sickly persons who desire to lodge out of the citty for the benefit of the air; but your Petitioners are not only deprived of that advantage, but find themselves very uneasy in their habitations from the troublesome noise and infectious smell which they are too often sensible cometh from the Dog Kennell near the Park gate, especially in the summer, which is the principal time they can propose to make profit by their Lodgings'. Thomas Burgh, engineer and surveyor general, viewed the kennels and, accepting that the noise and smell must be offensive to the petitioners, suggested that the said kennels might be removed into the Park, 'and placed by the pond near Scully's, where it would be more commodiously situated'. Was this the lake now in the Zoo, or that in the People's Garden? Rocque's 1756 map of Dublin shows what appears to be a Lake, in what is now the Department of Defence's grounds, immediately inside the wall at the bottom of Infirmary Road. The Phoenix Park was then a hunting ground for the Lord Lieutenant and these dogs, presumably, were used in the hunt.

In 1836 Arbour Hill (Cnoc an Earbair, the hill of the grass) consisted of St Paul's Widows' House, the Corporation of Carpenters' Alms house, the entrance to the Provost Marshal's, and the entrance to Richardston's fields, together with six residences. There was Mrs Marcella Ivie and her daughter Eliza, a dressmaker; John Walsh, provision dealer; Patrick Curtain, and the lodging house of Mrs Mary Dignum. This lady's surname, variously rendered Dignam, Dignan and Duig(e)nan is from the Irish Ó Duibhgeannáin. This was one of the more important literary families of Ireland, being bards and ollavs to the leading septs of the country now comprised in Cos. Leitrim, Roscommon and Longford – the MacDermotts, the MacRannels (now Reynolds) and the O'Farrells. The Ó Duibhgeannáin principal residence was Kilronan, Co. Roscommon, of which parish they were erenaghs. They are listed 30 times in *Annála Ríoghachta Éireann*, the so-called Annals of the Four Masters, between the years 1296 and 1578. Indeed one of those Masters was Cuchonnacht Ó Duibhgeannáin, *anglice* Peregrine O'Duigenan, who died in 1664. Maghnus Ó Duibhgeannáin (*c.*1415) was the chief compiler of the Book of Ballymote, and Dubhthas óg Ó Duibhgeannáin annotated the original Book of O'Hara, which was compiled in 1597. They had a bardic school at Castle Fore, Co. Leitrim, this being recorded as their residence in 1636. And when it came to piety, they were hard to excel. Maolpeadar O Duigenan (d. 1290) was described in the Book of Magauran as 'that holy man, peer of saints, who surpassed even Paul'. There were but three of the name in the *Phone Book* of Northern Ireland; there were 64 in the Dublin area directory, and 80 in the remainder of the country, while five-sixths of the country's 129 Dignams were in the Dublin area.

GRAFTON STREET

Bernard de Gomme's 1673 map of Dublin city names Grafton Street as 'the Highway to St Stephens Green', and what is now King Street South at the Green end of Grafton Street, was called Leather Lane. The 'Highway' was subsequently named after the duke of Grafton who served as Lord Lieutenant from 1721 to 1724. On the proroguing of the Irish Parliament in 1706 Grafton warned the members to keep a watchful eye on the papists, and in 1723 he warmly supported an Act proposing that all priests should be compelled to leave the kingdom, and if they refused to do so they should be taken and castrated. When, in 1722, William Woods, an ironmonger of Wolverhampton, was granted a patent to coin copper half-pence and farthings, Grafton, assisted no doubt by Jonathan Swift's Drapier letters, 'realized that the granting of the patent was a disreputable transaction, with fraud as its source and plunder its object; he knew that the Irish were in the right and were determined not to yield; and he advised that the patent be declared void' (E.A. D'Alton, *History of Ireland*). 'He [Woods] was a wretched ironmonger, an impudent hardwareman, a rat, a sharper, an incorrigible, wretch, avaricious, insolent, dishonest'.

In 1773, a committee appointed to inspect Dublin city leases that were then near expiring was empowered to set 'by public cants to the highest and best bidders several lots of ground in Grafton street and Harry street, formerly called

Flint's Croft ...'. The forty listed properties ranged from 3*s*. 3*d*. to 19*s*. per foot. The rebuilding of the houses was to be completed by September 1776; 'the front, rear, and outside walls to be 14 inches thick at least, the window stools and copings to be of mountain stone, the houses fronting Grafton street to be four storys high and the houses in the new intended streets to be three storys high, a raised footway flagged in Grafton street at least 6 inches high and 4 feet wide ...'. The Flints, after whom this area had once been named, came from England in the 13th century and settled in Dublin. A document of 1326 concerning the manor of St Sepulchre numbers Elena Flynte among the freeholders at Ardmacanock. This place was also known as Stokken, being situated behind St Kevin's church, according to Liber Niger Alani (also called Archbishop Alen's Register), a pre-reformation document that ranges from 1172 to 1534. Ardinatanoke (?) appears to have been part of the one-time suburban district named Newland, which also included the neighbourhood of St Kevin's church. It is interesting to note that the *Dublin Directory* of 1850 shows James Flint residing at 15 Peter Street, not very far from where Elena had lived more than five hundred years previously. A Lieutenant Thomas Flint was listed in the 1659 *Census* as a titulado of Cork city, but apart from that sightings of persons of this surname are rare indeed.

A Mr Flint features largely in the Account of Secret Service Money, Ireland (published in Gilbert's *Documents ... 1795–1804*), from 14 December 1802, when, by direction of Marsden, he disbursed £20 English. The next payment was in September 1803 when he provided £20 'to send to E'. Altogether he made 19 payments up to his final transaction when he made out £13 7*s*. 6*d*. for Lacy. Others to receive payments and expenses through him were Fleming, Finnerty, Murphy, Farrell and Doyle. In December 1803 he paid £5 13*s*. 9*d*. 'to Terence Coligan's wife by desire of M.F'. The largest was £200 paid to Murphy in February 1804. And rare as the Flints are in documents down through the centuries, they are still so. Current telephone directories show two Flints in Co. Antrim, and one each in Cos. Kildare, Limerick and Waterford.

BRIDEWELL

Lincoln Place at the east end of Dublin's Nassau Street, and its continuation to Fenian Street across the bottom of Westland Row, was once named Patrick's Well Lane, from a well so-named located there. Not too far away, according to Peter Somerville-Large's *Dublin*, was St Brigid's Well from which the 1575 pest-house, the Bridewell, was named. This was on Hoggen Green, now called College Green. Dictionaries, giving it as dating from 1552, define Bridewell as 'a house of correction: a lock-up', named from St Bride's Well in London. This was near where stood a royal lodging, given by Edward VI for a hospital, and converted later into a house of correction. Bíodh san mar atá (be that as it may). Dublin's Bridewell (Tobar Bhríde) shown on Speed's 1610 map of the city directly in front gate of Trinity College, provided a prison for any unfortunate vagrant that was rounded up. A year after it was built, it was moved farther out to a section of city property at All Hallows. In 1776 the Bridewell held fettered lunatics. Two years later Joshua Mecum was listed as keeper of Bridewell, and in 1780 a Dublin Corporation committee, set up to enquire into 'the duty of inferior city officers',considered a petition against Joshua Mecum. They reported that 'the charges therein set forth not having been supported, no person appearing for that purpose,we were of the opinion that he be acquitted of any misconduct in that respect'. Though we have gone back over three years of the Corporation minutes, we have been unable to discover the nature of the complaint laid against him. Daily complaints were made at that time against one John Giles 'for permitting almost every person arrested by him to go at large … on receiving some pecuniary or other gratuity contrary to his oath and bond …' In some places of detention there were complaints of forced payments to officials.

Regarding the handling of debtors, this committee reported: 'We also find that the officers in general when an unfortunate debtor is arrested by them, that such a debtor is conveyed by them to a sponging-house, where they are kept oftentimes several days before their friends or relations know where they are, and in such sponging-houses considerable sums are extorted from them for their diet and lodging, drink and keepers, whereas if the serjeant committed the prisoner to the city Marshalsea (which by his oath he is obliged to do), in such cases the prisoner would be treated with humanity …' First used in 1700, 'sponging-house' was a house kept by a bailiff or sheriff's officer, formerly in regular use as a place of preliminary confinement for debtors. From as far back as 1693 'to sponge' meant to live parasitically on others.

The Bridewell Garda Station is in Dublin's Chancery Street, which street was previously named Chancery Lane, and before that Bridewell Lane. At 31 Chancery Lane in 1850 was 'Police Office'.

Mecum, the name of the 18th-century Bridewell keeper, may be the English surname variously spelled Meacham, Meachem, Meachim, and the west Midland and New Zealand variant Meacheam. One of the rare sightings of this name was that of John Macham/Machem, a 1673 butcher in the city of Waterford, and one of the wardens of the company of skinners and cordwinders the following year. MacLysaght's *Surnames* does not list this name, though a few of the names are to be found in Ireland. There are five telephone directory entries spelled Makim in five different counties, and of the six Makems in the *Phone Book* of Northern Ireland, four are in Keady, Co. Armagh. Best known of this surname is the ballad singer Tommy Makem.

OFF LANE

Like a child that marks its name on wet cement, or carves it on a school desk or church seat, Henry Moore, earl of Drogheda, in the early 18th century bestowed each component of his name and title on some street in his land on the north bank of the River Liffey in Dublin. There was Henry Street, Moore Street, Earl Street, Drogheda Street and, believe it or not, Of Lane. And as Drogheda Street changed to Sackville Street and thence to O'Connell Street, so Of Lane become Off Lane and later Henry Lane. In 1836 it comprised of eight houses and led to the entrance of Cow Pock Institute. It was rumoured that Luke Gardiner, who bought this property from the earl, had begun his career as footman to a banker and by eavesdropping on his master's conversations picked up useful financial tips which he turned to good account. This we read in John O'Donovan's fascinating book *Life by the Liffey*. O'Donovan doubts this and suggests that it was likely that Gardiner was the natural son of nobleman who settled a small capital sum on him to help him get a good start on the ladder. 'Among Luke Gardiner's earlier acquisitions was land in the Sir John Rogerson's Quay area, where presently one of the streets was named with discreet ambiguity after Saint Luke'. His first major development was in Henrietta Street in the 1720s, considered the most majestic street of its size in these islands. Charles, Luke's son, preferred music to land development, accepting a doctorate of music from Trinity College.

Gardiner, one of the Anglo-Norman surnames formed from employments, trades, personal characteristics and nationality, is found in medieval Irish records and derives from the occupation 'gardener'.(Our Gardiner acquaintances are fine traditional Irish musicians.) There were but two of the name on Taylor and Skinner's *Maps* (1783); one was Rt. Hon. L. Gardiner, whose residence in the Phoenix Park now houses the Ordnance Survey. Of the eight listed in the 1814 *Dublin Directory* six were in Co. Mayo, largely in the Killala area. One was John Gardiner, Farmhill, and in *Owners of Land* (1876), Hariett Gardiner was at Farmhill on a sizeable 4,073 acres. The other Mayo Gardiner had 280 acres at Rashowen. There were nine Gardiner holdings in Co. Antrim, mostly of modest size; with holdings in Cos. Louth, Meath, Laois, Cork, Leitrim, Roscommon and Tyrone. This last mentioned county had the biggest Gardiner estate, 5,506 acres, then at the Court of Chancery in Dublin. The many Gardiners in the Killala area of Co. Mayo in 1814 were probably the descendants of John Gardner (also spelled Garner), who is listed in the Co. Mayo entries in the Book of Survey and Distribution (1636–1703) as owner of land at Ballygowan (also spelled Ballynegowne) and Donnarrow (also spelled Duncanarew), both in the parish of Kilfian. Now rendered Ballygowan, this townland name is not listed in Nollaig Ó Muraíle's excellent *Mayo Places*.

There were ten of the name in the 1836 *Dublin Directory* – a bookseller and stationer; a dressmaker; a grocer and wine merchant; a tobacco and snuff manufacturer; a printer; a chair and cabinet maker; two surgeons and two attorneys. None so-named lived in Church Street, the address of a Mr S. Gardiner in 1794. Described as an 'opulent citizen', he was accused of being an active disturber on the occasion of the 1794 acquital of Dr Drennan, the Presbyterian United Irishman from Belfast. When the verdict was announced, the court 'rung with indecent and vociferous plaudits, huzzaing, clapping of hands, and throwing up of hats'. Current telephone directories show 266 north of the Border (of which 92 Gardners), and 124 to its south (27 Gardners).

DAWSON STREET

In 1713 it was decided that it would be 'for the honour and advantage of this city, and a convenience to the Lord Mayor' that there should be a permanent Mansion House. A house erected by Joshua Dawson in Dawson Street ten years previously was bought from the owner for £3,500. Dawson particularises the furnishings that he would sell with the house: all the brass locks and marble chimney pieces, as also the tapestry hangings, silk window curtains and window seats and chimney glass in the great bed chamber; the gilt leather hangings, four pair of scarlet calamanco window curtains and chimney glass in the walnut parlour; the Indian calicoe window curtains ... in the Dantzick oak parlour', and similar fittings in the 'large eating room'. Originally a two-storey red-brick building, it continues to the present day as the site of the residence of Dublin's lord mayor. In 1770 a committee was appointed 'to consider what ought to be provided for the said house, and what immediate repairs are necessary to be made therein, and that they direct the same to be provided and done in the cheapest manner, the expense of the said furniture and repairs not to exceed the sum of £100'. Nothing appears to have happened, and in 1775 another committee was formed for precisely the same purpose, with the same limitation of £100. On 21 July of that year Henry Hart, the lord mayor, with the sheriffs, treasurer, masters of the works, Alderman Dunn, Alderman Faulkner, and six of the commons to be named by the commons or any five of them were commisioned to forward the matter. The nominated commoners were Messrs Vierpyle, Haughton, Dickinson, Worthington, Ward and Ould. Later that year the latter became one of the city's sheriffs. However, the assembly rolls of the corporation of the city of Dublin for 2 April 1776 note that 'Fielding Ould, esquire, one of the High Sheriffs of the city of Dublin died lately in his office of Sheriffalty ...'

We presume that Ould is the same as Old, an exclusive Cornwall surname denoting 'old, senior'. It appears almost certain that this Fielding Ould was the son of Sir Fielding Ould, the man who, in 1759, succeeded Bartholmew Mosse, the founder and first Master of the Hospital for the Relief of Poor Lying-in Women, at George's Lane, Dublin. This man was celebrated in the following Dublin rhyme: 'Sir Fielding Ould is made a knight./He should have been a Lord by right, /For then the ladies cry would be, /"O Lord, good Lord, deliver me!"'

No doubt it would be unfair to suggest that the Revd Fielding Ould, curate of Lucan, was a subscriber to Lewis' 1837 *Topographical Dictionary* merely to see his name in print and to be listed along with his 'betters'. If such was the case he was disappointed: his name is not among the 'seated' gentry in the Lucan entry. The *Dublin Directory* of 1850 has the Revd D.F. Ould as residing at 12 Charles Street, Great. In all of this island's currrent telephone directories there is but a single entry of this surname, that being in Co. Meath.

PALMERSTOWN

Some people have been known to add, or delete the letter 'e' to or from their names; or to capitalize some internal letter, or decapitalize the initial letter, all in an effort to be, or to appear to be different. It is sad then that those Mayo people with such a unique name as Mullover, derived from the even more unique Irish Ó Maolfhomhair (*fomhar*, harvest), should have changed it to the English name Milford. Palmer also was occasionally used as a synonym of Mullover, and one must suppose that the Mullovers are now concealed in the under the names Milford (found only in the Northern Ireland *Phone-Book*) or Palmer.

This English surname of Norman origin, le paumer, the palmer or pilgrim, has been on record in Ireland since the 13th century. Six members of this family were Comissioners for the Poll-Money Ordinances of 1660 and 1661 for the counties of Kilkenny, Cavan and Mayo, as well as being tituladoes for Ardfinnan, Co, Tipperary; Ballilogue, Co. Kilkenny; and the parishes of St Andrew's and St Audoen's in the city of Dublin.

Of the twenty-three Palmer residences listed in the 1814 *Directory*, three were in Co. Mayo – Roger Palmer Esq., Carromore, Killala; William Palmer Esq., Richmond, Killala, and William H. Palmer Esq., Palmerstown, Killala. The thirty-five landowners named Palmer listed in 1876 (*Owners of Land*) were fairly evenly spread throughout the four provinces, but by far the largest holding was that of Col. Sir Roger William H. Palmer, Bart., of Kenure Park, Rush, in Co. Dublin. He was owner of 80,990 acres in Co. Mayo; 9,570 in Co. Sligo, and

3,991 acres in Co. Dublin. The baronetcy was created in 1777, and the holder listed in 1836 was William Henry Palmer, the family's residence then being Rush House.

There are two parishes named Palmerstown in Co. Dublin, one south of the Liffey in the barony of Uppercross, and the other to the north of the county in the barony of Balrothery. The first was originally Teach Guaire, and the other was called Gleann Uisce, but towards the end of the 11th century both took the name Palmerstown from their owners, Ailred the Palmer and his wife. The latter is now gaelicised as Baile Phámar. Sometime after 1080 the Palmers, who lived outside the West Gate (afterwards known as the New Gate), being childless and having no direct heirs, resolved to devote themselves and their wealth to the care of the poor and the miserable. As well as their residence, they owned Teach Guaire in Fingall and Gleann Uisce in Uí Dunchadha, each being about 1,500 acres, and these they bestowed on the hospital which they founded on their curtilage outside the West Gate. The Palmers took monastic vows, and, with the fellow-workers they had gathered about them, they lived in the religious house that they had built beside the hospital. This institution was organised to be a house of Canons Regular of St Augustine, though afterwards it adopted the rule of the Cruciferi, Cross-bearing or Crouched Friars. A tower stood until around 1800, when it was pulled down, and the site was in great part covered by the buildings of John's Lane Distillery, and partly by the Church and Monastery of SS Augustine and John, belonging to the Order of Augustinian Hermits. Judging by entries in telephone directories there are more Palmers in the North than in all of the South.

DEANRATH

A list of persons indebted to the Revenue Commissioners was recently published in newspapers, giving the size of the indebtedness and the occupation of those listed. 'Gentleman' was the listed occupation of some. One wonders if being a baron or a lord might reasonably be considered an occupation. The surnames Bar(r)on and Lord are listed by Basil Cottle in his Penguin *Dictionary of Surnames* as 'Occupational' names, though suggesting that either might have derived through service in the household of a baron or a lord, or through having acted the part in a play, or from uppish behaviour, pride or haughty bearing. And while bishops or deans in the past might not have over-strained themselves at work, they were nevertheless 'jobs', and surnames deriving from them could be properly described as 'Occupational'.

The surname Dean(e) has two clear origins, one being 'Occupational', and the other deriving from a word meaning 'valley', and once preceded by 'de'.

Those derived from the occupation were once preceded by 'le', and the le Den family was one of the 'Tribes of Galway'. Ambrose Deane was a member of this family, once owners of extensive property in Tuam, Co. Galway. He had collected his rents here in 1777 but mysteriously disappeared on his way back to Dublin. A well in a demense, five miles from Tuam, is curiously associated with this disappearance. *Owners of Land* (1876) lists two Dean holdings in Co. Galway, one of two acres and the other of 294. Hardly extensive.

Deansrath in the Co. Dublin parish of Clondalkin is listed in the 1654 Civil Survey as Deane Rath, wherein the dean of St Patrick's held one hundred acres. Deane was among the principal Irish names in the Co. Tipperary barony of Lower Ormond in the mid-17th century and were tituladoes in Cos, Limerick and Waterford, and also in Dublin City and the Co. Dublin barony of Newcastle & Uppercross. Thomas Dean was a 1660 Poll-Money Ordinance Commissioner for the Co. Meath town of Athboy, and Alexander Dean was a Co. Waterford Commissioner for the years 1660 and 1661.

The *Calendar of State Papers: Ireland, 1509–1573* refers to a letter of Alexander Craik, bishop of Kildare, from Deanerath, dated 26 October 1562, wherein he repeats his desire for discharge of 'my fyrst frewtes which was promesyd to be remyttyd me afore I cam from London'. He requests that he might enjoy his deanery without trouble from the law, and prays to be disburdened of his bishopric, of Kildare, as he cannot understand the Irish tongue.

Breach-Ghaeltacht is the name of an area where there is a mixture of Irish and English spoken and, though it is equally a *breach-Ghalltacht*, one has never heard it so described. This condition of language mixture and language change was written about by Richard Stanihurst in 1577. He said that 'the meaner sort spoke neither good English nor good Irish, but rather a mingle mangle of gallimaufrie of both languages'. This we quote from Peter Somerville-Large's *Dublin*. Elsewhere this is given as 'mingle mangle or gallimaufrie' (our italics). Cad is gallimaufrie ann? The *Phone Book* (NI), *An Eolaí Telefóin* 01, and the non-01 directory (1982) list *c.*100 Dean(e) subscribers each.

SANTRY

The Welshmen who came to Ireland from a place in Wales named Barri were known as de Barri, a name that in time became Barry, and with their complete hibernicization it acquired the Irish form of de Barra. They arrived here following the Anglo-Norman invasion, and Philip de Barri obtained extensive grants of land in the Co. Cork baronies of Barrymore, Orrery and Kinelea as early as 1179. Philip's posterity prospered and multiplied, and the several branches of the family formed septs somewhat in the Irish fashion, the chief of which were the important Barry Mór, Barry Óg, Barry Roe, while minor branches became Barry Maol (bald) and Barry Láidir (strong). The Barrys of Rathcormac, Co. Cork, adopted the surname Mac Adam, taken from one Adam Barry, Adam being a common first name in Anglo-Norman families.

It is almost certain that Sir John Barry, Protestant, listed as a landowner in the Co.Dublin book of the 1654 Civil Survey, bore this same Norman surname. He owned 770 acres a Sterminstown, Ballcurris, Ballystrowan, Silloge and Santry, all in the parish of Santry. Upon his land at Santry was 'a Dwelling house of stone wth. a barne & an old stable, Thatcht, ye walls of a house & a garden & 2 orchards. Also a small slated house wth.six thatcht Cabbins valued by ye jury at 300li. Also ye parish Church of Santry'. This placename derives from Seantrabh, the meaning of which is 'plain enough' according to P.W. Joyce in *Irish Names of Places*, when he takes *Onomasticon Goedelicum*'s alternative form *sen-trebh* to mean 'old dwelling' or 'old tribe'.

In 1739 the 4th baron, Henry Barry, Lord Santry, appeared on a murder charge before his peers in the House of Commons in Dublin, there then being no regulations regarding the trial of peers. The previous year the young Lord Santry had killed a footman named Loughlin Murphy 'out of mere bad temper' when drunk in a public house in Palmerstown. He was found guilty, sentenced to hang, and his estates forfeited to the Crown. However, his peers unanimously recommended mercy and after obtaining a reprieve, and later a full pardon, he withdrew to England. Two years later he had his estates restored.

Listing this affair, the 1836 *Directory* informs us that that same year there had been a severe frost which lasted from 29 December until 8 Feburary. It would appear that these weather conditions were not confined to Dublin, for in Bennett's *History of Bandon* we read: 'All rivers in Cork were frozen over; whilst so severe was the frost in Cork, that the ice on the Lee was found capable of supporting tents, shows, booths etc. Lough Drippel, near Dunmanway, was the only piece of water in the South of Ireland upon which the frost had no effect'. Also reporting this frost, Smith's *History of Cork* locates this lake at Mohana a mile south of Dunmanway. It would appear to be on a tributary of the Dirty River which in turn joins the Bandon River just south of Dunmanway.

There are 2,828 Barry entries in the telephone directories in the South, with 84 in the North. The Irish *de Barra* is listed 24 times.

Kildare

On his being summoned to England to be arraigned before Henry VIII, the earl of Kildare appointed his son Thomas, known as Silken Thomas, to act in his place as head of government in Ireland. Thomas shared his father's fears about the outcome of this visit and, as a result of a report spread by his enemies, he proceeded in June 1534 with a retinue of 140 horsemen to St Mary's Abbey where the Council was sitting. There he flung the Sword of State on the council table and declared that he was no longer Henry's Deputy but his foe. Among, those who took refuge in Dublin Castle was Archbishop Allen/Alen of Dublin, the compiler of 'Archbishop Alen's Register of Early Church Documents, 1530–32' a bitter enemy of the Geraldines. While Thomas and his followers swept angrily through the district of Fingal, the archbishop, fearing that if Dublin Castle was captured he would receive no mercy, stealthily took ship for England. Whether it was due to weather or treachery, the vessel in which he was travelling was driven on the beach at Clontarf, and the terrified prelate took refuge in a friend's house in the neighbouring village of Artane. His hiding-place was soon discovered and, despite his pleas for mercy, he was butchered by Thomas's soldiers. It is most likely that the archbishop was of the Scottish or North English family of this name, it being derived from a Welsh saint's name. However, the surname Allen is also the anglicised form of the Irish Ó hAillín, particularly in Cos. Offaly and Tipperary, and it is more than likely that John Allen of Tipperary, who was on trial for his life in 1921, charged with being in possession of a revolver some ammunition and a document entitled 'Night Fighting', was of this latter clan. Sir Neville Macready, Commander-in-Chief of the British Forces in Ireland, on the grounds that actual war was raging, claimed, in the martial law area, despotic powers of life and death. Allen and five other young Irishmen were executed on 28 February 1921. The first execution, on 1 February, under the new ordinance was that of Cornelius Murphy, his brother also being executed on the grounds that he failed to inform on him. In 1640 John and Richard Allen, Irish papists, had land in the Co. Kildare parish of Oughterard, and we wonder which of the named townlands in this parish at that time – Oughterard, Bishop's Court, Catlewarneing,

34

Huttonread, Collinhill, Clonaghins, Ballicoman, Terrils Mill, or Lyons – was subsequently given the present name of Boston. This also names townlands in Cos. Limerick, Tipperary, Clare and two in Laois.

FEAR ENGLISH RIVER

Presumably 'The sweep of Carbury' shown on Taylor and Skinner's 1783 map of Co. Kildare, just north of the village of Carbury and south of the hill marked Knockirr (?Knockcor), is Clár Chairbre, given in *Onomasticon Goedelicum* as being situated 'round Carbury of Birmingham country in Kildare'. The name of the parish of Dunfierth, located in Clár Chairbre, is given in the above book as Dún Firchert, with reference to the Birminghams of Dún Firchirt. Meyler Birmingham came to Ireland from Warwickshire, England, with Strongbow in 1170; and his second son Piers, the only one with recorded issue, is the ancestor of the now-spelled Berminghams of Ireland. In 1640 John Bermingham had 3,400 acres at Dunfierth, and 96 at Garrisker, while the following members of the name had land in adjoining parishes in this barony of Carbury: William of Parsonstown, 490 acres; John of Rahin, 183; John of Carrick, 510; Edward of Ballinedrummy, 70; John, Morrice and Garrett, 262 at Garrisker; and Edward of Grange, 218. All, being Irish papists, had their land confiscated, except Edward of Grange, of whom the Civil Survey of 1654–6 reports: 'Edward of Grange retourned a Protestant by the Jury whoe being demanded why they soe retourned him (hee having beene by some of us whoe did know him & took him for a papist) were answered that he came before them & swore he was a Protestant wch. was the ground & reason of their so retourning him.' It was recorded that there was one house upon the 'lands of Dunfearth', with 'two acres of Ash Saplins' valued at £3. The personal name Cairbre may mean 'a charioteer', and Cairbre Lifeachair, given in *Irish Personal Names* (Ó Corráin & Maguire, 1981) as meaning 'Liffey-Lover', was the son of Cormac Mac Airt. Another Cairbre, son of Niall of the Nine Hostages, was founder of a royal dynasty and gave his name to the barony of Carbury, Co. Kildare. Indeed, it not only names the barony but also a village, a townland and a civil parish. Sidh Neachtain, the ancient name of the hill of Carbury, is regarded as the source of the River Boyne. Another river which rises in this locality is the Kilcooney, and our Ordnance Survey map ($\frac{1}{2}$"= 1 mile) shows it as it flows west, actually crossing another river! This other river, with the strange name of Fear English River, flows northwards to join the Blackwater at Johnstown Bridge, before this in turn flows on to join the River Boyne.

KILCOCK

De Latocnaye in *A Frenchman's Walk through Ireland 1796–97* expressed surprise that the Irish drank infinitely less than he could have believed, and indeed what we understood to be the case, though he did not deny 'that there are such things as drinking parties where one may get straightforwardly drunk …' The Englishman Arthur Young in *A Tour of Ireland 1776–79* writes that whereas 'drinking and duelling were two charges long alleged against the gentlemen of Ireland, … the change of manners which has taken place in that Kingdom is not generally known in England. Drunkenness ought no longer to be a reproach …' He claimed that every person drank as much or as little as they chose, and said that he had never been pressed to drink a single glass more than he had inclination for. He asserted that hard drinking was very rare among 'the people of fortune', despite the fact that they sat much longer at table than in England. This moderation did not extend to the graziers of the rich lands of Limerick, who neglected the drains, fences, weeds etc. … Young blaming this on 'the idleness and dissipation so general in Ireland'. These gentlemen, he said, were 'too apt to attend to their claret as much as to their bullocks, live expensively, and being enabled, from the nature of their business, to pass nine tenths of the year without any exercise of industry, contract such a habit of ease, that works of improvement would be mortifying to their sloth'. Despite the apparent fall in drinking, distilleries abounded, and when Young reached Kilcock, Co. Kildare, he was informed by a Mr Jones of Dollerstown that the town of Kilcock contained six distilleries for making whiskey. Mr Foster of Branchale, some distance from the town, had 'a more complete distillery', and both he and the town distillers used the wash and used grain in fattening 'either hogs or beasts, generally the latter'. We have failed to locate Branchale, but a 'Foster Esq.' is shown on Taylor and Skinner's *Maps* (1778) as residing at 'Courtown' some distance south of Kilcock, this being the home of Peter Read Esq. in 1814. Kilcock, as well as being the name of this town, also names townlands in Cos. Kerry, Roscommon and Kildare, the latter being Cill Choca, 'the church of Coca' this being a rare early name.

NAAS

In 1577, according to Samuel Lewis in his *Topographical Dictionary of Ireland* (1837), betwen 600 and 700 thatched houses were burned at Naas in Co. Kildare, on the night of a festival, by Roderick Oge O Moore and Cormuck O Connor, at the head of a party of insurgents from the country west of the

English Pale. At the time of writing, Lewis gives the total number of houses in the town as about 600, some hundred less than that of 280 years earlier, and housing a population of 3,808. Variously known as Nás Laighean, Nás na Ri, and An Nás, it is now officially An Nás, *nás* being defined as 'omen, augury; fate, forfeit; commemoration, a commemorative assembly, a fair'. It was called Nás na Rí, Naas of the kings, because this was the seat of the kings of Leinster until the year 904, when Cerball, king of Leinster, was killed. P.W. Joyce in *The Irish Names of Places* writes that 'a great mound of the palace still remains just outside he town'; and Lewis states that 'The rath in the centre of the town is a high conical mount, where the states of Leinster are said to have held their general assemblies …'. About a mile south of the town are the remains of 'the gaunt-looking mansion of Jigginstown, with a 380 foot long frontage'. This was begun in 1636-7 by Thomas Wentworth, earl of Strafford, Lord Deputy of Ireland from 1633 to 1640. He intended it as a summer house for himself, and as a palace for Charles II, if and when he came to visit Ireland. It was left unfinished when Strafford was called to London and beheaded in 1641. On being elected President of the Royal Society of Antiquaries of Ireland in 1916, Thomas Johnson Westropp gave an address on 'The Progress of Irish Archaeology', a lengthy and enlightening review of a hundred years of Irish archaeology. In it he attacked the spurious claims of Dr Molyneux and Major Vallency that Irish was identical with Sanskrit, Greek, Hebrew, Persian, Arabic, Chinese and Japanese. Of Vallency Westropp charitably writes: 'Few men have suffered so much gross flattery and cruel abuse as did this learned, honorable but injudicious man.' The seal of the town of Naas has a serpent at its centre, with the motto 'Prudens ut Serpens' below, and this Westropp attributes to 'some other savant', in designing the seal, equating Naas with *nahash*, a serpent.

MULLAMAST

Pride, covetousness, lust, anger, gluttony, envy and sloth, the seven listed deadly sins, which ordinary mortals are prey to, and indulgence in which is prohibited. Not so kings going by the five prohibitions of the king of Leinster, is listed in the 11th-century *Geasa agus Buadha Ríogh Éireann*. These kings apparently were not subject to such weaknesses of the flesh, but we cannot say if they had constant and uncontrollable desires to indulge in that which was prohibited to them, to wit: (1) go round Tuath Laighean left-hand-wise on Wednesday; (2) sleep between the Dobhair (Dodder) and the Duibhlinn, with the head inclining to one side; (3) encamp for nine days on the plains of Cualann; (4) travel the road to Duibhlinn on Monday; and (5) to ride on a dirty, black-heeled horse across Magh Maistean. Magh Maistean, 'the plain of Maistiu', lies east of Mullach Maistean, 'the summit of Maistiu' now the name of a townland in the Co. Kildare parish of Narraghmore, anglicised Mullamast. Maistiu was a mythical maiden, the daughter of Aengus the Firbolg chief who gave his name to Dún Aengus of Inishmore, Aran. She was the embroideress to the great Dedannan chief Aengus of Brugha on the Boyne.

Atop the conspicuous hill of Mullamast is the great fort of Rathmore (An Ráth Mhór, 'the big fort'), which is about two hundred feet in internal diameter. It was here in 1577 that 'a horrible and abominable act of treachery was committed by the English of Leinster and Meath upon that part of the people of Offaly and Leix that remained in confederacy with them, and under their protection. It was effected thus: they were all summoned to shew themselves, with the greatest number they could be able to bring with them, at the great rath of Mullach-Maistean; and on their arrival at that place they were surrounded on every side by four lines of soldiers and cavalry, who proceeded to shoot and slaughter them without mercy, so that not a single individual escaped, by flight or force' (*Annála Ríoghachta Éireann*). Some of the three or four hundred murdered were of the Seven Septs of Laois, together with some gentlemen of the Keatings. One account says that an O'More escaped, but the common tradition of the country was that many more escaped through the advice of one Harry Lalor.

A favourite site for a Norman motte-and-bailey was on a natural gravel ridge or mound (usually an esker), but in several instances there are indications either from early historical references or from finds, that the mottes were built on ancient burial mounds or on other existing earthworks. Burials were found under the motte of Rathmore.

Despite Daniel O'Connell's stated views on Irish rights not being worth the spilling one drop of blood, he issued what subsequently became known as the 'Mallow defiance' in 1843, when he challenged the British government to stride to victory over his dead body. More demonstrations followed, among which were the 'historically resonant' meetings at Tara, seat of the ancient high kings, and Mullamast, the site of the above massacre. At this latter O'Connell offered his 'own heart's stream' for Ireland.

The current Ordnance Survey map shows Daffy Lodge close by Mullamast, and wondering what was the origin of Daffy (excluding the possibility that it was merely a 'fancy' name), we searched the *Index of Townlands* to find that it names neither a townland nor a parish.

(O) Daffy, Ó Deabhthaigh: Woulfe suggests the modern word *deabhthach*, quarrelsome, for its derivation. Essentially a Co. Clare name. Telephone directories of the island list 26 Daffy entries, almost entirely in Co. Clare, and some in adjacent Co. Limerick.

WATERGRANGE

The Civil Survey of 1654 lists Charles Lord Moore as the owner of 60 acres at Gransclare and Grans Inisky, in the Co. Kildare parish of Gransclare. More accurately represented today by Grangeclare, this, according to P.W. Joyce in *The Irish Names of Places*, is the gráinseach of the *clár* or plain. We failed to find the second-named place, though we trawled the *Index of Townlands*, hoping to find some variant spelling. It appeared to be Gráinseach an Uisce, and eventually we found it in translated form as Watergrange. The 1659 Census lists the Moores as among the principal Irish names in one barony each in Cos. Roscommon, Meath, Longford and Kilkenny; in two baronies each in Cos. Down, Waterford, Carlow, Louth; in three baronies in Cos. Antrim, and Derry; in four in Co. Dublin; in five in Co. Kildare, and in six in Co. Laois. On top of that the Moores were tituladoes in Cos. Down, Derry, Limerick, Tipperary, Kildare, Louth, Meath, Roscommon and Sligo, as well as in Dublin City. In 1985 there was an estimate 16,500 Moores in the country, the great majority, outside of the metropolitan area, being in the provinces of Ulster and Munster. 'It is practically impossible', says MacLysaght, 'to say what proportion of these are of Gaelic Irish origin and what proportion of English extraction, for Moore is also indigenous in England and very common there (it is thirty-ninth in their list)'. Indeed, it would be more correct to say Anglo-Norman rather than English, since it was Anglo-Norman Moores who established themselves in Munster after the invasion. These eventually took the Irish form de Móra. The Old Irish Moores are Ó Mórdha (*mórdha*, noble, stately). These were one of the Seven Septs of Laois, and it can be seen above that they were most numerous in Laois in 1659. In 1641, according to H.B.C. Pollard's *The Secret Societies of Ireland*, 'there was then organised among the people an association known as The Defenders, whose ruling spirit was the celebrated insurgent leader, Roger Moore, celebrated in legend as Rory O'Moore.' Well, Roger Moore or Rory O'Moor, was Ruairí Ó Mórdha, a staunch ally of Owen Roe O Neill in the subsequent war.

Transplanted to Connaught in 1654–8 were William Moore, of Barmeath, Co. Louth, who was to get 533 acres in the parishes of Claregalway and Kilkilvery, Co. Galway and Melchior Moore, Cregganstown, Co. Meath who was to get 460 acres in the parish of Ballynacourty, Co. Galway, Col. Garrett Moore, Brees, Co. Mayo was to get 2,993 acres in the parish of Ballintober, and 2,993 at Balla, Crossboyne and Kilcolman, jointly with Richard Burke, in the same county; John Moore, Barmeath, Co. Louth, to share 320 acres in the Co. Mayo parish of Kilcolman.

Owners of Land (1876) shows the Moores to be in every Leinster county except Carlow; in every Munster county except Clare and Kerry; in all of

Connaught's counties except Leitrim and Sligo, and to be in every one of Ulster's nine counties. A high proportion of those in Ulster, however, had very small holdings, the largest being the 8,242 acres of James Stewart Moore, Ballydinnity, Dervock, Co. Antrim. The largest Munster holding was that of Arthur Moore, Mooresfort in Co. Tipperary, who had 10,199 acres; tops in Connaught was the 12,371 acres of George A. Moore, Moore Hall, Ballyglass, Co. Mayo, but the biggest of the lot was the 16,609 acres of the marquis of Drogheda, Moore Abbey, Newbridge, Co. Kildare. On 27 June 1791 Charles Moore was created marquess of Drogheda, earl of Drogheda, Viscount Moore, Baron Moore of Mellifont (Baron Moore in England), his address being Moore Abbey, Co. Kildare.

CALFSTOWN

A certain class of Englishman addresses one of his own class gruffly and impersonally by his surname. When used in Irish, however, it was the title of the chief of his clan, that is, Ó Néill, Ó Dombnall and Mac Murchadha. This was translated to English as The O Neill; The O Donnell; The Mac Murrogh. In 1335 the English, perforce, acknowledged Muiris Mac Murchadha as The Mac Murrough, the lawful chief of the Leinster Irish, and gave him 80 marks annually, on condition that he would not molest the possessions of the English colonists. This man was the descendant of Domhnall, bastard son of Diarmaid Mac Murchadha, Diarmaid na nGall. Diarmaid, having no legitimate male heir, bequeathed his castle and lands, and, as far as he could, his authority over Leinster, to his daughter Aoife, and her husband Strongbow. This was not acceptable to the clans of Leinster, as a female ruler was unknown among the Irish chiefs, and anyway they would not accept a foreigner who had made war upon them and robbed many of them of their possessions. Hence the selection of Diarmaid's bastard son, Domhnall the Handsome.

Diarmaid, the successor of the above Muiris, died in an English prison in 1369 and Art Mac Murrough became king of Leinster, and in time was recognised as The Mac Murrogh. On his death he was succeeded by his son Art, who continued to receive the 80 marks Black Rent. However, when the English confiscated the lands of his Anglo-Irish wife, Elizabeth le Veele, because of her breaching the Statute of Kilkenny by marrying an Irishman, hostilities ensued. The surname le Veele appeared in mediaeval documents soon after the Anglo-Norman invasion and the first of the many recorded in the Ormond Deeds is for the year 1294. Norman in origin, the name is from *le veel*, the calf, and in several documents both le Veele and Calfe are used to denote the same person. The 1659 Census lists Veale among the principal Irish names in the Co. Waterford barony of Decies with Isaak Calfe being a titulado for Kinsale, Co. Cork. Almost all Irish people of the name today belong to Co. Waterford families. Walter le Veele was Bishop of Kildare from 1300 to 1322, and the name had a continued association with that county and the manor of Norragh (An Fhorraach), the disputed land mentioned above. A touch of scandal attended Elene Callfe daughter of Callfe of Mocklone, when, during an examination in 1547 regarding ownership of land at Fynnaghes and Cultrym, it was questioned whether Margaret Leye, daughter of the above Elene, and one of the disputants, was 'mulery' begotten or not.

This surname was not confined to south Leinster. In 1365 Richard Calf was Bishop of Down, and the *Register of Wills and Inventories of the Diocese of Dublin 1457–83* gives the 1472 will of Alice Cassell of Lusk, Co. Dublin, wherein she ordained and constituted John Callf, her lawful husband, and her son Richard Callf executors of her testament or last will.

We have not come across any of the name Calf(e) in any document since that time, and the great majority of those bearing the name Veale today are to be found in Co. Waterford. The name has been gaelicised de Bhial (*de* erroneously replacing *le*), and Tomas de Bhial, who was born in Rinn ó gCuanach, ring in Co. Waterford, was the author of *Gleann an Áir, Tóraithe agus Ropairí*, but probably best-known as the translator of the works of Canon Sheehan and Alice Stopford Green.

Calfstown in the Co. Kildare parish of Mylerstown, is Baile na Chalbaigh in Irish.

FURNACE

'Six oxen, or six horses in summer to a plough, or four in winter, do about half an acre a day' related Arthur Young in his *A Tour in Ireland 1776–79* when writing of his visit to Mr Nevill at Furness Co. Kildare. Nevill had 220 acres and kept 22 horses. 'He is a landlord remarkably attentive to the encouragement of his tenantry,' wrote Young. This English agricultural experimenter and journalist says that he was to have gone to Wexford to call upon Mr Neville MP, to whom he had a letter of recommendation, but found that he was away in England.

Neville is the name of an aristocratic English family, though ultimately French, derived from Neuville, 'new place'. It was used in Ireland for Ó Niadh (*niadh*, champion) in Co. Limerick, and occasionally for Nevin in Co. Clare. Ó Niadh has been anglicised Nee and Knee. The Nevilles of Cos. Kilkenny and Wexford are of English origin. The first of the name to settle in Wexford was

Theodore de Nevel, who held Ballycanew in 1247, and the family's long association with Ballycanew is perpetuated in the townland Nevillescourt. In 1324 Symon Neville, who had married Isabel, daughter of Sir Thomas de Lyvet, lord Rosegarland, Co. Wexford, obtained the knight's fees in Rosegarland, thus beginning the long occupation of that estate by the Nevilles. Richard Neville MP for Wexford town from 1771, he whom Arthur Young was to meet in 1776, died in 1822 'in rather peculiar circumstances'.

The 1659 Census lists Nevill among the principal Irish names in the North Liberties of Cork City, and in the Co. Wexford barony of Bargy. Thomas Nevill was titulado of the High Town ward of Kilkenny City and Liberties, and Richard Nevill was titulado of Maynham, Co. Kildare. The Co. Wexford book of the Civil Survey (1654) shows Walter Nevill on 180 acres at Ambrosetown, and Robert Nevill sharing 15 acres in the parish of Clonmines. The Kildare Nevilles were in Furnace when Taylor and Skinners *Maps* came out in 1778, and the 1814 *Directory* shows R. Neville MP there. Other Nevilles listed herein were at Ballyclamper, Co. Down; Bawnmore, Co. Wexford; Gardenstown, Co. Roscommon, and at Annamult and Marymount, Co. Kilkenny.

None of the Neville holdings listed in *Owners of Land* (1876) exceeds a thousand acres, though there were holdings of 797, 776, 733 and 710 in Cos. Kilkenny, Tipperary and Roscommon. The Co. Wexford holding at Bawnmore was but 164 acres. We are not informed of the location of the 392 Co. Kildare acres, as their owner, Thomas Neville, lived at Tudor Lodge, Kingstown, Co. Dublin.

The place-names Furnance or Furnish, according to P. W. Joyce's *Irish Names of Places*, are a memory of iron-smelting funaces of the Anglo-Normans and English, and sometimes an English translation of Sorn Furnace names a townland in Co. Leitrim, and two each Cos. Galway and Mayo. That of Co. Kildare names neither a parish nor a townland being but the name of a residence in the parish of Forenaughts. Is Furness/Furnace a variant anglicisatin of Forenaughts? Joyce gives Forenaughts as coming from fornocht, 'a bare, naked or exposed hill'.

There are but three Knee entries in the telephone directories (Cork, 2, Kerry, 1) and 110 Nee entries, almost all in Connaught and Donegal. The 4.24 Neville entries are largely in south Leinster and Munster.

Kilkenny

A grant of 1388 reads: 'Henry Lang, chaplain, vicar of Jerpoint, gives and grants to Thomas Seys, chaplain, Robert Kyng, chaplain, John Shorthals and Roger Ragyt all his lands, tenements, ponds and fisheries which he has in Jerpoint and Gowlan (?Gowran). To have and to hold to them and their heirs of the chief lords of those fees for ever' (What heirs did chaplains have?) There was no further mention of a Ragyt in the Ormond Deeds until year 1420, when in a deed of that year Elizabeth Calfe granted Walter Marcos and John Raggyt, chaplains, her manor at Norragh with all its demenses, lordships, rents, services and possessions, together with advowson of churches reversions of dower, suits of court, attendances of free tenants there, and wardships, reliefs, marriages, escheats and all other rights pertaining to the said manor, to have and to hold for ever to them and their heirs and assigns …' Two years later Chaplain Raggyt granted his manor of Norragh to Edmund de la Freyne. In 1430 John Ragit and Richard Hunt, chaplains, were involved in another land transaction, when they made a grant of 30 acres at Castledogh, Co. Kilkenny. This land lay along the bank of the river Nore. The same John Raggyt, chaplain, gave evidence in 1441, when he was fifty years old or more, as to the legitimacy of one Edmund le Freyne, and later that year he quit-claimed land in the borough of Kilkenny. In 1445 John Raghit, though not named a chaplain, was a witness to a grant of land at Caston (?Catstown, Baile na gCat, in the parish of Aghavillerin), the tenement of Tascoffyne, to Richard Boneys and Rosina Fawkiner his wife.

Umfrey Ragyt and Walter his son, paid 2s. 6d. for seven and a half acres, and 2s. 8d. for eight acres at Dunfort in 1443. In 1454 Thomas Raggyt witnessed a grant, and Nicholas Raget is mentioned in 1493. Right up through the decades this family featured in the Ormond Deeds as witnesses and signatories of deeds, indentures, grants of land etc. Sometime before the turn of the 17th century Piers Ragged paid 6s. 8d. for the upper rooms over the castle gate in Kilkenny, and in 1600 Nicholas Ragged, sergeant, was paid 19s. 2d. for work done for the town. The last entry in the Ormond Deeds regarding this family was when Dermod Ragged witnessed an indenture in 1603. In 1571 the earl of Ormond granted Piers Ragged of Walisloghe (Wallslough), serjeant of the said earl, the town or village of Archerstown, Co. Kilkenny with 'all the meases, lands, tenements, etc., thereto belonging, except all conies, pheasants and partridges.'

The Penguin Dictionary of Surnames gives the surname Ragget as meaning 'counsel', or perhaps 'gate for roe-deer', but adds that another gives it as 'ragged, shaggy'. MacLysaght's *Surnames* gives it as deriving from 'le ragged, untidy', adding that it was one of the 'Tribes of Kilkenny'. In 1639 Dr William Petty, when he was doing his Down Survey of Ireland, employed a Dr Ragget, who 'was already conversant with these parts', to undertake the surveying of North Kilkenny and Ormond. Ballyragget castle, built in 1495, with its rounded turrets complete with wishing chair and sunken bawn was, according to legend, the work of Maighréad Ni Ghearóid, the turbulent countess of the Mountgarret family. Before it became Ballyragget, Béal Atha Ragad, 'Ragget's ford-mouth', it was called Tullabarry, from Tulach Ó mBairrch, mound of the Ó Bairrche tribe. This place had been the stronghold of the Raggets as early as 1220. Today three of the five listed in the telephone directories are in Co. Kilkenny.

FRENEYSTOWN

Deriving from the Old-French meaning 'ash tree', and variously rendered de la Freygne, de la Freynge, de Freigne, Freigne, Frenyne and Frene, this surname, repeatedly occurs in every collection of documents relating to Cos. Kilkenny and Tipperary from the year 1302. Eventually it became Frayne and Frain, and in some cases the final 'e' was sounded, making it into the bisyllabic Freney or Freeney. Freeney and Frayne are by far the most common and are largely found in Cos. Wexford, Kilkenny, Waterford and Cork, Mayo and Roscommon. Irish telephone directories list three Frains, two in Roscommon and one in Mayo, and there were but eight Freeneys/Freneys. Fulc de la Freigne was seneschal of Kilkenny in 1302, an office frequently held by members of this family, as was the similar post in Co. Tipperary. Frequent mentions of this surname, in its many and varied spelling, are to be found in the Ormond Deeds, relating to grants, deeds, and indentures. In 1357 Patrick, son of the above Fulc de la Freigne, knight, released and quitclaimed for ever the lands and tenements of 'le Rowyr', Co. Kilkenny. Now the parish of The Rower, the name is the anglicised form of An Robhar, '?reddish land'.

In 1441 Thomas (Barry), bishop of Ossory, was asked to pronounce on the legitimacy of Edmund le Freyn. 'There lately appeared before us in our cathe-

dral church of St Canice Kilkenny, Edmund le Freyn, lawful son of James le
Freyn of happy memory and Elisia Power, who laid a complaint that certain
sons of ambition and iniquity, not having God before their eyes, declare that
same Edmund was born illegitimate and in concubinage, etc.' These were the
le Freyns of Clone in the Co. Kilkenny parish of Rathbeagh. Witnesses to the
marriage which took place some thirty years previously, being not 'moved by
bribe, hate, love or fear and not corrupted or suborned', gave evidence in support of Edmund, and the Bishop so found.

There is but one Frayne in the 1814 *Directory*, this being at Birrmount/
Burrmount, Enniscorthy, Co. Wexford. Two of the family are to be found in
Owners of Land (1876) – the Revd Nicholas Frayne, Common, Newbridge, Co.
Kildare, with 14 acres, and Patrick Freany, Callan, Co. Kilkenny with 19 acres.
(The Barons de Freyne of Frenchpark, Co. Roscommon, wealthy landowners,
bore the surname French).

The form Freney is best-known on account of the exploits of James Freney,
of Co. Waterford, a noted highwayman. His autobiography, written about 1750,
is a remarkable document. William Carleton, the novelist, attended the hedge
school of Pat Frayne at Skelgy : 'A schoolhouse was built for him – a sod house
scooped out of the bank on the roadside – and in the course of a month it was
filled with upwards of a hundred scholars, most of them males, but a good
number of them females'. Skelgy is the spelling found in Dowling's *The Hedge
Schools of Ireland*, where Towney is given as the place where Carleton lived. We
presume that these are Skelgagh and Townagh, townlands in the Co. Tyrone
parish of Clogher.

Freneystown, a townland in the Co. Kilkenny parish of Tiscoffin, is given in
Owen O'Kelly's *Place-Names of County Kilkenny* as Baile na bhFréineach, while
the Co. Wicklow parish name of Freynestown is derived from the family name
of de Freigne, according to Liam Price in his *Place-Names of Co. Wicklow*,
though he does not give an Irish version of the name.

EARLSTOWN

Cailleach means a veiled or celibate woman; *cailleach dhearg* means a red poppy
or corn-rose; *cailleach breac* is a grey seagull, also a dogfish, also the fish Peter-
nine-eyes; *cailleach rua* is the loach, and *cailleach dhubh*, apart from meaning the
cormorant, also menas a nun, especially any order wearing black drapery.
Cailleach is also taken to mean a hag or witch, and though not contained in Ua
Duinnín's *Foclóir Gaeilge agus Béarla, cailleach bhán* is used to mean a 'white
witch'. The famous Biddy Early of Co. Clare, who died on 14 December 1874,

was described as 'a white witch'. It is very likely that Biddy's surname was not the English one, but the Irish Ó Maolmhoicheirghe (now shortened to Ó Mochéirghe), anglicised as Mohery and Mulmoher. O'Donovan's anglicised form in his translation of *Ánnala Ríoghacta Éireann* is O'Mulmoghery, when he records the death of Muircheartach O Maolmhoichéirghe, noble bishop of Ui Briuin-Breifne in 1149; the death of Matha Ó Maolmhoichéirghe in 1226; that of Braon Ó Maolmhoichéirghe, abbot of Kells, Co. Kilkenny, in 1277, and the drowning of Aodh Ó Maolmhoichéirghe, coarb of Dromlane in 1512. As mocheirghe means 'early rising', Ó Maolmhoichéirghe was anglicised as Earley, an English name meaning 'ploughing field', but also possibly 'manly, like an earl'. In Co. Armagh the name became Fields through the mistaken presumption that Moghery was from *machaire*, a plain.

In 1247 Henry de Erlegh owned unspecified land in 'Nova villa (et) in Cullaki'. This latter is believed to be the ancient borough of Coilleach, so called from its woods, according to Eric St John Brooks in his *Knights' Fees in Counties Wexford, Carlow and Kilkenny*, though Owen O'Kelly's *Place-Names of Co. Kilkenny* renders it Cúlach, 'big back-land'. John de Erlaye (de Erley) was listed as owning Nova villa de Erley & Nova Coyllagh in 1317, and in 1355 the heir of John Derley is listed as the owner of Erleyston & Nova Coyllagh. Newtown (Nova villa) of Erley became Newtown Erley, then Erleystown, and now Earlstown (Baile an Earlaigh in Irish), a parish in Co. Kilkenny. The family which gave name to this town in turn took its name from Earley in Berkshire, which manor as well as other property in Somersetshire they held, the latter by service of acting as royal chamberlain. John de Erley, known as the White Knight, who came of age in 1292, served towards the close of the century in the wars in Scotland, and his grandson, also John, was with the Black Prince at the battle of Najera in 1367. Taken prisoner in Spain with the Black Prince, John is said to have had to sell much of his estate to pay his ransom. By 1381 the manor of Earlstown had been conveyed to John Sweetman, the Sweetmans thereby becoming barons of Erley. John Earlev was listed as titula-does of the parish of St Bride in Dublin city in the 1659 Census, and we find a Fras. Eardley at Dolly-villa, near Castledermot in Co. Kildare in the 1814 *Directory*. *Owners of Land* (1876) lists the four acres of John Earley, Dublin, he being the only Earley possessor of land in the whole country.

Spelled Early and Earley in current telephone directories, there are over fifty north and fifty south of the Border, and over eighty in the Dublin area. No anglicised form of Ó Mochéirghe now appears to exist.

DANGANMORE

Mary Comerford (1893–1982) is how Dorothy Macardle in *The Irish Republic* names the Dublin-born woman who was wounded and imprisoned during the Civil War. Though she later changed her first-name to Maire, she never adopted Comartúm, the gaelicised form of her English surname. Neither her wounding nor her imprisonment are very surprising, for she was as brave as she was dedicated. Macardle tells of her riding her bicycle along the bullet-swept streets and quays at the start of the Civil War, keeping communications open between the Four Courts and the headquarters of the Brigade. When the room in the Four Courts which had been turned into a hospital came under heavy fire, Máire was sent out to negotiate about sending the wounded away. She remained a passionate Republican until the day of her death. In 1850 there were Comerfords living in Dublin's Nixon Street, Townsend Street, North King Street, and in Peter's Row, but we cannot say if Máire was descended from any of those. Her lasting memorial is one small but invaluable book, *The First Dáil*, published in Dublin in 1969. The quartermaster of the Kilkenny Brigade during the War of Independence was Eaward Comerford, an Irish teacher.

In Ireland since 1210, the Comerfords have been one of the most distinguished families, especially in Cos. Kilkenny and Waterford. The name is still most numerous in Co. Kilkenny, followed by Co. Tipperary, spreading out to Cos. Waterford, Cork, Wexford, Carlow and Kildare. Listed among the gentlemen of the jury of the shire of Kilkenny in 1637, the head of the family in 1572 was the baron of Danganmore, a Palatine title. An Daingean Mór 'the large stronghold', is a townland in the Co. Kilkenny parish of Dunnamaggan. Junior branches were seated at Ballybur, Callan, Inchibolaghan Castle and Ballymacka. Indeed, Thomas Comerford of Ballymacka in that same year was attainted for his part in resistance to Elizabethan aggression. Waterford, it was said, was famous for its intellectual wealth at the close of the 16th century, and among those who gained that reputation for Waterford were the Comerfords. In 1592 a memorial of sundry things was issued 'commanded by her Majesty to be well considered by the Lord Deputy &c … Through the whole Realm, yea and in the English Pale, there are Jesuits and seminarie Priests … in many places openly maintained in the houses of some noble persons, and in many gentlemen's houses disguised in apparel of servingmen …' Listed among a number of merchants believed to be retaining Sir Morren, priest, was R. Comerford. Another was 'Belle Butler, wife unto T. Comerford of Waterford, merchaunt, who is himself in Spain these 12 months, and one J. Myller, and J. White FitzWilliam, merchaunts, do retain one Sir John White, priest.' The Revd E. Langton, R.C.C., owner of the 'stone house' of Langton in Kilkenny, and F. Langton

Esq., listed as representatives of the Langtons and Comerfords, were descendants of Alderman Langton MP (1562–1632), a gentleman who fathered 12 sons and 13 daughters. As our set of the Ormond Deeds is short Volume 1, we can only say that there are innumerable references to the Comerfords throughout the other five volumes, the earliest being 1411.

Despite their long prominence and noted intellectual wealth, the Comerfords had scant acres in 1876 judging by *Owners of Land*. Nicholas Comerford, Bullockhill, had 196 Co. Kilkenny acres, and in the same county James Comerford, Mooncoin, had 11 acres. John Comerford, Parknakyle had 20 Co. Carlow acres; James Comerford, Rathdrum, 45 acres in Co. Wicklow, and biggest of the lot was Isaac Comerford, Galway with 444 acres there.

BARTONSFARM

The English surname Goslin(g) is named from the fowl so-called, and in Ireland it has been usually located in east Leinster, according to Mac Lysaght's *Surnames*. There are ten Goslins in the Dublin area telephone directory, three in the *Phone Book* of Northern Ireland, and half of the ten Goslings in the South are in Co. Louth. It gave name to the townland of Goslingstown in the Co. Kilkenny parish of Castleinch (this being Ghuais línigh in Irish). One of the two tituladoes of this townland listed in the 1659 Census was George Barton, gent. Other tituladoes were Colonel Barton Esq., Gortecorgan in Co. Fermanagh; Henry Barton, gent., of Bwellynan-arge in the Co. Offaly barony of Aglish; William of Ratoath Co. Meath, and William of Macaross, Co. Monaghan.

The surname Barton is an English toponymic derived from 'barley farm' in Old-English, or in Middle English 'demense farm kept for the lord's use, grange for storing his crop'. Gaelicised de Bartún, this name is in Ireland since the 13th century, but the leading family, mainly identified with Straffan, Co. Kildare, came in 1599. And while none of the name appears on Taylor & Skinner's 1783 *Maps*, the 1814 Directory shows them residing in Cos. Tipperary, Fermanagh; Cork, Leitrim, with four in Co. Kilkenny. *Owners of Land* (1876) shows this family located in three Ulster counties – Fermanagh, Tyrone and Donegal, and in this latter county were the 8,017 acres of Baptist Johnson-Barton Greenfort, Croaghross, Milford, the largest Barton estate in the land. In Co. Fermanagh was the 2,659 acre holding of Edward Barton, Clonelly, Kesh, who had a further 348 acres in Co. Longford. They had holdings in eight Leinster counties, the largest of which was the 5,044 Co. Kildare acres of Hugh L. Barton, Straffan House. Samuel H. Barton, Grove, Fethard, whose 5,119 acres was the largest of three Barton holdings in Co.

Tipperary, was the only Barton to reside therein. When first we leafed through Frances Gerard's *Picturesque Dublin: Old and New* (1898), we were struck by the ninety-one drawings therein by Rose Barton. At first they struck us as black-and-white reproductions of very competent watercolours, but in fact they were grey wash drawings. We wonder where are the originals. Rose (1856–1929) was the daughter of Augustine Barton, a lawyer of Rochestown, Co. Tipperary. In 1874 she travelled with her mother and sister to Brussels, where she received drawing and painting lessons. She exhibited widely during her long professional career and was firmly established in London by 1906 where she settled. Another artist of the name was Mary Georgina Barton who was born in Farrandreg, in the Co. Louth parish of Castletown. Born in the late 19th century or early 20th, she studied in London and Rome and settled in England.

Robert Childers Barton (1881–1975) was reared with his cousin Robert Erskine Childers on the 1,542 acres at Glendalough House. Commissioned in the British Army during the first World War, he had distinguished himself in the eyes of Michael Collins by his kindness to prisoners and their relatives in the aftermath of 1916. He converted to republicanism and was several times imprisoned for his republican activities. He was elected as Sinn Fein representative for Wicklow to the first Dáil, and was first Minister for Agriculture. And though he was a member of the team which negotiated the Treaty, and voted for it in the Dáil, he took the anti-Treaty side in the Civil War. He retired from politics at the end of hostilities to manage his extensive Co. Wicklow estate.

Bartonsfarm, in the Co. Kilkenny parish of Aghavillar, is Feirman Bhartúnagigh in Irish, and Bartonsfarm, a townland in the parish of Aghaviller, is Farm an Bhartúnaigh.

OWNING

Lewis *Topographical Dictionary* (1836) informs that the Co. Kilkenny parish of Owning is also called 'Beaulieu or Bewley'. (The *Index of Townlands*, 1851, lists Bewley as the name of a parish in neighbouring Co. Waterford.) One might reasonably presume that Beaulieu/Bewley is what P.W. Joyce in his *Irish Names of Places* calls 'a fancy name', given by some local landlord to his residence which in turn replaced the original parish or townland name. Not so. A document of 1434 gives Bewley as its alias, and a land grant of 1440 reads: 'Malachius O Fynyne and Anastasia Datoun his wife give and grant to James, Earl of Ormond, his heirs and assigns one acre of land in Villa de Ownyng alias Bewles'. In 1446 Nicholas son of David Hynberye received a grant of land, part of which was 'the manor of Owenyn'. In 1453 there was a transfer of 40 acres in tenemento de Owning called Monerothe (elsewhere rendered Monero and Moynroo) from Robert Daton to his brother Patrick. In 1504 there is a reference to a grant of land from Richar Henebre to Peter Butler, knight, and his wife Margarte Gerot, part of which was Ownynge. *Liostaí Logainmneacha: Chainnigh/Kilkenny* (Brainse Logainmneacha na Suirbhéireachta Ordanáis, 1993) gives Ónainn as the Irish for Owning. This book merely lists the Irish for each name, and we must await the publication of the fuller version to discover their meanings.

The above surname Daton is of Norman origin, being originally d'Auton. It was prominent in Co. Kilkenny from the 13th century. It is now usually made Dalton by assimilation. No all, however. Spelled Daughton, two are listed in the Northern *Phone Book* and there is one each in Cos. Limerick and Cork, with two listed for Co. Kerry. The name Henebry, originally de Hindeberg, also has been continuously in Cos. Kilkenny and Waterford since the 13th century. It has been gaelicized de Hionburgha. Nowadays it is largely spelled Henebry and Heneberry, though also Hennebry, and Henneberry. Judging by telephone directories the name is exclusively in all six Munster counties, largely in Co. Waterford, but also in Co. Kilkenny.

In 1876 Owning , Piltown, Co. Kilkenny, was the location of the 205 acres of Thomas Bowers according to *Owners of Land*. Indeed persons bearing this surname then held no land outside Co. Kilkenny. Thomas Bowers, Mooncoin, possessed 5 acres; Thomas Bowers, Graigavine, had 351 acres, and the 1,568 acres of Maunsell Bowers (minors) was in the hands of the receiver E. Roberts, Waterford. Was the latter name the sameas Mainsell Bower, one of a 1794 committee for the erection of a bridge across the Suir to replace the ferries at Granny and Ferrybank? A witness to the 1804 will of John Blunden, Kilmacoliver, was Maunsell Bowers, Clogga, in the Co. Kilkenny parish of Pollrone, and the widow Bowers was one of the recipients of small bequests in the1796 will of Alexander David Brown, 'late of Townsend Street but then of Ranelagh, Co. Dublin'.

And like Henebry and Daughton, the name Bowers has a long and continuous association with Co. Kilkenny. Thomas Bowers was one of the 1661 poll-money ordinance commissioners for Co. Kilkenny. The 1982 'combined rural' telephone directory lists four of the name still in the Piltown area of Co. Kilkenny – two in Co. Cork and one each in Cos. Waterford, Clare, Meath and Westmeath. These last two show the northwards drift of this surname, and the current *Phone Book* of Northern Ireland has 44 Bowers entries. There are 20 in the Dublin area directory. This name is not listed in MacLysaght's *Surnames*, nor is it in *The Penguin Dictionary of Surnames*. The latter, however, gives Bowers as the plural of Bower or 'of (i.e. at) the Bower'. The surname Bower (which had in one above instance been interchanged with Bowers) means 'dwelling, chamber, woman's room'.

KILBLINE

Local tradition had it that 'the founders of Boran's union were seen as a couple of cross-bred bainins from Clogh and a few half-idiots from Moneenroe'. The union was the Irish Mines and Quarry Workers Union, launched in late 1930 with Nixie Boran as its first chairman. The Kilkenny Miners' Federation, founded in 1908, had been the first stage in the formal unionisation of the Kilkenny mines workforce, though there is no record of their participation in formal negotiations with management. Prior to that the Gazebo Brass Band and Benefit Society, founded in 1881, appears to have been the earliest representative body for miners, but there is no evidence to suggest that it had any formal role in negotiating working conditions. The mines were part of the property that had been inherited by Richard Henry Prior Wandesforde in 1904, though now he was dependent on coal and urban rents, subsequent to the Land Act of 1903, when he was divested of land at his Castlecomer estate. Charles B.C. Wandesforde, Castlecomer, is listed as owning 22,232 acres there in 1876.

Sir Christopher Wandesforde was MP for the years 1692 to 1707, and the family 'attempted to create a stable rural society of miner-farmers by parcelling out part of Moneenroe in regular, freehold plots in the 1770s' (*Kilkenny: History and Society*, edited by William Nolan and Kevin Whelan). Taylor & Skinner's 1778 *Maps* shows the earl of Wandesford at Castlecomer; and the Hon. Charles H. Butler Southwell Wandesforde, Castlecomer, was a deputy lieutenant for Co. Kilkenny in 1836.

In the late 1920s the miners, who had contributed some six thousand pounds in weekly amounts of sixpence for the building of a new Catholic church in Moneenroe, had numerous deductions from their wages for such items as candles, gelignite and detonators, and those of them that had company houses were subject to payment of rent. Nixie Boran's republican socialism had developed from his reading of James Connolly, and from his astute perception of local conditions. 'To counter the threat of parochialism Boran and his associates initiated contacts with the British Communist Party in the late 1920s. The existence of some form of embryonic communist cells in the colleries was highlighted by Boran's attendance at the Red International of Labour Unions in August 1930' (*Kilkenny: History and Society*). Needless to say, this led to increasing concern among the local clergy, and denunciations from the altar. Bishop Collier visited Clogh church in December 1932, when the activities of Boran and his associates were pronounced the work of the devil, and the assembled congregation were called upon to renew their baptisimal vows through renunciation of Satan and all his works and pomps. By early 1933 the Miners' Union had been stamped out, despite a gritty and courageous Boran.

The surname Boran, sometimes spelled Burrane, is from Ó Bodhráin (probably from *bodhar*, deaf) and belongs to east Limerick and west Tipperary and indeed *Griffith's Valuation* (1852–6) shows families in the Tipperary parishes of Clonbulloge, Donohill, Emly, Ballyshehan and Dangandargan. Was William Burran who, in 1364, was paying 2*s.* 6*d.* per annum for his burgage in the vill of Kilbline, in the Co. Kilkenny parish of Tullaherin an Ó Bodhráin? The Irish name from whence Kilbline is *Cill Bhleidhin*.

OSSORY

In a deed of 30 September 1571 'Mary Fitz Gerald of Ballylinch, Co. Kilkenny, widow, was named as "administratrix of the goods and chattels of Oliver Grace, late of the same, Richard Strong of Waterford, merchant, his wife Katherin Walshe, sometime wife of Richard Laules of Kilkenny, and Lettice Courcye of the same, widow, executors of the last will of the said Richard Laules'. What with relations, living and deceased, and same addresses, this would need considerable mental concentration to untangle. Wives appear to have retained their own names. However, it did not seem to have fazed John Bale, late bishop of Ossory, who was witness to the said grant of land. Bale had been appointed to Ossory in 1552, and, unlike many of the leading officials in Ireland who displayed little enthusiasm for the more radical changes of the Reformation promulgated in England, he insisted on preaching in his diocese in accordance with the far-reaching changes laid down by the second Book of Common Prayer. Official reaction among clergy and laity was hostile, though Bale did find some response among Kilkenny townspeople, especially the youth. He was very much involved in the then practice of staging plays in churches, somewhat akin to the introduction of modern song, dance and mime in many Roman Catholic churches in the past twenty years, and perhaps this might have been the reason for his poularity among the youth. According to O'Grady, *Stafford and Ireland* (1923) these plays were quite a feature of the period, comic as well as sacred being associated with the Church. Dr Jones, the bishop of Meath, fell into grave disgrace for attending a comedy, one Sunday afternoon in the church, where actors, dressed in women's caps, 'challenged to themselves the names of Her Majesty's Commissioners', 'rising up and making courtesies', and 'going in a disguised sort of way through the streets, crying "room for Her Majesty's Commission"', to the horror of all loyal subjects, and the delight of the ribald'.

In 1559 a letter from Queen Elizabeth referred to the books and writings of John Bale, late bishop of Ossory, 'a man that hath byn studious in serche for the history and antiquities of this our realme' which he had left behind him 'in the tyme of our late sister Quene Mary when he was occasioned to departe out of Ireland ...'

Thomas Bale, gent., titulado for Copper Alley in Dublin City, was the only one of that name in the 1659 Census, and current telephone directories show Ireland's half dozen or so Bales in the city of Dublin, with one person named Bales listed in Northern Ireland's *Phone Book*. Basil Cottle's *Penguin Dictionary of Surnames* gives Bale(s) as a variant of Bail, meaning 'outer court of a castle', from residence/authority therein, but MacLysaght's *Surnames* does not list it.

Ossory originally stretched from the Slieve Bloom Mountains to the sea, and from the river Barrow to Magh Feimhin, with the Roman Catholic diocese of Ossory now including most of Co. Kilkenny, and portions of Cos. Laois and Offaly. The Irish of this name is Osraí, and Ossory Hill is Cnoc Osraí.

POLLRONE

On 10 June 1355 at Waterford an 'indenture witnessing that on Wednesday in the vigil of St Barnabas in the 29th year of Edward III, it was agreed between Stephen Marreis, knight, of the one part, and John son of David Meiller of the other that Stephen has granted to John half the manor of Polrohan which David Meiller, John's father, formerly held for his life by enfeoffment from Richard de Rocheford (excepting 30 acres of arable land lying in the said manor), until John shall be paid by Stephen his heirs or attorneys 29 marks in silver or gold in one day or in various terms at the will of the said Stephen. And when the said sum has been fully paid, then John his heirs, assigns shall return to Stephen and his heirs the half manor of Polrohan.' This we presume to be the now-spelled Pollrone, of which there are two – both in Co. Kilkenny, one in the parish of the same name, and the other in the parish of Tullahought, in the vicinity of Carrick-on-Suir. Poll Ruáin, 'Ruan's hole', is the origin of this name It is this latter that we think was in question, as it was in this area that we find subsequent references to the Meiller/Mayler/Meyler/Meiler family. (Mac)Meyler, a Welsh name found in Ireland since 1200, has been gaelicised as Maoilir and Mac Maoilir.

One of the witnesses at a hearing at Ardclone on 25 November 1352 regarding land at Rathgulleby (?) was Maurice Meyler, and we believe that Meyler lived in the vicinity of this townland in the Co. Kilkenny parish of Fiddown. And what is 'Frisca Forcia'? It is 'recent ejectment', and in June 1376 an assize was held at New Ross to decide whether Matthew Shirwode and Isabella his wife 'unjustly by frisca forcia disseised Christiana Arlonde of her free tenement there, namely one garden with appurtances'. One of the twelve jurors there was John Meiler. At a court held at Crumpstown in September–October 1417 John Meyler of Balliclerchan was one of eight charged with debt or trespass. This we take to be Ballyclerahan in the vicinity of Clonmel, Co. Tipperary. In 1430 Schane Meiller is listed – with others – regarding tenure at Listerlin, in the Co. Kilkenny parish of the same name and in the vicinity of Carrick-on-Suir. In a petition to the Queen in 1570 Walter Meyler prayed to surrender his manor of Pryst's Town, as he is too poor to defend it against 'the savage nation of the Kavanaghs, and to have reversion of the rectory of Downcormouke'.

In the Co. Wexford barony of Shelmaliere in 1640, according to the Civil Survey, Richard Meyler, The Dirr, had 180 acres, and Nicholas Meyler had a share in 60 acres and 800 acres in the parish of Tagmon. Nicholas Meyler (we know not if he is he same one) owned 400 acres at Old Ross and Nicholas Meyler (!) owned 160 acres a Duncormuck. All were Irish papists. The 1659 Census lists the Meylers among the principal Irish names in the Co. Wexford baronies of Forth and Bargy.

The *Book of Survey and Distribution* for Co. Mayo showing landowners for *c.*1640 lists three MacMoylers in the barony of Murrisk; one in the barony of Clanmorris, and six in the barony of Kilmaine. The largest property here was the 95 acres of Thomas McMoyler, Knockmullengee, in the parish of Kilmolara. Knockmullengee? The hill of the windmill?

The *c.*thirty Meylers in the 1982 combined country telephone directory were almost exclusively in Co. Wexford, and the six MacMylers were in Co. Mayo.

THE GARRANS

Though of no particular importance or eminence, we know the precise whereabouts of James Purcell's three sons, Philip, Robert and Redmond on the night of 25 January 1542. At the request and instance of their father, James Purcell, gentleman, of the Garrans in the county of Kilkenny, evidence was taken before Miles, bishop of Ossory, and Master Richard Clinton, doctor of divinity, to determine their whereabouts on that night. There would appear to have been some suspicion that the three Purcells, or their servants, had something to do with a fire at St Mullins, Co. Carlow that night! Though he was one of the examiners, Master Richard Clinton nevertheless gave evidence and swore 'uppon the Holy Ewangelist' that he had been that night in the Garrans with the father and three sons. Sir John Fynnelle, a chaplin, also swore that he was at the Garrans, and that the said Philip, Robert and Redmond were present with him from the beginning of the night until the morning after. 'And he further deposith that the said iii sonnes at that tyme there was ii of them, Redmonde and Robert lay in one bed in the grete house in said Garrans, and Phillip lay yn abede in the cheambr of the said house with othr gromes.' James Derre, porter to James Purcell in the Garrans, 'deposith that he did nott lett none of the said iii sonnes the said nygth oute ower the gate of said Garrans; the cause why he hade the key of gate in his custody the said nygth as he was accustomide to hawe'.

The whereabouts of two of James Purcell's grooms was also investigated, and Sawe Ynywoe, widow, said that the grooms were lodged that night in her house 'till it was day uppon the morrowe'. She said that she saw the fire but thought that it was at Brownystowne, 'land all thie while thie said gromes lay within in one bed'. Among the other supporting witnesses was Jowane Ynywryne, who claimed that the two grooms were in said Sawe Ynywoeis house. In another deposition, to consider the whereabouts of Derby Keally, 'Gillpatrick Odolyng deposith that the said Derbyis wiff, gossope to said Patrick, was sore seke that nygth, and that his wife More Ynywryne was to and fro hir, and when the deponent hard the crye of the warnyng the fire, he thought it was the woman was dede, and went out of his doores – for his house was bye the said Derbis house – and when he entryd into the house he sawe said Derby sitting by the fire in his owne howse the said tyme and nygth.' More Ynywryne? More Yn Y Wryne? Mór Iníon Uí Riain? Sawe Ynywoe. Sawe Yn Y Woe? Another witness was Ande Ynywridane. Ande Yn Y Wridane?

Purcell Puirséil (French, *pourcel*, little pig). This Anglo-Norman family is one of those which became completely hibernicised. They distinguished themselves in the wars of the 17th century and later a branch went to Cork. The name is found mostly in Cos. Tipperary and Kilkenny.

The Garrans, Na Garráin, 'the groves', must have been reasonably close to the river Barrow on the east of Co. Kilkenny where it borders Co. Carlow, to be able to see the fire at St Mullins across the river. No such place now exists as a townland or parish name.

Laois

BALLYADAMS

Killing a person who was 'escaping under the suspicion of a felony' was an acceptable excuse in 1596 to acquit and pardon the perpetrator. Pardoned in that year was 'Rob. Boheme alias Rob. Bowen, sen., of Balliadams, Queen's co., gent.) for the murder and homicide of Rich. Stanton (late of Moylerstown, Co. Kildare, gent. He was said to have 'procured and incited John Bohene or Boheme, Tho. Maris or Marice, and Luke Wafer, of Ballyadams, gentlemen, to murder Stanton, whom they attacked and mortally wounded at Ballybeg, Co. Kildare. Stanton had since been proven to have taken arms with the rebels in Mayo, and at the time he met his death was escaping under suspicion of a felon.' (A Francis Wafer of Adamstown was listed in the Co. Wexford Civil Survey as owning land in Adamstown in 1641). More than a hundred years later a descendant, John Bowen, was known as 'John the Pike' for his zeal in piking the Irish. This man had erected 'a very pretentious monument' in the church at Ballyadams which had been built by his father at the end of the 17th century.

The surname Bowen is used as a synonym of the Irish Bohane, but the first of the name to settle in Laois was a Welsh soldier, John ap-Thomas ap-Owen (Bowen). He was constable of the castle of Ballyadams in November 1549, and a year later he obtained a lease for 21 years of 'Ballytobrid, Ballytarse alias Cronagh, Ballynlegerrot, Ikalle and Dirrentwo'. Canon John O'Hanlon in his *History of Queen's County* writes that he believed that this man, who died in 1569, was the one styled by the Irish as Shawn-a-Ficha – Sean an Phíce, 'John the Pike'. However, in another place in his book O'Hanlon says that it was Sir John Bowan, he who kept possession of the country during the insurrection of 1641, that was known as Sean an Phíce. In July 1578 Robert Bowen surrendered Ballyadame, Rathgilbert, Aghetobride, Ballentobride, Monascerbane, Derrearowe, Crenaghe, Balleatrsne, Kyllganer, Donbrenne, Ballyentle Kylmohide, and Farraghmore, in order to obtain a new grant thereof.

The 1659 Census lists Stephen Bowen as tituladoes of the Co. Laois townland of Killeshin; and the tituladoes for the parish of Ballyadams were George Bowen, William Bowen and Lady Ellis Bowen, while William was a 1660 commissioner for the poll-money ordinance for Co. Laois. Matthew

Bowen was titulado of Castlegrace in the Co. Tipperary parish of Tullaghorton. Jumping forward more than two hundred years we find the Bowens owning land in four Leinster counties; in four Munster counties, three in Ulster, and only in Mayo in Connaught. The largest Bowen landowner as listed in *Owners of Land* (1876) was Robert Cole Bowen, Bowen's Court, Kildorrery, Co. Cork, where he had 1,680 acres, and a further 5,060 in Co. Tipperary. The only one of the name owning land in Laois was Captain Charles H. Bowen, Kilnacourt, Portarlington, and 13 Longford Terrace, Monkstown, Dublin, the possessor of 1,420 acres. The only living descendant of the Bowens of Ballyadams known to O'Hanlon in 1907, was the Honble. and Revd William Bowen, eldest son of Charles Lord Bowen, who was descended from Thomas Bowen of Liskellin, Co. Mayo. In 1876 the Revd Christopher Bowen, Isle of Wight, owned 621 acres in Co. Mayo, and Francis C. Bowen, Hollymount, was the owner of 181 acres.

Ballyadams names a townland in Co. Kildare, Co. Meath, and two in Co. Laois. One of the latter is in the parish of Ballyadams (Baile Ádams), in the barony of Ballyadams. The barony of Ballyadams comprised the greater part of the ancient territory of Críoch Ó Muighe. There are 27 Bowens listed in the *Phone Book* of Northern Ireland; 34 in the Dublin area, but with 35 Bowens in Co. Cork.

BALLYDERMOT

In 1645, quelling mutinies and travelling around forty miles for that purpose seemed to be all in a day's work for an army officer. While stationed at Castlelyons, some few miles south of Fermoy in Co. Cork, Lord Broghill took a detachment of his troops to Youghal to supress a mutiny (we know not what road he travelled), did his suppressing, and was back at Castlelyons the following day. No doubt he might rightly have felt that he deserved some rest after such exersions, but on his return he found Colonels Ridgeway and Bannister, whom he had left the charge of the troops, so drunk, that he was amazed at it...' (Smith's *History of Cork*). No doubt one might consider oneself fortunate to be visited by a lord's amazement rather than his anger. Perhaps his anger was defused because it happened 'by the artifice of an Irish sutler, who brought to the camp a cask of ale made of ryley, a grain which produces that intoxicating quality'. The earliest use of the verb 'rile', an American and dialectic variant of 'roil', was 1590, being defined as 'to render (water or any liquid) turbid or muddy by stirring up the sediment'. Of course, it is still used in its other meaning, 'to disturb in temper; to vex, irritate, make angry'. In an ensuing battle Broghill's soldiers were twelve hours involved in marching, drawing up or fighting. Smith says that Ridgeway, though drunk, killed nine that day with his own hand. One would have thought that twelve hours of work might have had some sobering effect on the colonel.

The surname Ridgeway is derived from the name of a place, meaning 'ridge road', and the first of the name to come to Ireland was Sir Thomas Ridgeway (d. 1631), later the first earl of Londonderry, who came of an old Devonshire family. The Council of Ireland formed in 1606 included 'Thomas Ridgwae Knight of Warrs'. He took a very active part in the plantation of Ulster, obtaining for himself 2,000 acres in Co. Tyrone, while a relative of his acquired a large estate in Co. Cavan. In 1615 the Irish House of Commons considered the case of Mr Paul Sherlock, who had offered to bribe the chancellor; and Lord Mountmorres in his *History of the Principal Transactions of the Irish Parliament from 1634 to 1666* comments: 'This circumstance must bring to recollection, the memorable instance of corruption in England about this period…' That same day Sir Thomas Ridgeway was appointed vice-treasurer of the commissioners from the House 'charged with the affairs of the comonwealth, before the king and the English privy council'. A nephew of Sir Thomas was Captain John Ridgeway, who was very prominent in opposition to the 1641 insurgents. As an Ulster family the Ridgeways died out, but a younger branch settled in Laois in the 17th century, and two of the name were tituladoes for Kilkenny city in the 1659 Census.

Owners of Land (1876) lists Henry Ridgeway, Newtown, Co. Waterford with 48 acres in Co. Kilkenny; while in Co. Offaly Henry W. Ridgeway, Bristol, had 627 acres; Thomas Ridgeway, Geashill, had 438 acres, and John Ridgeway, Ballydermot, in the parish of Clonsast, had 1,684 acres. Ballydermot also names townlands in Cos. Donegal. Wexford and Derry, and Ballydermody in Co. Tipperary is officially Baile Dhiarmada. The Dublin area telephone directory lists 22 of the name Ridgeway; there are four in Northern Ireland and of the eleven in four counties in the remainder of the country, there are four each in Cos. Cork and Laois. Sir William Ridgeway (1852–1926) was an archaeologist and scholar, and William Ridgeway LLD (1765–1817)was the author of *State Trials in Ireland*.

ABBEYLEIX

On the basis that it is a male personal name, it is accurate to say that Laoiseach means 'man of Laois', though as Muimhneach might mean either a female or a male of Munster, so might Laoiseach also be a male or a female of Laois. Though we have a personal dislike for the anglicisations, as regards Ultonians and Connachtians, for Ultach and Connachtach, at least it can be said in their favour that they are not sexist. Rather crudely anglicised as Lucius, Lewis and Louis, Laoiseach was a favourite among the O Mores of Laois, and also occurs among the O Farrells. Laoiseach Canvore (*ceann mhór*, big head), son of Conall Cearnach, chief of An Craobh Rua, the Red Branch Knights, was granted land in north Leinster for his assistance in expelling the Munstermen who had settled in that province. Thus the area took the name Laois from Laoiseach. O More/Moore is the anglicised form of Ó Mordha (*mordha*, majestic), the name of one of the 'Seven Septs of Laois', a people who descended from Laoiseach. This area was designated Queen's County by an Act of Parliament in 1556 and writing in 1873 in the first volume of *Names of Places*, P.W. Joyce says: 'The name of this principality has altogether disappeared from modern maps, except so far as it is preserved in that of the town of Abbeyleix ...'. He could not have anticipated the achieving of independence and the old name of Laois replacing that of Queen's County. As indeed in the replacing of Maryborough by the much-mispronounced Port Laoise (three syllables, please!).

Abbeylix is from Mainistir Laoise, 'the abbey of the territory of Laois', a name that came from the monastery founded there in 1183 by Conor O Moore. The abbey, with twenty acres of arable land, was granted to Thomas, earl of Thomond in 1562, for thirty-seven years. The holding, subsequently increased to 820 acres, was afterwards assigned to Sir John Vesey, ancestor of the family which derived the title Lord De Vesci. Arthur Young in his *A Tour of Ireland, 1776–1779* tells of passing within sight of Lord De Vescey's plantation in 1777, and in the second volume of *Queen's County* (edited by the Revds E.O. Leary and M. Lalor), published in 1914, we read of Lord De Vesci's fine modern mansion, a replacement, we presume, of the mansion of Abbeyleix House, the seat of Viscount De Vesci, which was built in 1774: 'The modern town called at first New Abbeyleix, to distinguish it from the former collection of thatched houses, was laid out by Lord De Vesci, after the middle of the eighteenth century. Since that time, old Abbeyleix – a little distance from it and towards the south-west – was levelled, and it has fallen into decay'.

MacLysaght's *Surnames* does not list the surname De Vesci, nor is it in any of his other books on surnames. Taylor and Skinner's *Maps* (1783) shows Lord Viscount De Vesci at Bray, south-east of Athy, as well as being at Abbeyleix, but the 1814 *Directory* has the viscount only at Abbeyleix House; as indeed had the *Telephone Directory* of 1991–92; he now resides at Knapton Cottage, Abbeyleix.

'It seemed incredible', wrote Fynes Moryson in 1600, 'that by so barbarous inhabitants, (as the people of Leix) the ground should be so manured, the fields so orderly fenced, the Townes so frequently inhabited and the high waies and paths so well beaten as the Lord Deputy here found them – the reason whereof was that the Queene's forces during these warres never till then came among them.'

DYSART ENOS

John Edward Pigot (1822–71) is described in *A Dictionary of Irish History 1800–1980* (editors, Hickey and Doherty), as 'Young Irelander and poet', whereas in the same book Richard Pigott (1828–89) is given as 'journalist and informer'. Of the latter, born in Co. Meath, we read: 'A supporter of nationalist causes for a period, he was imprisoned for sedition. Pigott had a poor reputation and was at various times a pornographer and a blackmailer'. He is best remembered for the forged letters, supposedly written by Parnell, ostensibly supporting the 'Phoenix Park murders'. John Edward Pigot, born in Kilworth, Co. Cork, using the pen-name 'Fermoy', contributed articles to *The Nation* and *The Spirit of the Nation*: he was a member of Young Ireland and the Repeal Association and was active in the Irish Confederation. He was joint honorary secretary of the Society for the Preservation of the Melodies of Ireland (1851). 'In this capacity he travelled throughout the country collecting old Irish airs and tunes which were used by George Petrie and Patrick W. Joyce in their published collections. Pigot's manuscripts in the Royal Irish Academy include some 2,000 tunes'. Interestingly, Kilworth was also the birthplace of another collector of Irish songs, Liam de Noraidh (1888–1972).

Spelled Pigot, Pigott, Piggott and Piggot, and nowadays largely the latter, this surname is 'well-known in Ireland since the 16th century, where it has been located in many parts of the country, and has been conspicuous on both sides in the centuries-long struggle between Ireland and England' (MacLysaght's *Surnames*). We are informed that the Co. Cork Pigots were originally Becket. In the year 1577 Robert Pigot obtained an extensive grant of lands in the Co. Laois parishes of Dysart Enos and Kilteal, and in 1606 by patent of Queen Elizabeth, Sir Robert Pigott of Dysart, was additionally granted the 'rectory of Kilcolmanbane together with all its churches, chapels etc.' Among the commissioners of the 1660 and 1661 poll-money ordinances, the Piggots were also listed as tituladoes in the town of Kinsale, in Cos. Kilkenny and Cork, with three in Co. Laois. Herein the name was among the principal Irish names in the barony of Maryborough. The 1814 *Directory* lists Piggots at Camira and Capard in the Co. Laois parish of Rosenallis, and Slevoy Castle, in the Co. Wexford parish of Taghmon. Now rendered Dysartenos, it is from Dísert Aenghusa, the hermitage of Aenghus. This was Aenghus the Culdee (Céile Dé), author of the celebrated *Féilire Aenghusa*.

The Pigotts were still strong in Co. Laois in 1876 according to *Owners of Land*. Robert A.R. Pigott, Capard, Rosenallis, possessed 4,932 acres there, while H.A. Robert Piggot of the same address had 3,477 acres in Co. Limerick. In the same county Lady J. Piggot, Leixlip, had 505 acres, and William Piggot, Ryevale, Leixlip, had 364 acres, with a further 262 in Co. Offaly and 32 at Ryevale.

William Piggot, St Catherine's, Leixlip, had 393 Co. Cork acres, and there was another holding there of 483 acres. This family had land in seven Leinster counties, the other sustantial holding there was that of the Piggots of Slevoy Castle, Taghmon,who had over 1,600 acres in Co. Wexford and 626 in Co. Cork. Piggots of Oakpark, Portumna, owned almost 600 Co. Cork acres.

During Lord Macartney's governorship of Grenada, one Mr Arthur Pigott sought the appointment of Attorney-General of Tobago but Macartney wrote to warn the secretary of state, stating that Mr Pigott was 'a very troublesome, contentious man, and extremely improper for any appointment under the crown'. Today the name is largely spelled Pigott, and the telephone directories of the island list 42 in the North, and 46 in the South. Of these there are 16 in the Dublin area; otherwise the greatest concentration is the Cork/Limerick area.

WOODBROOK

Though in his pastoral letter of 1831 he acknowledged rack-rents, ejection from lands and houses, as well as unemployment, Dr Doyle, bishop of the diocese of Leighlin, aimed his principal remarks against the 'deluded persons illegally combined under the unmeaningful appellation of "Black feet" and "White feet". The most active and prominent among you are old offenders, thieves, liars, drunkards, fornicators, quarrellors, blasphemers ... God has ordered us to honour the King, and obey those who are sent by him. Let us be Christians, not in name, but in fact, and give honour and obedience to those whom Providence has sent to rule over us.' Among those rulers 'sent by Providence' were the county magistrates and grand jurors. In the years 1831 and 1832 in Queen's County these gentlemen bore surnames such as Staples, Poole, Adair, Despard, Johnson, Stubber, Cosby, Osbourne, Blackney, Manning, Kemmis, Sandys, Trench, Ansell, Binning, Wray, Scott, Thacker, Jervais, Cote, Pigott, Vicars, Hampton, Chetwood and Wilmot. In 1784 Robert Roger Wilmot married Elizabeth Hester Chetwode of Woodbrook, Portarlington, in the county which has since reverted to its original name of Laois. Taylor and Skinner's *Maps* (1783) shows Woodbrook as the residence of 'Chetwood, Esq.,' and the 1814 *Directory* has Jonathan Chetwood there. In 1836 Jonathan Chetwood, Woodbrook, was listed among the magistrates for Queen's County. However, Woodbrook was listed as a Wilmot residence for the years 1831 and 1832.

In 1708 Knightley Chetwood was among the Queen's County magistrates, and in 1753 Valentine Knightley Chetwood was listed in the same capacity. Jonathan Cope Chetwood was among the grand jurors of 1810 and 1820 for that county, while Edward Wilmot Chetwood held a similar position for the years 1840 and 1850. *Owners of Land* (1876) shows Knightley Chetwode, Woodbrook, as owner of 1,389 acres in Co. Laois, and 464 acres in Co. Limerick. The rather strange first-name and the variant spelling of the surname goes back to 1601 when Anne Knightley married Sir Richard Chetwoode.

In 1746 Chetwood's *Tour through Ireland* was published, and in 1828 Eustace Chetwood, the British grand secretary of the Orange Order, visited Ireland, giving 'the signs and passwords to the Irish Orangemen'. And though the resident of Woodbrook in 1832 is given as Edward Wilmot in O'Hanlon's *History of the Queen's County*, the index thereof lists him as E. Wilmot Chetwode. This gentleman was involved in the successful wresting of the borough of Portarlington from the Dawson family influence in the election of 1832. The successful Liberal candidate was Thomas Gladstone, eldest brother of the future prime minister, W.E. Gladstone. A pamphlet addressed to the Free Voters asked if they were to vote for the family which 'had extinguished their Municipal Rights and embezzled their Corporate Property', and continue under the tyranny of those 'who, not content with peculating your undoubted property, have been in the habit of bartering with Jews, and Enemies to your Liberties …'.

In Basil Cottle's *Dictionary of Surnames* we read: 'Chetwood. Chetwode L[ocative] 'wood wood' British + OE, tautologically; place in Bucks.' Presumably the 'wood' in the name of the Brookwood residence was coincidental. Woodbrook names townlands in Cos. Galway, Roscommon, Tyrone and Wexford, so we presume that that of the Chetwood's residence must have been 'a fancy name' imposed by that family. Sir John Bentjeman's wife was an Irishwoman, Penelope Chetwood. There is none of the name in any of this island's telephone current directories.

LOUGHMANSLAND GLEBE

If the ordinary rules were adhered to, the surname Loughman would be pronunced 'Lockman'. But it is not. Nor does it follow the pronunciations of 'bough', 'cough', 'dough' and 'rough', which would render it 'Bowman', 'Coffman', 'Doeman', or 'Ruffman'. We considered this when we started to look at the surname Loughman. We do not know how it is pronounced elsewhere in the country, but in Co. Tipperary it is pronounced not following any of the above samples – but as if spelled 'Lukeman'. It is, however, exclusively spelled Loughman in the island's telephone directories, nor have we come across any instance of its being spelled Lukeman. The Dublin area telephone directory lists 26 Loughmans; there is but one in the *Phone Book* of Northern Ireland, with 30 in the remainder of the country. The furthest north are two in Co. Monaghan, with the remainder in Cos. Carlow, Laois, Kilkenny, Galway, Westmeath, Cork, Limerick, Tipperary and Kildare. It is in the latter two counties that this name is most numerous.

There is an English surname Lukeman, a rare form of Luckman ,'Luke's Servant', but of Loughman Edward MacLysaght in his *Surnames* says: 'While I have not got quite conclusive evidence I have little doubt that this name is a corruption of Loughnan, which was the anglicised form of Ó Lachtnáin in Kilkenny and adjacent counties in the sixteenth century, as we know from the Ormond Deeds.'

A 1564 fiant of Elizabeth I lists the pardon of John Mothell, of Kilkenny, merchant, especially for the death of Margaret inny Loughman (Iníon Uí Lachtnáin); a fiant of 1574 numbers John Loghnan among a large number of pardoned persons; among another group of the pardoned in 1585 in Cos. Tipperary and Limerick was Nicholas Loghnane, and a 1601 fiant includes Joan ny Loghmane of Ballinowe, Co. Kilkenny, among the pardoned.

The 1654 Civil Survey of Kilkenny City shows Nicholas Loghman as sharing a house on the north side of the Dominican abbey, built upon the town wall behind Deans Gate. The house was divided into two, one portion having stone walls and a slate roof. There were five rooms in this part and two in the other. The 1659 Census lists Loghman among the principal Irish names of Kilkenny City, and of the Co. Laois barony of Ossory; Loughnan of the barony of Shelburne in Co. Wexford; Loghnane in the barony of Middlethird in Co. Tipperary, and O Loghnan in the barony of Athlone in Co. Roscommon.

Though Loughman is nowhere to be found in *Owners of Land* (1876), some of the listed Loughnans may have been Loughmans. They had modest enough holdings in Cos. Dublin (13 acres); Kilkenny (10; 63; 216; and 274); in Kilkenny City (4 and 13); in Cos. Offaly (18 and 18 at Dromakeenan); Kerry (204), and Roscommon 189 acres.

Ó Lachtnáin (*lachtna*, grey), anglicised (O) Loughnane, names several small Connaught septs. In Meath, where it may be classed as Oriel, it has been changed to O'Loughlin, thus hiding the identity of an old family there. Similarly it is disguised as Lawton in Co. Cork.

Loughmansland Glebe is the name of a townland in the Co. Laois parish of Lea; the name derives from Mánsa Lé (manse-land of [the parish of] Lea).

DURROW

A Belfast visitor to the Kerry Gaeltacht, wishing to send a postcard, and not having the wherewith to inscribe it, went into a shop and enquired 'An bhfuil peann agat?' (Have you got a pen?). In Ulster *peann* is pronounced 'pan', and the girl in the shop asked our Belfastman if it was a frying-pan he required! People in the south of this island know that 'pen' was — and indeed still is betimes — pronounced 'pin'. We wonder was it some scribe from the south of the country that drew up the 1792 will of Mark Flower, Church Street, Dublin, when he gave his occupation as a 'Penmaker'. The 1836 *Dublin Almanac* lists Mark Flower, 176 & 177 Church Street, as a 'pin manufacturer'.

One of the Protestant dissenters, 'called Quakers', who in 1695 'was admitted etc., upon grace especiall, and for the fine of three pounds, sterling, paid to the treasurer of the citty for the use of the citty, and haveing subscribed the said declaration', with a payment of 12*d*. per annum, was Henry Flower, weaver. This man's will, dated 24 December 1700, describes him as 'clothier'. The inventory of his belongings lists ratteen, camblet, corleroy, tammy and druggett — materials of different sorts and mixtures. Camlet was originally a costly eastern fabric but subsequently named various combinations of wool, silk, hair and latterly cotton or linen. Originally Drugget(t) named a kind of stuff, all of wool, or half wool, half silk or linen, used for wearing apparel.

When Sir George Carew was appointed lord president of Munster in 1600, the sergeant-major of that province was one George Flower. *Pacata Hibernia*, listing the garrisons at Dunkerron, Kinsale, Baltimore and Bantry, says: 'Great were the services which these garrisons performed, for Sir Richard Percy and Captain George Flower, with their troops, left neither corn, nor horn, nor house unburnt between Kinsale and Ross'. *Description of Ireland anno 1598* informs that Sir George Flower, a distinguished Elizabethan officer, appeared to have settled in Kilkenny. The 1659 Census lists Col. Henry Flower as titulado of the Dublin parish of St Michan's, and John Flower, gent., titulado of Haystown, Co. Dublin. William Flower was a 1661 commissioner for the poll money ordinance for Co. Kilkenny, while at the same time Peter Flowre was comissioner for Co. Carlow. Also a 1661 commissioner was Sir William Flowre, for both Cos. Laois and Kilkenny. William Flower of Durrow was a Tory MP from 1715 until 1727. Henry Jeffrey Flower, Baron Castle-Durrow, was created Viscount Ashbrook in 1751. In his *A Tour of Ireland 1776–79*, Englishman Arthur Young was in the Durrow area in October 1777: 'Enter a fine planted country, with much corn and good triving quick hedges for many miles. The road leads through a large wood, which joins Lord Ashbrook's plantations, whose house is situated in the midst of more wood than almost any one I have seen in Ireland'. Indeed, the name Durrow tells of trees. Naming townlands in Cos. Galway, Waterford, Offaly, and Laois, the official Irish for the latter is Daru. This is the modern rendering of the original which consisted of *Dair* and *magh*, 'the plain of the oaks'.

Owners of Land (1876) shows a John Flower, England, having 844 acres in Co. Tipperary, and Lord Ashbrook, The Castle, Durrow, with 4,515 acres.

Flower is listed seven times in the Dublin area telephone directory, with two in the *Phone Book* of Northern Ireland, and one each in Cos.Westmeath and Longford.

The surname Flower might derive from the occupation of 'arrow-maker', but also might indicate 'fragrance/delicacy/smooth skin' – or the occupation of maker of flour, as flower and flour were once the same word.

LACKA

One might reasonably have presumed that it was some time after the publication of his *Unconquerable Ulster* in 1, with its foreword by Sir Edward Carson MP, that Herbert Moore Pim ceased being a Unionist and joined the Republican ranks. Not so, as this man, along with Denis MacCullough and Ernest Blythe had, as Volunteer officers and instructors, being served with expulsion orders in July 1915. Having ignored these and remained on in the country, they were arrested and were sentenced to terms of imprisonment. Pim, a Protestant, was born in Ulster in 1883 and died on some unknown date after the publication of his last book *New Poems* in 1927. He was already the author of two novels and other works.

In September 1919 a Sinn Féin gathering at Enniskillen, Co. Fermanagh was addressed by another Protestant Republican, Enniskillen-born George Irvine, who had just been reprieved from a death sentence. A monster rally was planned for the following month, to be addressed by Arthur Griffith, founder of Sinn Fein, Eoin MacNeill, co-founder of the Gaelic League, Darrell Figgis, and Herbert Pim. The police banned the proceedings, which were to have been held in the County Hall and, when they were then switched to the Gaelic Field, the police blocked the West Bridge. Undeterred, the speakers made their way to the field by boat.

The surname Pim, prominent in Quaker records, came to Ireland in the mid-17th century, and has been identified with Cos. Laois and Dublin. The first Quakers came to Rosenallis, Co. Laois, three years after their arrival in Ireland in 1656. These were the Jacksons, Moons, Thompsons and Pims, led by the father of the Irish Quaker movement, William Edmundson. The Pims had a breast-shot rape mill at Fancourt and another at Lacka, in the parish of Offerlane. And at Rushin in the same parish Jonathan Pim built a tollhouse. The *Directory* for 1814 lists a Jonathan Pim at Rushin and a Moses Pim at 'Lackey'. Lacka derives from An Leacach (place of slabs). Altogether twenty-nine Pims attended the Quaker School at Ballytore, Co. Kildare, in its 110 years existence. Bancroft Pim started there on the year of its opening in 1726, and James H. Pim was one of the last pupils there in 1836, the year it closed down. Very popular first-names among the Pims were John, Joseph, Jonathan, Samuel and James.

Of the four Pims that owned land in Co. Carlow in 1876, three held in excess of 100 acres; five had land in Co. Dublin, three of which were less than 20 acres, and two less than 100. The largest Pim holding was of Joshua Pim, Rathgar, Co. Dublin, who had 1,045 acres in Co. Laois. Six others of the name had land in this county, with the smallest being Mrs Anna Pim, Clonlask, Edenderry, with a single acre. Three more had land in Co. Offaly. Today's telephone directory shows four Pims in Dublin, and only one in the South, naturally in Co. Laois.

COLDBLOW

A large part of the opposition to the proposed 1800 Act of Union between England and Ireland was based on commercial considerations. Towards the end of 1799, as it became apparent that plans for the Union would not be abandoned, loss of confidence in the business world caused a marked commercial recession in Dublin. Several cotton manufacturers, each of whom claimed to have invested between £30,000 and £40,000 in an industry which normally gave employment to up to 4,000, attested that trade had become so slack over the winter of 1799–1800 that they were obliged to dismiss many and to keep others on only for charitable reasons. The lack of success in the promotion of the linen industry in the south of Ireland was attributed to 'the injudicious attempts to introduce large-scale methods in a peasant society'. (Would the success in the north of the country mean that the people there were not peasants?) In the twenty years after 1780 some success attended the attempts to establish cotton manufacture in the south in place of linen.

Fears were expressed that, in the event of the Act of Union being passed and the high protective tariffs removed, the British manufacturers would dump their produce in Ireland during hard times, fatally undercutting the local industry. Nor were they much impressed by arguments that free trade would benefit the consumer. Eventually representatives of the cotton trade were offered an extension of the period of full duties on cottons and calicoes from five years to seven, with subsequent progressive reductions.

In Co. Laois, Queen's County, at that time, there was a cotton factory at Cullenagh, a factory for thicksets (a coarse twilled cotton fabric) at Ballylinan, another at Abbeyleix, others at Kilmoroney near Athy and Portarlington, and 400 cotton looms in Mountmellick, employing 800 artisans. Stradbally, Co. Laois was the site in the early 19th century of Calcutt's cotton factory.

The English surname Calcutt/Calcott is from a place of that name, and means 'cold cottage/hut' or 'coal-shed', or also possibly 'Cola's cottage', and there was but one person of that name in the 1659 Census. That was Richard Callcatt who was named a titulado for the west quarter of Carrickfergus, Co. Down. The 1814 *Directory* shows James Calcutt as residing at Coldblow, with Mountrath, Co. Laois as the post-town, and no doubt James was one of the cotton factory family. Not a single person of the name is listed as owning a single acre in Ireland in 1876, and the current directories of Ireland have – like the 1659 Census – but one entry of this name, that being in the city of Dublin.

Coldblow, which names neither a townland nor a parish in Co. Laois, is located less than a mile south of Mountrath, on the road to Castletown. However, it does name townlands in the Co. Dublin portion of the parish of Leixlip; in the Co. Offaly parishes of Aghacon and Kilcomin, and in the Co. Wexford parishes of Ladyisland and Tacumshin. We do not know the origin of this unusual name, and can only presume that it refers to a cold, windy place, *áit scéirdiúil*. Equally strange is Cold Winters, the name of townlands in the Co. Dublin parishes of Castleknock and Lusk. This latter is also found in the 1659 Census.

TINNAKILL

Lord Mountjoy, lord deputy of Ireland, wrote in 1607 to the English privy council regarding the O Moores and their fellow-rehels, that 'the notablest disturbers of the peace of the kingdom, shooting at the recovery of their lands taken from them for their rebellion and bestowed upon the English' should be banished into some remote parts of the other provinces. The O Moores and the Lalors, two of the Seven Septs of Laois, whose territory was in the vicinity of the Rock of Dunamase, Co. Laois, were destined for Co. Kerry. The agreeement for the transplanting of the septs, signed at Muileann Uí Leathlobhair (Lalor's Mills) in 1609, included numerous conditions, promises, and pledges regarding the remaining members of the transplanted septs. But the agreement was not honoured and the survivors of the septs, men, women and children, were dispersed. For several days the officials of James I were busily employed throughout Leix (now Laois) in 'destroying the people remaining there, in seizing their cattle and all they possessed, while a savage order had been issued to hang any of them found in their ancient principality'. Among the eighty-seven of the Lalors killed were: Hugh, and Domhnal Mac Seaghan O'Lalour, Donough and Hugh Mac Diarmuid O'Lalour, Domhnal Mac Theig O'Lalour, and Donough Mac Domhnal O'Lalour.

The above spelling of this surname is closer to the original Irish Ó Leathlobhair, *leath*, half, *lobhar*, sick person, though now generally taken to mean 'leper'. The name is variously anglicised Lalor, Lawler and Lawlor, and while today all versions are numerous, the latter, the most numerous, though located throughout the country, is mostly found in Co. Kerry. Lalor is most common in Co. Laois. The earliest mention in the Annals of the Four Masters of the personal name Leathlobhar, from whence the surname, records the slaying of Leathlobhar, son of Eochaidh in the year 707.

Ó Leathlobahair is a most numerous family, being among the principal Irish names in eight Co. Laois baronies; five Co. Kildare baronies; four Co. Kilkenny baronies, and one each in Cos. Dublin and Carlow. Only one of the name was listed titulado, that being David Lawlor Esq. for Ballyallia in the Co. Clare parish of Templemaley. The descendants of those who had been transplanted fared better, if one goes by the acreage shown in *Owners of Land*, compiled in 1876. Two Lawlors in the Killarney area had each over a thousand acres, and one at Tralee had 420 acres, while the four Lalors listed in Co. Laois had but 1, 2, 18 and 42 acres respectively.

Patrick Lalor, born in 1781 at Tinnakill, in the Co. Laois parish of Maryborough (now Portlaoise), raised the flag in 1831 to declare open the campaign against the tithe system. The bailiff had seized sheep to the value of the sum owed to the local clergyman, a certain Mr La Touche. When the auction was called, the sheep were driven to Mountrath with the word 'Tithe' in large pitch capitals on both sides, but no buyer could be found for them. A wrong, according to Patrick Lalor, no matter how long sanctioned by custom or tradition was still a wrong, called to him, personally, for redress. Indeed, the rights of descendants to goods or property illgotten by some ancestor, has never been legally proclamined upon, or indeed considered at all. Also born at Tinakill was his famous son, James Fintan Lalor (1807–49), patriot and political essayist. Tinakill names two townlands in Co. Laois, one in the parish of Ardea, and the other, the birth-place of the Lalors, in the combined parishes of Clonenagh & Clonagheen. It derives from Tigh na Coille, house of the wood, and to the present day there are Lalors living here.

Telephone entries are as follows: Lawlor 904, Lawler 180, and Lalor 209. All three are most numerous in Dublin, and south Leinster and Co. Tipperary.

TULLY

The principal Irish gentlemen for 'Queen's Countie alias Lease' (now, of course, Laois), according to the Carew Manuscripts for 1589 to 1600, were Cosby,

Harpoole, Bowen, Brierton, Pigott, Barrington, the earl of Kildare, Hovenden, Colclough, Loftus, Whytney, Hugh Boy Clan Donnell, MacDonnell, O Dempsey, and Hetherington of Tully. Tully is given as Towlough in a fiant of 1562–3 when Patrick Hetherington was granted lands there. A fiant of 1568–9 granted to Jenken Ederington 'a ruined castle, the lands of Ballyrone etc.', but an inquisition of 1570 notes that 'Ginkene Hetherington, late of Ballyrone, is found to have died seized of the castle of Ballyrone, and towns and lands in that locality amounting to 484 acres'. 'David Hederington is the sonne and heire of the said Gynkin, and is of the adge of 22 years and above'. In *The Calender of State Papers* for 1509–1573 we learn of David Hetherington having been sent to Knockfergus (later Carrickfergus) in January 1568, and of his return in February with his report on the North. In March in a letter to Sir William Cecil, secretary and treasurer, Captain Nicholas Malbie writes: 'Neither honours nor rewards will bring the North to obedience; it must be the sword'.

William and Richard Hetherington, gents, were listed in the 1659 Census as tituladoes for Cloghpook, in the Co. Laois barony of Stradbally (this is now in the Co. Kilkenny parish of Kilmadum), and Arthur Hetherington Esq. was the titulado for Athlumney in the Co. Meath barony of Skreen. He was also a Co. Meath commissioner for the 1661 poll-money ordinance. Remarkably then that none of the above members of the Hetherington family were listed as owning land in any of these districts in 1640.

However, on 3 April 1655, one Mr Edward Hetherington of Kilnamanagh was hanged, with placards on his breast and back, 'for not transplanting'. He had been sentenced for a breach of the declaration concerning transplantation of the previous November, and also for his disobiedience to several subsequent reminders. 'And likewise it did appear by an original examination had from the High Court of Justice, by the positive oath of two Englishmen that in the year 1641 he was a Tory, and (with others) had taken them prisoners at the Naas, and had confessed to them that he had that day killed seven Englishmen, with many other circumstances likening the truth thereof. And the said court have unanimously sentenced him to die as a spy, according to the penalties of the said declaration of the 30 November last.' So it appears that if he was not a non-transplanter, he could be guilty of being a Tory, and if that did not stick he might be found guilty of being a spy.

Tully is now neither a townland nor a parish name in Co. Laois, but the 1659 Census shows it in the barony of Ballyadams, Co. Laois. In 1778 'Hetherington Esq.' resided at Knightstown, between Portarlington and Mountmellick, and the only Hetherington that we could discover as owning land in Ireland in 1876, was Francis Hetherington with 142 acres at Blackhills, in the Co. Laois parish of Abbeyleix.

The 53 Hetheringtons in telephone directories in the South are mainly in Dublin and south Leinster, but also in north Leinster, and some in the

Donegal/Sligo/Leitrim area. The *Phone Book* of the Northern Ireland contains *c*.100 Hetheringtons.

COOLBANAGHER

It is not uncommon for someone setting up as a hairdresser to assume a French name, for however worthy a hairdresser that person might be, the French connection is presumed to enhance the hairdresser's worth. In 1836 Jean Baptiste Fleury, hair dresser, 1 Sackville Street, entrance Eden Quay, described himself as 'from Paris'. The name is genuinely of French origin, but we wonder if Jean Baptiste might in fact have been a Dubliner. The only other bearer of the name was Robert Fleury, esq., 18 North Cresent, Mountpleasant. The *Dublin Directory* of 1850 has but one of the name, that being Revd Charles M. Fleury, 24 Upper Leeson Street.

This surname is an occasional synonym in Co. Galway of Furey, but in Co. Cork Fleury derives from a French placename. Current telephone directories list none of the name north of the Border; there are a half-dozen in the Dublin area, and four of the twelve in the remainder of the country are in Co. Cork. The five in Laois/Offaly might well be Fureys, for this sept, a branch of the royal O Melaghlins, was early located in neighbouring Co. Westmeath. They later migrated across the Shannon to Co. Galway where they are mainly located today.

And whereas the Catholic religion was banned and the Irish language severely discouraged, French Protestants in Ireland were to receive every assistance in practising the liturgy and administrations of the Church of Ireland in their own language. To this purpose a formal document was addressed to the duke of Ormond: 'We haveing taken into our consideration that there are many Protestant strangers of France and other forreign nations now residing in this Cittie of Dublin and Kingdome of Ireland, and for that it is hoped the number of them will receive great increase from the incouragement that is given to strangers by a late Act of Parliament to the Protestant religion … it being alsoe by us seriously considered that most of the said strangers are not capable of joining themselves in communion with us … in the English tongue but would cheerfully and with much advantage to the good of their soules frequent these ordinances in a language better known to them.' For political and personal reasons the Duke readily assented, and so was set up the French church in the Lady Chapel of St Patrick's Cathedral, Dublin, in 1666. It was to continue until 1816.

The very first minister appointed here in 1666 was Jacques Hierome DD and sixteenth in line was Amaury Philippe Fleury, appointed in 1716. Born in

France in 1673, he continued in the service of Dublin's French church until his death in 1734. His son, Antoine replaced him in 1730 and continued there until 1736 when he was appointed to the rectory of Coolbanagher, Co. Laois. Cúl Bendchuir is how *Annála Ríoghachta Éireann* renders this, and Joyce's *Names of Places* quotes 'Irish authorities' as giving this as Cúil Beannchair. Beannchair is defined a 'abounding in peaks', while *cúil* is 'corner or angle'. On his death Antoine Fleury was buried in the graveyard attached to the French church of Portarlington, of which town he had been made a freeman in 1737. His son George Louis Fleury became archdeacon of Waterford in 1773, and several descendants have been clergymen of the Church of Ireland. Charles William Fleury, appointed a minor canon of St Patrick's in 1890, was most likely a descendant, though we have no information to the effect. He vacated the office in 1902 and died in 1917.

Longford

On looking at a motte and bailey one cannot but wonder at the manpower that went into its construction. How many men, how many days, did it take to transport all the material that was required for the average-sized motte, five metres high and 20–25 metres across its diameter. And one wondered why the builders of the motte at Co. Tipperary's Donohill did not avail of the eminence across the road, where stands the ruin of a church, but clearly this structure was already there when the Normans set about selecting their site. A hollowed-out section of this hill appears to have been the source of some, if not all, of the earth and stone for the motte and bailey. What is believed to be the largest motte in the country is at Granard, Co. Longford, which, with an extensive bailey, is surrounded by a deep ditch and bank. Like the remnants of a stone structure on the motte of Donohill, Granard's motte is topped by what Peter Harbison in the *Guide to National Monuments of Ireland* describes as 'an incongruous statue of St Patrick erected in 1932'. The motte is a flat-topped mound, somewhat like a child's sandcastle, surrounded by a ditch, attached to which, and eccentric to it, is a space – the bailey – enclosed by a bank and fosse (trench). They were built by the Anglo-Normans after their arrival in Ireland in 1169, for the purpose of securing the captured lands. Granard is given offically in *Gasitéar na hÉireann/Gazeteer of Ireland* as Gránard, Granard in the Co. Limerick parish of Croom, is given by the recently published *Logainmneacha na hEireann: Contae Luimnigh*, as Garrán Ard, 'the high grove'. The Census of 1659 names only three tituladoes for the barony of Granard, Co. Longford, they being Thomas Flood, Richard Kenedy and William Langford, with the mosst numerous of the principal Irish names being Réilly, Kernan, Farrell and Brady. In 1876 one Kennedy and three Floods had land in this county, but it was the descendants of the old Irish who had the largest holdings in the county, after Right Hon., the earl of Granard, Casteforbes, Newtownforbes (his family name, of course, being Forbes), with 14,978 acres. Three (O) Reillys had three-figures holdings while one had 2,464 acres; four (O) Farrells had 1, 4, 61 and 590 acres, but the second biggest landowner in the county was Lord Annally, residing at Woodlands, Clonsilla, Co. Dublin, with 12,160 acres. The O Farrells (Ó

Fearghail, from *fear*, man, and *gail*, valour), princes of Annally, who became Lords Annally, had maintained their sovereignty until the reign of Queen Elizabeth, when Annally was formed into the County Longford by the lord deputy Sir Henry Sidney. Anghal or Anghaile was the tribe name of the Conmaicne, sept of Uí Fhearghail. The third largest landowner in Co. Longford in 1876 with 10,319 acres, was George Machonchy, Cadwell, Torquay, England. This surname, now largely spelled MacConkey, and mainly found in Co. Monaghan, but with a number in Co. Limerick, derives from Mac Dhonnchaidh (son of Donogh), being a sept of the Scottish clan Robertson. Basil Cottle in *The Penguin Dictionary of Surnames* gives the spelling as McConachie, McConachy and McConagh(e)y, being forms of McDonaugh.

AGHAREAGH

The sale of surplus and obscure minor 'Irish titles' and their purchase by foreign persons with more money than sense, came to mind when looking up the Irish surname Ó Maolainbhthe/Ó Maolanfaidh. Failing initially to locate any of this name in the telephone directories of Ireland, we thought that if it were no longer 'in use', it would be a wonderful name to acquire by somebody in need of an ancient, dignified and meaningful 'title'. *Maolainbhthe/Maolanfaidh* means 'chief of the storm', anfadh being defined as 'a storm, a tempest, a disturbance in the elements, especially at sea'. Partly the reason for our assumption that there were no longer any persons of this name surviving, is due to the fact that it has been anglicised in so many different ways. The Tithe Applotment Books and Griffiths Primary Valuation (1824–60) has it in Co. Tipperary parishes in the baronies of Ormond Upper and Lower, Owney and Arra, Iffa and Offa, Middlethird and Slievardagh. It was variously rendered Malompey, Malomphy, Molamphy, Moleemby, Molanphy, Mullamphy, Mullanphy, Mullamby and Mullumby. MacLysaght's *Surnames* says that it is seldom met outside north Tipperary. When we finally opened our eyes we located five Molamphys entries in the telephone directory in the Nenagh region of north Tipperary, and one at Shannon, Co. Clare.

The *Surnames of Ireland* says that Mullaniff(e) is a north Connaught variant of Mullanphy, and we have come upon but one mention of this. Among the Co. Longford Lay Activists of the Catholic Association in 1825 was listed Henry Mullaniff, Esq., Augharea House, a £50 freeholder. He was listed in 1828 among the Social Composition of Longford Town Activists of the Catholic Committee, and was appointed a magistrate in 1840. Aghareagh names townlands in the adjoining Co. Longford parishes of Street and Templemichael. Joyce's *Irish*

Names of Places says Ahgareagh derives from _achadh riabhach_, 'grey/brindled/tan-coloured field.'

Mullanphy Hospital, Mullanphy Asylum, and Mullanphy Orphanage, all in St Louis, USA, attest to the wealth and generosity of one of Co. Fermanagh's most distinguised emigrants. Born near Enniskillen in 1758, John Mullanphy served in the Irish Brigade in France until the Revolution. He returned to live some four years in Ireland, and in 1789 he landed in Baltimore, USA, with his wife and three year-old son. He helped defend Fort McHenry in 1814 and fought with Jackson's men in New Orleans in 1815. 'During the war he bought up all the cotton and stored it in New Orleans … After the war Mullanphy sold the cotton in England at thirty cents a pound. He had paid four for it' (Peadar Livingstone, _The Fermanagh Story_). Finally settling in St Louis, Mullanphy became a great benefactor of the Church, donating land to the Sacred Heart nuns for their second convent in the USA; he founded the church of St Ferdinand at Florison, a convent of Loreto, helped the Jesuit Novitate, and when he died in 1833 he left 22,000 dollars to the twelve American bishops to open a children's orphanage. 'His only son, Brian, became mayor of St Louis in 1847 and this man did much to help Irish emigrants on their journey to the West.'

NEWTOWN FORBES

Is there a single person named MacFirbis in all of Ireland today? Writing of this famous Connaught family of antiquarians and hereditary historians to the O'Dowds in _The Surnames of Ireland_ (1980), MacLysaght says that 'the name is now almost entirely replaced by the Scottish Forbes'. Almost?

Mac Firbhisigh, the original Irish of this name, may mean 'son of man of property'. Giolla Íosa Mór MacFirbhisigh, who died in 1262, was described as _ollamh_ or professor of Tireragh, and another MacFirbhisigh of the same name was the main compiler of the Book of Lecan (1417); in the year 1362 is recorded the deaths of Auliffe, _ábhar ollaimh_ (literally 'the material of a professor'), in Tireragh; and also John, son of Donough MacFirbhisigh. The last mention of this family in Annals of the Four Masters is to the death in 1379 of Firbhisigh MacFirbhisigh, a learned historian. Tireragh from Tír Fhiachrach, 'Fiachra's land', comprised of the Co. Mayo baronies of Carra, Erris and Tirawley, and the Co. Sligo barony of Tireragh and part of the barony of Carbury in that county.

No doubt the MacFirbises were around in the year 936, but perhaps a little too far west to have seen a strange sight, that of Olafr Cenncairech (_ceann caireach_, 'scabby head'), the leader of the Limerick Norsemen and his army, transporting their fleet overland on their return journey to Limerick from Lough Erne, where they had been raiding. It is suggested that his easiest route would have been via Lough Oughter or Lough Gowna and from there overland to the River Black, which leads into the Shannon. The manoeuvre is a fine example, not only of the Viking command of inland waterways but of the ability of Norse armies to move longships overland even in the depth of winter. Having reached Lough Gowna, we imagine that he would have headed due north to Arvagh. Here he would enter Lower Lake, go west along the present boundary between Cos. Longford and Leitrim, then south-west through the string of small lakes, still on the boundaries of Longford and Leitrim – Beaghmore Lake, Tully South Lake, Gortermone Lake, Doogary Lake, Lough Nabelwy, Clooncose Lake, Lough Cornacullew, Fearglass Lake – and from there to the upper reaches of the Black River. This joins the Rinn River, and flows into the Shannon at Lough Forbes.

The Forbes, a very important family in Scotland, settled in Co. Longford in 1620. Sir Arthur Forbes, Bart (b.1623) was elevated to the peerage in 1673, as Baron Clanhugh and Viscount Granard, and was created earl of Granard in 1684. The new town built by the family was named Newtown Forbes and is in the parish of Clongesh. The Irish name for the town is An Lios Breac, 'the speckled fort'.

In 1876, according to *Owners of Land*, A.K. Forbes had 1,140 acres in Co. Meath; three Forbes had modest holdings in Co. Antrim, with one similar holding in Co. Down. James Forbes had a single acre in Galway city, and Col., the Hon. William Francis Forbes, had 1,584 acres in Co. Leitrim. Lady Adelaide Forbes, Johnstown Castle, Wexford, beat the lot silly with her 15,216 acres there. Again going by telephone directories, we find almost 150 of the name in Northern Ireland's *Phone Book*, and twenty in the 01 *Eolaí Telefóin*, lying between 'An Foras Riaracháin' and 'Forbidden Planet'. In the remainder of the country the greatest majority are in Co. Cork. There is one in Co. Longford and one in Co. Wexford.

EDGEWORTHSTOWN

We have heard of a small, bald publican who made no secret of the fact that he had a wig; he was in the habit of hanging it casually on a hook behind the bar, clapping it down on his head when he was going out, or when the humour struck him. Nowadays men have no hesitation in dousing themselves in perfume – so long as it is called by some *macho* name, and neither men nor women concern themselves too much in concealing the fact that they are

dyeing their hair. But there the openness ends. There is no public acknowledge-
ment by the bald of their wearing a wig/hairpiece/toupee, nor are acquaintances
encouraged to remark upon the fact (behind his back, of course, there will be
comments, sneers even, the cosmetic appendage being referred to as 'the sliding
roof', 'the rug' etc.). Maria Edgeworth (1767–1849), the celebrated writer, was
gone very thin in the hair in her later years and, despite the fact that she was
understandably embarrassed, she did not wear a wig. William Allingham in his
Diary retells a story of Edward Fitzgerald's (*Omar Khayyam*), who used to know
'old Miss Edgeworth' and her 'turban': 'One day by some mischance a strange
gentleman came into the room and found her writing with her almost bald pate
plainly visible. Miss E. started up with the greatest agility, seized her turban
which lay close by and darted through an opposite door, whence she quickly
reappeared with the decoration upon her head, but unluckily turned the wrong
side foremost.' There are five Edgeworths listed in *A Biographical Dictionary of
Irish Writers* – Richard Lovell Edgeworth (1744–1817), Henrv Essex Edgeworth
(1745–1807), Michael Pakenham Edgeworth (1812–1881), Francis Ysidro
Edgeworth (1845–1926), and Maria (1767–1849).

Listed among the 16th-century families of Co. Longford, the Edgeworths
had settled in Ireland around 1583. Edward Edgeworth, Esq., 'preacher of the
word of God', is mentioned in a fiant of 1594. In 1619 Francis Edgeworth was
granted land at Cranalaghmore and – beg, at Lissard and Goorte. Taylor and
Skinner's *Maps* (1778) shows 'Edgeworth Esq.', at Kilshruley in the Co. Longford
parish of Clonbroney; Thomas Edgeworth was shown there in the 1814
Directory, and in *Owners of Land* (1876) the Revd Essex Edgeworth was then
resident there on 1,565 acres. He had a further 296 acres in Co. Meath. Michael
Pakenham Edgeworth, Mostrim House, Anerly, London, possessed 1,659 Co.
Longford acres, and Edgeworthstown, the place named for this family, was then
the home of Antonie Edgeworth, with 3,255 acres.

Of his four marriages Maria's father fathered 22 children, and the 19 who
survived is one more than the number of Edgeworths listed in the island's
current telephone directories. He was a good landlord, spoke and worked for
parliamentary reform and Catholic emancipation, and voted against the Act of
Union.

The surname Edgeworth derives from 'Worth (an enclosed place, a home-
stead) on an edge)'. Edgeworthstown had previously been Meathas Troim,
which is now the Irish name for this place. This was anglicised Mostrim, and
names a Co. Longford parish. Ua Duinnín's *Foclóir Gaeilge agus Béarla* lists
meathas as a component of place-names, but does not explain it. This is followed
by *méathas*, 'fat, fatness'. Ó Dónaill's more recent *Foclóir Gaeilge-Béarla* only has
méathas, directing us to *méathras* 'fat, fat meat … richness'. *Troim* is the genitive
singular of *trom*, the elder tree.

LONGFORD

It tells its own tale when *gynaeceum* – the word for 'the women's apartments in a house' or a 'building set apart for women' was in the time of the Roman empire defined as 'a textile manufactory'. The Irish for such a building was *long na mban*. Long is nowadays generally taken to mean 'a ship', but is defined as 'a vessel, a bath, a ship, a house, the setting of a jewel …'. *Long suain* means a dormitory.

The element *long* in An Longfort, the original Irish of Longford, the name of the Leinster county and town, was once erroneously taken to be the English word 'long', a translation of the Irish word *fada*. From this it was assumed that the original Irish was Áth fada, 'the long ford'. Longford the name of townlands in Cos. Limerick and Offaly are also An Longfort, and probably such is the case of Longford in Cos. Galway, Mayo, Meath, Laois, Roscommon, Sligo and Tipperary. At least one of the four townlands so-named in Co. Tipperary does mean 'the long ford'. That which is in the parish of Tipperary is referred to as 'the foord of Aghfadda' in the Civil Survey of 1654.

The 'seated' gentry of the town of Longford in the county of the same name, listed in Lewis' *Topographical Dictionary* (1837) were Lefroy, Jessop, Armstrong, and at a distance of two miles was the earl of Granard at Castle Forbes.

No Bond was among those seated gentry in 1837, but the Bond's holdings in 1876, were more numerous (and in general larger) than the previously 'seated gentry'. Persons of this name had 77 and 235 acres at Ardglass; 516 acres at Cartroncard; 597 and 5,977 acres at Farra; 179 acres at Castlecon, and 299 acres at an unnamed location in Co. Longford, the property of a London-based Bond. Willoughby Bond, Farra, had a total of 8,559 acres in Cos. Longford, Meath, and Westmeath. There were also Bond holdings in Cos. Dublin, Kildare, Louth, Meath, Laois, Westmeath (where there are five Bond holdings), Tipperary, Antrim, Armagh (five holdings) Donegal, Down, Derry, Monaghan, and Tyrone (four holdings).

The surname Bond comes from the Anglo-Norman le Bonde, meaning 'unfree tenant'. This surname is in Ireland since the early 14th century and is now to be found in small numbers in all provinces. However, going by the current telephone directories the greatest concentration is to be found in Ulster, where there are over 60 entries. Three of these are described as 'reverend', and unlike entries in directories south of the Border, a number to its north have indicated the person to be a farmer. And while it may sometimes be necessary to so proclaim one's line of business, one cannot understand why army officers (foreign and native, and often retired!) see the need to add 'Col.' etc., to their names. (We have yet to see 'corporal' or 'sergeant' after a telephone entry. And while we're at it, why do Irish radio and television commentators feel it necessary to refer to the native army as 'the Irish army'.)

Probably the best-known bearer of this surname was Oliver Bond, the Dublin woollen merchant who was condemned to death for high treason for his part in the rising of 1798. An appeal to save him resulted in a three-day reprieve, but 'a stroke of apoplexy snatched Bond from his friends, after they had rescued him, as they thought, from the grave'.

GRILLAGH

Oscar Wilde's remark that the Irish were a fair people – 'they never spoke well of each other', would appear not to have been entirely true in early Ireland when the first-name Fearghal, meaning valorous, was extremely popular and was conferred on a great number of males. It was borne by the High King Fergal mac Máele Dúin, ancestor of the O Neills, who died in 722, and was a favourite name among the Uí Ruairc (O Rourkes) and the Ui Fhearghail (O Farrells).

Indeed, the surname Ó Fearghail derived from the first-name Fearghal, being variously anglicised O'Farrell, O'Ferrall, Farrell, Ferrall, and variations with double or single r's and l's. Uí Fearghail became a numerous and important sept of Annaly, whose chief seat was Longford, formerly called Longphort Uí Fhearghail, that is, O'Farrell's fortress. Here there were two branches of the family – the O'Farrell Bawn (Ó Fearghail Bán) in the north of Co. Longford, and O Farrell Boy (Ó Fearghail Buí) in the south. And if the first-name Fearghal was numerous, so also was the surname. It features – under a variety of spellings – 359 times in *The Irish Fiants of the Tudor Sovereigns*, 1521–1603; the O'Farrells in the index of the Annals of the Four Masters fills seven columns, so important were they, and the *Census* of 1659 lists them among the principal Irish names in 17 counties – Donegal, Armagh, Waterford, Kilkenny, Carlow, Dublin, Kildare, Kilkenny, Offaly, Longford, Louth, Meath, Westmeath, Laois, Wexford, Leitrim and Roscommon. They were in each of Leinster's twelve counties. *Owners of Land* (1876) shows them with land in 22 of the 32 counties of Ireland, including all Leinster counties.

But when did persons bearing this surname begin to drop the 'O'? There were twice as many without the 'O' as with it among these 1876 landowners; current Southern telephone directories list 3,137 Farrell entries to 472 O'Farrell: north of the Border there are 220 Farrells to 15 O'Farrells. (The original Irish name features 13 times.) Indeed the 'O' was already being dropped by the beginning of the 16th century. And though the spelling Ferrall may appear somewhat closer to the original Fearghal, it was the rendering adapted by the more affluent and probably most anglicised of the family, though strangely it was those who most retained the 'O'.

It is most interesting then to peruse the current telephone directory of San Juan, the capital of Puerto Rico, and to note that there are 63 O'Farrells listed (albeit with considerable variety of spellings), to a single Farell entry. Did the first to bear this name leave Ireland for Puerto Rico before the 'O' began to be shed?

The largest single holding in the 1876 *Owners* was the 9,731 acres of John Nolan Farrell, Logboy House, Ballyhaunis, Co. Mayo. The Rt. Hon. R. More O Ferrall, Ballina House, in the Co. Kildare parish of Cadamstown, had a total of 5,159 acres in Cos. Kildare, Longford, Meath, Carlow, and in Dublin City. Other large holdings were the O'Ferrall 1,354 Co. Kildare acres at Kildangan; the 1,689 Co. Longford acres of C.F.J.F. O'Ferrall, Lissard; John Arthur Farrell's 4,084 acres at Moynalty, Co. Meath; the O'Ferrall 5,131 acres at Dalystown, Co. Galway, and the 1,287 Co. Sligo acres of Ed. Farrell, Capel Street, Dublin. Though the five Farrell holdings in the Co. Longford parish of Ardagh were most modest, it was here that the greatest concentration of the name was to be found mainly in the townland of Grillagh. P.W. Joyce's *Names of Places* gives *greallach*, 'miry or marshy place; ground beaten or trampled on, a slough', as the origin of this name.

CLOONSELLAN

Early grammarians, we are informed, called the letter S *bainríon na gconsain*, the queen of the consonants, being the sixteenth letter in the Irish alphabet and the fourth in the ogham alphabet, its Irish being name *sail* (willow). Each letter of the ogham alphabet had 'tree' names – A *ailm* (pine) B *beith* (birch) C *coll* (hazel) etc. *Saileán*, the diminutive of *sail*, means 'willow-bed, osier-bed', and is found in the place-name Cluain Saileán. Anglicised Cloonsellan, this names a townland in the Co. Longford parish of Killashee (Cill na Sí). In 1876 all its 243 acres were the property of Joseph M'Gaver as listed in *Owners of Land*, while the single acre of the Very Revd Edward M'Gaver was, presumably, the ground whereon the parochial house was built. The largest M'Gaver holding was the 566 acres of Nicholas M'Gaver, Cloontha. This latter derives from *cluainte*, 'meadows', and is also in the same parish of Killashee.

MacGaver would sound exactly the same were it written MacAver or MacCaver, a matter that had to be kept in mind when trawling different sources, seeking its original Irish. MacLysaght's *Surnames* does not list this surname or anything resembling it: De Bhulbh's 1997 *Sloinnte na hÉireann / Irish Surnames* lists the fairly rare Mac Avera which derives from Mac Aimhréidh (*aimhréidh*, disordered, untidy). And then there was MacGaver, Mac Éibhir, from the old first name Éibhear now anglicised Ivor. Ivor, however, is a common 'English' form for Ímar: Ímhear, a borrowing of the Old Norse Ívarr. 'There was an Ímar who was king of Northumbria and of Dublin and the name was borne by a number of Viking leaders in Ireland. The name was soon adopted by the Irish' (Ó Corráin and Maguire, *Irish Personal Names*). In the same book we find: 'Éber: Éibhear. In the early documents this name is borne by legendary and pseudo-historical personages such as Éber, son of Míl, leader of the Goidelic conquest of Ireland. It occurs among the later medieval O Neills and MacMahons and, in the form Éibhir, it survived in Derry and Oriel down to the end of the nineteenth century in the families of Magennis and O Lafferty. It has been anglicized Heber, Harry and Ivor.' It is indeed likely that at least some whose name was originally Mac Éibhir might now be known as MacIvor, or indeed MacKeever, both of which are based on that Norse forename Ívaar. M'Awfir and M'Avir (of the Moreis? Co. Wexford), listed in a fiant of 1602 appear to be anglicised forms of this latter.

The above Revd Edward MacGaver was defended by Daniel O'Connell in 1827 in a case over a disputed will, and whether MacGaver was impressed by the man (he won his case) or by his policies, he was to become an important local O'Connellite priest. When the Longford Liberal Club was set up two years later, McGaver was to second a resolution in praise of the 40-shilling freeholders 'for the manly and uncompromising patriotism by which they wielded that mighty engine, the Electoral Francise'. Indeed, Fr MacGaver, parish priest of Granard, was to become the most prominent cleric to engage himself in the political affairs of the county since the 1820s.

In an article entitled 'The Emergence of the Political Community in Longford, 1824–29' (Longford: *Essays in County History*, Lilliput Press, 1991), Fergus O'Ferrall remarks that a Maynooth education was not a prerequisite for political activity: less than half of the activist priests attended Maynooth; 'Out of the six priests who were active in the first phase of the collection in 1824 and 1825 only one can be found in the Maynooth lists'. Fr MacGaver had not attended Maynooth. He is listed among the subscribers to Lewis' *Topographical Dictionary* (1876), being then Parish Priest of Carrickedmond, Colehill, Co. Longford.

The *Census* of 1901 shows MacGavers at Cloontamore, and Cloonsellan in the parish of Killashee; at Bridge Street, Longford Town, and Sr. Rose at Revd Mother Hampson's of Aghafin.

Telephone directories of the island list but three MacGavers, two in Dublin, and one in Co. Clare. However, some of the 186 (36 in the South) MacIvors, or the 380 (176 South) MacKeevers may have originally been MacÉibhir.

Louth

The claim that Lord Rokeby was benevolent and anxious to give employment to the peasantry of the country would appear to be borne out by the fact that he left the considerable sum of £12,000 in his will for various charitable purposes. This man, Dr Richard Robinson, transferred from Kildare to become archbishop of Armagh in 1765, and considering that the Established Church found in him a vigilant guardian of her legal rights and privileges, one wonders if his charity extended only to those of his own religious persuasion. 'Lord Rokeby was a man of tall stature, robust, yet of dignified form, penetrating eye, and commanding aspect. To his friends and to those whom he esteemed, he was affable, mild, attentive and polite. The unworthy and obtrusive he repelled with a frown'. He belonged to the Robinsons of Rokeby of York, and in 1751 he arrived in Ireland, accompanying the duke of York, who held him in high esteem.

In 1777 he was created Baron Rokeby of Armagh, and in 1785, on the demise of his brother William, he succeeded to the title of baronet. Apart from erecting habitations for the incumbents, he built a very elegant mansion contiguous to the town of Armagh in 1770; the following year a public library, and in 1772 Lisnadill church. Besides these improvements in Armagh, Lord Rokeby erected a very handsome mansion-house and offices at Marley, near Dunleer. The last public building erected by Primate Robinson was the Observatory, which was beautifully situated on a hill, at the north east side of the city. 'It is furnished with a complete astronomical apparatus, and contains very convenient accommodation for an astronomer' (Stuart's *Historical Memoir of Armagh*). In the 1760s Archbishop Robinson, a temporal as well as spiritual peer in Ireland, was a principal shareholder in and developer of the Drumglass colliery, on the Co. Tyrone part of his estate. In 1836 there were 180 persons employed by the Hibernian Mining Company, then under lease from the lord-primate, raising 500 tons of coal per week.

The Surnames of Ireland informs us that Robinson is an English name comparatively recently in Ireland, and has become very numerous, especially in Ulster. Nowhere listed among the principal Irish names in the 1659 Census, they were tituladoes in Cos. Fermanagh, Cork, Dublin, Kilkenny, Longford, Roscommon, Westmeath, Meath, and Thomas Robinson was a commissioner of the poll-money ordinance of 1660 for Co. Longford. Of the fifteen listed in *Owners of Land* (1876) for Co. Antrim, only three exceeded a hundred acres – 132, 146 and 120, and of the eleven in Co. Armagh, only the Revd George Robinson, Armagh (340 acres), and the Revd Thomas R. Robinson, also of Armagh (265 acres), had in excess of one hundred acres. They were to be found in six other Ulster counties, but all being modest holdings. In Munster the Robinsons generally had bigger holdings, but in Connaught there was but a single Robinson landowner, having a mere two acres in Co. Sligo. They were in nine Leinster counties, the largest being that of Sir John S. Robinson, Rokeby Hall, Dunleer, with 2,941 acres in Co. Louth. Rokeby, no doubt named for the place in England, was to become the name of a townland in the Co. Louth parish of Marlestown. Marlestown and Marlay have the same Irish, that being Baile Bhearlaí.

LAWLESSTOWN

On 18 November 1789, Valentine Browne Lawless, of Maretimo, Blackrock, Co. Dublin; Lyons, Rathcoole, Co. Kildare; and Abington, Co. Limerick, was created Lord Cloncurry. Writing about the surname Lawless in his *Irish Families*, Edward MacLysaght says: 'The best-known family of Lawless is that of Cloncurry, Co. Kildare, originally of Herts., England. Nicholas Lawless, who conformed in 1770, was created Lord Cloncurry in 1789'. Lord Cloncurry's seat is not listed in the 1814 *Directory*, and there are but two Lawlesses therein – Peter Lawless, Esq., Cherryfield, Tallaght, Dublin, and B. Lawless, Esq., Cherrywood, Bray, Co. Wicklow. In the 1836 *Dublin Alamanac and General Register of Ireland* Lord Cloncurry, Lyons, is among the deputy lieutenants of Co. Kildare, and Valentine, Baron Cloncurry, Lyons, is among the magistrates of the county. Valentine 2nd Baron Cloncurry (1773–1852) was a member of the United Irishmen in 1798 and a protagonist of Catholic Emancipation, and John Lawless (1773–1837), author of *A Compendium of the History of Ireland* and *An Address to the Catholic of Ireland*, was so violent a speaker on behalf of Catholic Emancipation that O'Connell regarded him with distaste, calling him Mad Lawless. William Lawless (1772–1824), a professor of Anatomy, was outlawed as a member of the United Irishmen. He later became a distinguished general in Napoleon's army. An earlier *non grata* Lawless was Patrick who was exiled after 1691. He became Spanish ambassador to London and afterwards to Louis XIV of France. Another writer of the name was the Hon. Emily Lawless (1845–1913), born in Kildare, third daughter of Lord Cloncurry. She wrote historical studies, novels and poetry. There were Lawlesses with fairly modest holdings listed in *Owners of Land* (1876) – in Cos. Dublin, Wexford, Cork, Galway and Roscommon. The largest Lawless holding was that of Lord Cloncurry, Lyons, Hazelhatch, with 6,121 acres there.

We wonder if 'the Lawless brothers from Cork', Clement and Paul, who arrived in Australia in 1840, were connected with Clement F. Lawless, Kilcrone, Cloyne, Co. Cork who owned 192 acres there in 1876? They moved their cattle into pioneering Queensland in the 1850s, amassing runs of nearly 300 square miles, and used their Queensland empire as a base for an aristocratic lifestyle in Ireland. 'Sharing the commonly held Irish view that colonial women were inferior, they both returned to Ireland to marry, and thereafter commuted between Ireland and Australia, and died in Ireland' (Patrick O'Farrell, *The Irish in Australia*). Mount Lawless in Australia is named after this family.

The surname Lawless, from the Old-English *laghes*, meaning 'outlaw', was variously anglicised Laweles, Laghles, Lachles, Laules etc., and is gaelicised Laighléis. It was introduced into Ireland after the Anglo-Norman invasion. One branch settled in Kilkenny City and became one of the 'Tribes of Kilkenny.' The 1659 Census lists Lawless among the principal Irish names in a barony each in Cos. Dublin, Meath, Louth, and two in Co. Kilkenny. Lawlesstown names a townland in the Co. Louth parish of Cappoge, and two in Co. Tipperary in the parishes of Kiltegan and Rathronan.

The Irish for Lawlesstown is *Mullachan Laighléisigh*.

PEPPERSTOWN

In a bond of 20 June 1557, signed by Patryck Sarsfeld, Walter Pepparde, esquire, 'who quietly enjoys the tithes of Carlow and Fassoughreban in counties Carlow and Kildare for a term of 11 years', was granted an alternative method of payment to his annual payment of £20. The bond states that at the end of first two years 'he shall pay annually between harvest time and All Hallows 40 pecks of corn, half wheat, half oats, and 20 marks in money ...'. A mark was equal to 13*s*. 4*d*. or two thirds of a pound sterling.

Peppard is the name of a Norman family, known when they came first to Ireland as de Pipard and Pipard, and it has been identified with Co. Louth since 1185. This surname has sometimes become Pepper, an indigenous English surname, particularly in the last century, though this is not an entirely modern innovation as the townlands of Pepperstown in Cos. Louth and Meath attest. In a letter of 20 October 1565 to Sir Henry Sidney, lord deputy of Ireland, Queen

Elizabeth wrote: 'Right trusty and welbelovid we greet you well. Where Walter Peppard of that our realme, esquire now deceased hath at sondry tymes contynued a long suitor unto us heere as well about the demaunnds of certain hereditaments in Lex named Ballaroan and Killmahid togethir with a certain ferme of his namid Slewmarge to be restored unto him ...'. In response Sidney claimed that the lands in question were the property of the queen through conquest, and questioned Peppard's 'doubtful service'. The queen returns to the subject in a letter of 7 October 1566, where she concedes that Peppard's widow's demands are 'very large and to conteyne muche doubtfulnesse in them', but suggests a settlement, because she was a widow and her children fatherless. She accepted Sidney's word that it was necessary to retain 'the spiritualities of Ballyroan and Killmahyde' for the victualling and service of the forts there, but in lieu of this 'some other spiritualtyes and tythes of lyke nature be searchid out in such convenient place as shall be most proffitable for us so as the same exceede not in the yerly valew more than the others of Ballaroan and Killmahyde ...'

The 1659 Census shows Major Peppard and his Company, of which thirty-nine were English and three were Irish, as among the tituladoes of the City of Drogheda and Liberties thereof, and William Peppard titulado for Peppers towne (now Pepperstown, Baile an Phiobaraigh) in the Co. Louth parish of Charlestowne. George Pepper gent., was titulado for Sarsfieldstown in the Co. Meath parish of Moorestown, and William Pepper was a commissioner for the 1660 poll-money ordinance for Co. Cavan. Indeed, the Peppards were regarded as Irish by English officals when they recorded them among the principal Irish names for the Co. Meath barony of Duleek.

Arthur Young in his *A Tour in Ireland 1776–1779* writes: 'Left Balbriggan and went to Ballygarth, the seat of – Pepper Esq., a place very agreeably wooded on a rising ground above a river.' Ballygarth names a townland and a parish in Co. Meath, and we wonder if this was the location of the 526 Co. Meath acres of Blundell Peppard, with an address in England, in 1876. Two Peppards of Salestown, Dunboyne, Co. Meath, had holdings of 278 and 93 acres in Co. Limerick. Other Peppers/Peppards had modest holdings in Cos. Kildare, Offaly, Louth and Armagh. Today's telephone directory lists six Peppers in the provinces of Leinster and Munster. The seven Peppards are found in Connaught and Ulster.

DROMGOOLESTOWN

In the distant past people who lived in Dromgoole in the Co. Louth parish of Stabannan in time became known as 'the Dromgooles', which appellation eventually became their surname and that of their descendants. Again in time, the place became known as 'the town of the Dromgooles', or Dromgoolestown. Of the 35 entries in the Southern telephone directories, 25 are spelled Drumgoole, 12 of which are in the Dublin area, with the majority of the remainder in Co. Louth and adjacent counties. The ten listed Dromgooles, outside the 01 area, are also found in Co. Louth.

In 1299 Robert de Drumgol went pledge for another man in a Louth law case, and Robert de Dromgol was coroner for Co. Louth, 1311–13. James Dromgole is mentioned in connection with the manor of Carlingford in Comitatus Lovid in 1540. John Dromgoole of Dromgoleston was listed among jurors in 1529 and 1530; Thomas Dromgoyll of Wodtoneston (now Wottonstown) was listed in a document of 1536; in 1562 Nicholas Dromgoll was among those granted the nunnery of Hogges, and other property in Dublin, and more at Clareston (Claristown), Co. Meath. Christopher Dromgoole and William Taffe of Dundalk, merchants, were granted land in Co. Louth in 1577, and in 1615 Richard Dromgowle of Dromgowlestown was among others seised of land at Remoreston alias Redmondton, near Brecknanston (? Brackenstown, parish of Swords, Co. Dublin).

The Irish Fiants of the Tudor Sovereigns (1521–1603) numbers Nicholas Dromgole of Walsheston (? Walshestown, Co. Louth parish of Rathdrumin) among those pardoned in 1560; a fiant of 1562 notes a pardon to Walter Brine of Dublin, butcher, indicted for burglary and stealing from Nicholas Dromgole, merchant, in High Street, Dublin. In 1582 Andrew Dromgole of Tyrow, Co. Louth, and Patrick Dromgole of Dromgoleston, Co. Louth, received pardons.

A branch of the Dromgooles belonged originally to Drogheda, 'where they resided in princely state in Dromgoole Castle, a portion of which has survived the wreck of ages, and is still (1865) to be seen as an evidence of the massive grandeur of the old Irish mansion in feudal days' (W.J. FitzPatrick, *The Sham Squire*). One of those who resisted Cromwell's attack on Drogheda was the founder of Dromgoole Castle, but when resistance failed he was taken out and hanged from the spikes of his own gate. His seven sons, during the sack of Drogheda, fled north and south. The historic records of time appear to have lost sight of this ancient sept until the wars between William and James, when one of them is again found living in stately grandeur with an income of £5000 a-year ... Dromgoole was dispossessed, and his fine property was 'parcelled out among the sycophants and adventurers who followed the fortunes of William'. Immediately after the battle of the Boyne another Dromgoole settled as a bleacher of linen on the banks of the Bann, at Bellevarlie, possessing an estate of several hundred acres of land. John, one of his four sons remained at the home place, and a scn of his was Dr Thomas Dromgoole MD (*c.*1750–1826). This man was occasionally the acting secretary of the Irish Catholic Committee and a leading supporter of Daniel O'Connell. During the time he lived at Water

Street, Newry, he held an honoured and faithful position in the Society of United Irishmen, and when he was subsequently balloted into a cavalry corps of yeomen he continued to make his position subservient to the interests of the United Irishmen. He was censured for a speech he made in 1812 in which he said Catholics were bound by their religion to subvert the established Church; thereafter he dropped into the background and ended his days in Rome.

Dromgoole is the anglicised form of Droim Gabhail, 'the ridge of the forked river/valley', and this is the Irish name of Dromgoolestown.

LOUTH

Before Louth acquired its present monosyllabic Irish spelling – Lú – the name was pronounced with two syllables approximating 'Lewy', from its older rendition variously spelled Lughmhagh, Lughmadh, and Lughbhadh in the *Annals of the Four Masters*. The name of a barony, county, townland and town, Louth is one of less than a dozen placenames in Ireland from which surnames are formed. Such surnames are known as toponymics. Best-known are Athy, Drumgoole, Finglas, Slane, Santry and Corbally. This latter names 49 townlands in 20 counties in all four provinces. It derives from An Corrbhaile, 'the noticeable town'. There are 44 Corbally surnames listed in the Southern telephone directories, two-thirds of which are in the Dublin area. The remainder are in the 04 area, largely in Co. Louth.

In 1540 Nicholas Corbally, late prior of BVM de Urso, Drogheda, was granted a pension of £5, issuing out of the possessions in Drogheda and Killaneryr (Killineer, Cill Ó nDaighre). In 1550 Thomas Corbally was among those who received a grant of land at Dunshaughlin, Co. Meath, and in 1556 Gilbert Corbally of Gareston (? Garrettstown), soldier, had his horse, valued at 10s., stolen. Corbally was listed in the 1659 *Census* among the principal Irish surnames in the Co. Dublin barony of Balrothery.

On the second Friday after Easter, 1610, having served their apprenticeship, the following were admitted to the franchise in Dublin: Anthony Enos, Garrott Barry, merchants, Francis Fyan, button-maker, Thomas Longe, tanner (Susan and Margery Usher, maidens, being the daughters of a deceased freeman), John Seyle, embroiderer, John Gore, musician, John Neill, tallow-chandler, Henry Wafer, sailor, William Tankard, smith, Thomas Whitseed, girdler, John Corballye, merchant, and Theobald Lowthe, carpenter.

MacLysaght's *Surnames* says that the surname Louth or Lowthe was 'probably an Irish toponymic when found in Ireland in mediaeval times (that is the four centuries after the year 1000), in later times it is usually an English one from parishes in Lincolnshire'. The fact that the name is found in Co. Louth is coincidental. It has been in Leinster since the fourteenth century. It meant 'loud/babbling (stream)'. Current telephone directories list ten Louth surnames – three in the Dublin area, three in Co. Wicklow, and one each in Cos. Cavan, Meath and Cork. There is a single Lowthe in Co. Meath. Neither of these surnames are to be found in Northern *Phone Book*.

*The Dublin Guild Merchant Rolls, c.*1190–1265 contains the names Willelmus Clericus de Loueth, Reginaldus de Luuethe, Nicholas Wydie de Louethe, Hugo Tannator de Louethe, and Robertus Saponarius de Louethe – a clerk, a tanner, and a soapmaker (?). *Crown Surveys of Lands 1540–41* lists Willelmi Louth among 'proborum et legalium hominum comitatus Midie'. This was in relation to the manor of Ardmulchan, Co. Meath. *The Irish Fiants of the Tudor Sovereigns* (1521–1603) lists but a single person bearing this surname, that being Thomas Louth of Newtown, who with a large number of others received a pardon in 1601. There are four townlands called Newtown in Co. Westmeath, but we think this is the one in the parish of Ballymore.

The first element of the older spelling of the Irish name for Louth is Lugh, the Celtic God of light and genius, son of Cian and Eithne, grandson of Balar, whom he slew, and foster son of Tailte. There is no certainty as to the meaning of the second element.

DURTY BATTER

In compensation for rebuilding a great part of the Tholsell for the corporation of Drogheda, Thomas Dixon, alderman, was granted, in October 1658, a sixty-one year lease on a small piece of land called 'the fflagery parke and the Greene Hills', with the corporation reserving to themselves 'the free liberty to carry sand from thence, as often as they shall have occasion to make use of any …' This lease was 'granted, assented, and consented unto' by the whole assembly, being added to his former grants 'of the Seller(cellar) under the Tholsell, the newe built shoppe on the north side of the same, the Bellcony, standings and a little wast room under the guild Hall stayres …' Herewith are some further names in Drogheda at that time, some of which have survived, albeit somewhat changed. 'Ye Green Batter' is now Greenbatter, a townland name, the second part being an anglicised form of *bóthar*, 'a road'. This is also found in 'ye Durty Batter', which, understandably, has not survived, although there is a townland named Dirtystep in Co. Kilkenny. *The Council Book of the Corporation of Drogheda* in another place writes of 'the aforesaid Lane of Batter', clearly indicating that 'Batter' was understood, and was not merely a name or part of a name. There was the Blinde buttes, and ye Blind gate; Laurence Gate and Laurence street; Sunday's Gate; Duleeke Gate; Saint John's land and Saint John's Hill; and 'the Dale' (Dales now names a townland in the old civil parish of Mayne). There was ye Rampire; ye Tholsell; ye Pound; ye friers Parke and Priors Park; St James St; Irish St; West St; Magdalen St and Maudelins St (the same?); ye water pump in Stockwell Lane; Rushy Lane; Letherway Lane; Tootinge Tower, and Cornmarkett Hill. There was Dobin's Park, and 'without the West Gate' was a place called 'the Ash Parke'. In November 1656 the corporation ordered: 'that Richard Burnell, Thomas Stoker, Alderman, Robt. Heely and Joseph Whirloe doe carry away their several proporcons of dunge lyenge upon the backe lane leadinge from Booth street to Saint Saviour's Church which is a comon nuisance and hurtful to theire neighbours at or before ye first of December next upon paine of forty shillinges to ye poor'. Talk about Durty Batter! At a meeting of the corporation in October 1658, Thomas Cockaine was granted interest in 'two little garden plotts ... adjoininge to the Towne walls, and the lane commonly called the name of the Scarlett lane ...' Currently Bárdas Droichid Átha are inviting tenders for the reconstruction of the 575-metre long Scarlet Street.

Durty Batter? *An Bóthar Salach*!

DUNDALK

Theobald and Wolfe might appear to be rather pretentious firstnames for the son of plain Peter Tone, a Dublin coachbuilder. It is thought probable that Theobald Wolfe Tone was the illegitimate son of one of the Wolfe family of landed gentry seated at Forenaghts, Co. Kildare. Theobald Wolfe Tone (1763–98), a Protestant, when about to write *An Argument on behalf of Catholics* in 1791, declared that he was not at that time acquainted with a single member of the Catholic community. The surname Tone derives from the Old-English word *tun*, meaning enclosure, and later village, and Anglo-Norman records indicate that it was unknown in Ireland before the 16th century, and no person of any note appears before Wolfe Tone. His writings acquaint us with the remarkable personality of the man, his honesty, his integrity and his bravery. His involvement in the United Irishmen is well known, as is his death in jail in October 1798. He was condemned to death by hanging and his plea to be shot like a soldier was refused. He was found dead in his cell, the authorities claiming that he had cut his throat. New evidence now challenges this claim.

Writing in his diary on 1 February 1798 he lists some of his fellow refugees in France, adding that 'all do very well except Napper Tandy, who is not behaving correctly. He began some months ago by caballing against me with a priest of the name Quigley, who is since gone off, no one knows whither; the circumstance of this petty intrigue are not worth my recording.' Shortly after five men were arrested 'in the most peculiar circumstances in a Margate hotel. The men had walked along the strand from Whitstable the previous day carrying a monstrous amount of luggage, including several boxes of papers, a mahogany trunk with a secret drawer, and a quantity of gold. On arrest two said that they were military gentlemen, with their servants.' But on examination the military gentlemen turned out to be Father Quigley, an Irish Catholic from Dundalk known to be a leader of the United party, and Arthur O'Connor, an aristocrat, revolutionary and bosom friend of Lord Edward Fitzgerald. (Lord Edward's comment on the arrest was 'O'Connor had nothing odd with him but twelve hundred guineas'.)

In early June 1798 holiday-makers assembled on Penenden Heath for that favourite spectator sport – a public execution. Fr Quigley, the United Irishman, was to be hanged. 'After making his devotions, and protesting his innocence in a lengthy speech to the crowd, he took out a penknife and calmly set about peeling an orange ...' After his execution, his head was removed by a surgeon and held up to the crowd: 'Behold the head of a traitor.' On the 20th of the month, Wolfe Tone records that it was his thirty-fifth birthday (and it may be added his last). 'Quigley has been executed, and died like a hero! If ever I reach Ireland, and that we establish our liberty, I will be the first to propose a monument to his memory ...'. Well, Tone did get back to Ireland, but liberty was not established, nor was Tone in a position to propose a monument to the memory of Fr Quigley. Tone is commemorated by a statue in Dublin, but has Dundalk a memorial to its patriot priest? Dundalk is the anglicised form of Dún Dealgan, 'the fort of Dealga'. Delga is said to have been the name of the Firbolg chief who built the fort.

And to briefly return to Tone. MacLysaght's *Surnames* says that the name Tone 'is now very rare if not extinct in Ireland'. There are 18 Tone entries in telephone directories, all in Leinster.

OMEATH

The 2,605 Co. Kilkenny acres of Edward Marsh, Springmount, Mountrath, was the largest Marsh holding listed in the 1876 *Owners of Land*. Apart from 206 Co. Leitrim acres, there were Marsh possessions in Co. Offaly – 38, 18, 304 and 192 acres. This latter holding was the property of the Revd Peter Marsh, who also owned 127 Co. Armagh acres; 904 in Co. Westmeath, and 259 in Co. Galway. His address was variously rendered O'Meath, and Omeath.

Omeath is from Ó Méith, a district in north Co. Louth between Carlingford
Lough and Newry. Ó Méith means the descendants of Méith. It now names a
village on the southern shore of Carlingford Lough. Apart from the 31 Marshes
listed in the Dublin area telephone directory, there are 24 in the *Phone Book* of
Northern Ireland, largely in Co. Down, followed by Cos. Tyrone and Antrim.
Of the 21 in the remainder of the country 13 are in Munster, particularly in
Cos. Clare, Cork and Limerick. This English surname, derived from 'marsh',
came to Ireland in the 17th century, and was prominent in the Protestant
ecclesiastical life of the country. Armiger and Vincent Marsh are listed in the
1659 Census as tituladoes of the Co. Cork parish of Ringrone.

Francis Marsh who had been Church of Ireland Archbishop of Dublin from
1682 until his death in 1693, was succeeded by Narcissus Marsh, who, incidentally,
was not related. Narcissus was born into a Wiltshire family who conferred strange
Christian firstnames on their children. In his diary Marsh mentions his brother
Onisephorous, and another brother, who became MP for Fethard, was named
Epaphroditus. Here also we read how he avoided matrimony for the love of God,
and of his occasional prolonged fasting. However, he is best remembered for
founding the first public library in Ireland, the building of which started in 1701.
Marsh's Library, St Patrick's Close, is there to the present day. At one time the
readers were limited to 'graduates and gentlemen', and they were locked into the
cubicles with rods and chains. While Provost of Trinity College, prior to becoming
archbishop, Marsh introduced the teaching of Irish. He translated to Armagh in
1703, and while there he formed 'an eleemosynary establishment at Drogheda,
for the reception of twelve ('poor decayed') widows of clerygmen who had
been curates in the diocese of Armagh ...'.

Sharing an interest in the Irish language, though perhaps for different reasons,
was an earlier archbishop of Dublin. This was George Browne, connexion of Anne
Boleyn's, who had been consecrated in 1536. He planned to 'set forth ... the word
of God ... in the Irish tongue ...' In a letter two years after his appointment
Browne confessed his failure to persuade the clergy of his diocese of which he was
archbishop, to preach the supremacy of the king. Neither secular nor regular priest,
notwithstanding the oaths they had taken, under compulsion, would obey Browne
in this matter. Part of that failure was the putting into force Henry VIII's 1530 Act
of Faculties. This forbade payment of the great sums of money claimed by the
bishop of Rome, 'called the Pope'. These comprised 'pensions, cences, Peter-pence,
procurations fruits, suits for provisions, and expeditions of bulls for archbishoprics
and bishoprics, and for delegacies and rescripts in causes of contention and appeals,
jurisdictions negative, and also for dispensations, licences, faculties, grants,
relaxations, writs, called rehabilitations, abolitions, and other infinite sorts of bulls,
briefs, and instruments of sundry natures, names, and kinds, in great numbers ...'.
This translation from the Latin almost has the native Irish joyous exuberance in
words and sounds.

CLOGHER HEAD

Though he gives reasons for not believing the story related by Cathal Maguire, archdeacon of Clogher, the compiler of the Annals of Ulster, regarding the meaning of the placename Clogher, P. W. Joyce in his *Names of Places*, forgivably relates the tale. He suggests that Maguire's statemant is merely a record, of 'an oral tradition', a tradition which says that Clogher comes from Cloch Óir, 'golden stone'. This stone which anciently existed at this place was worshipped as Cedmaed Celsetacht, the principal idol of the northern Irish. It was said to have made 'oracular responses', being the Devil pronouncing 'juggling answers, like the Oracles of Apollo Pythius ...' Maguire relates that the sacred stone was preserved in Clogher long after pagan times, being at the right of the entrance to the church. That this story is not found in any 'ancient authority' is one of Joyce's reasons for rejection, the other being that it is not unique but named over sixty townlands throughout the country. The Irish is Clochar, meaning 'stony land, a place abounding in stones, or having a rocky surface'. Clogher Head, Ceann Chlochair, is described by Joyce as 'a remarkable headland in Louth'.

In 1629 Bishop Spottiswood solicited Charles I to order the lord lieutenant to deliver letters patent making the town of Clogher a corporation 'for the better civilizing and strengthening of these remote parts with English and British tenants, and for the better propagation of the true religion'. The first Protestant bishop here was the famous – or infamous – Myler Magrath, a one-time Franciscan, who had been appointed by Pope Pius V as bishop of Down. After becoming a Protestant he was placed in Clogher by Queen Elizabeth in 1570, and was soon afterwards made bishop of Cashel.

Clogher Head is in the Co. Louth barony of Ferrard, and among the principal Irish names in this barony as listed in the 1659 Census was that of Rauth. Edward MacLysaght's *Surnames* says that Rath is a rare toponymic still extant in Leinster, especially in Co. Louth. The Civil Survey book for Co. Louth, listing the names of proprietors in 1649, has John Rath of Drumcashell with 50 acres at Clonkeehan in the parish of the same name being in the barony of Louth. *Owners of Land* (1876) lists but two of this surname in all of Ireland – Anne Rathe, Blackwater Post Office, Co. Wexford, with 81 acres, and Monica Rath, Clogher Head, Co. Louth with 206 acres. Of the 45 Raths listed in 'Republic' telephone directories, the majority were in Co. Wexford, but the two in Co. Lough were both in Clogherhead. The Northern Ireland *Phone Book* has seven Raths. Those in Co. Wexford may be a variant spelling of Rothe, gaelicised Rút, a name established in Co. Kilkenny in the 14th century and counted there among the 'Ten Tribes'. This name, which is a Norse word meaning red, has in modern times changed to Ruth and Routh. Today there are

40 Ruths in the telephone directory, and 13 Roths, almost all in southern Leinster and in Munster. Northern Ireland's *Phone Book* has two Ruths and seven Raths. MacLysaght informs that Rath is an occasional abbreviation of MacIlwraith in Co. Derry.

DOWDALLSTOWN

On 29 April 1543 George Dowdall was appointed archbishop of All Ireland by the king, which appointment received the approval of the pope on 1 March 1553. This was in succession to Robert Wauchop, whom the earl of Tyrone in a letter to George Dowdall in 1550, had referred to as 'the blind doctor who calls himself Primate'. In 1551 it is recorded that Dowdall took flight, writing that 'he wolde never be bushope where tholie mass was abolished'. It was deemed on 2 February 1553 that he had resigned and Hugh Goodacre was consecrated archbishop in his place. But as remarked above he was reappointed to the See the first day of the following month. In 1558, the year of his death, he brought charges against the lord deputy. Whether or not it was in anticipation of his demise, it was requested that he be speedily heard on his arrival, and ordered 'as appertaineth for sclaundering unjustly as a minister in so great a charge'. In a letter of 17 November the previous year he said that 'this pore realme was newer in my rememberaunce in worse case than it is nowe, except the tyme onely that Oneyll and Odonyll enwaded the english pale and burned a great pece of it'. On 30 May 1558 he submitted articles to the Privy council setting forth at length his reasons in support of the assertions relative to the evil condition and government of Ireland during the administration of the earl of Sussex: 'A man may ryde southe, west, and northe XX and XL myles and see neither house, corne, ne cattell', adding 'Many hundreth of men, wymen, and chilldren are dedde of famyne'. On 4 August, eleven days before his death at the age of 71, the queen in a letter to Lord Deputy Sussex, required him 'to suffer the Primate of Armagh, without peril of the laws, to exercise and use all manner of ecclesiastical censures against the disordered Irishry'.

Dowdalls, who had been prominent in the Pale since the Anglo-Norman invasion, had acquired Dubhdal as the Irish form of the name, and were listed among the principal Irish names in the 1659 Census in the Co. Dublin baronies of Balrothery and Nethercross; in the Co. Meath barony of Screen, and in the Co. Louth baronies of Dundalk and Ardee. In the same Census they were listed as tituladoes in Co. Limerick, Dublin city and county, in Cos. Longford, Meath, Westmeath, and Roscommon. The 1654 Civil Survey shows Lawerence Dowdall of Athlumney, Áth Luimní, to have been the largest Irish Papist landowner in the Co. Meath parish of Ardbraccan, with a total of 359 acres in Hallanstown, Gyanstown and Curraghtown. Lord Ranalagh, Protestant, owned the greater part of the parish with a total of 1,326 acres.

Taylor and Skinner's *Maps* (1778) shows Clown, the residence of Dowdall Esq., east of Trim and just north of the River Boyne. We wonder if this is today's Cloncarneel house? The 1814 *Directory* lists James Dowdall Esq., at Causestown, Co. Meath, and Mr Michael Dowdall at Strawberry Hill, Co. Galway. *Owners of Land of One Acre and Upwards* (1876) lists three Dowdalls in Co. Down, with 28, 34 and 114 acres, and one in Co. Dublin with 46 acres. There was but one in Co. Louth, that of John Dowdall, Lurgankeel, the owner of one single acre. Nearby, in the parish of Dundalk is Dowdallstown, a place where this family were once important enough to give their name. Over half of the forty Dowdalls to be found in telephone directories are in the South, with Co. Louth slightly ahead of Cos. Wexford and Cork.

The Irish for Dowdallstown is *Baile an Dódaigh*.

DOWDALLSHILL

Probably the most commonly used current Irish word for stream is sruthán, but it is also represented by sruill, sreabh, and sruthar. This latter, anglicised as Shrule, names townlands in Cos. Galway, Mayo, Laois, three in Co. Wexford, and one in Co. Longford. In this latter, Lewis' *Topographical Dictionary of Ireland* (1876) gives 'the bloody stream' as the meaning of sruthar, 'from a bloody battle fought here in 960'. It is defined in Ua Duinnín's *Foclóir Gaeilge agus Béarla* as 'a rapid stream'. Ballymulvey in this parish was then listed as the property of the Shouldham family, Moigh being the 'seat' of M. Shouldham. At a meeting in 1824 the local landlord, John Brady Shuldham, was thanked for his £100 donation for repairs to the chapel. Chairing that meeting was George Dowdall, one of a well-known family in this parish engaged in milling and farming at Terlicken.

In 1836 Molyneaux Shuldham was among the deputy-lieutenants of Co. Longford. *Owners of Land* listed John Shuldham, Kilgobbet, Cabinteely, as owner of 11 Co. Dublin acres, with an additional 253 acres in Co. Antrim; Alexander Shuldham, Derry, with 421 acres there; Major E.A. Shuldham, Coolkelure, Dunmanway, as owner of 13,039 acres, and John Shuldham, Gortmore, Ballybrocke, Co. Longford, with 2,571 acres. (We have not located either Gortmore nor Ballybrocke in Co. Longford.)

The surname Dowdall gaelicised *dubhdal* (*dubh* here is not the adjective meaning black), has been prominent in the Pale since the Anglo-Norman invasion. It was listed in the 1659 among the principal Irish names in the county and city of Dublin, and in Co. Limerick. Persons of the name were tituladoes in Cos. Meath, Westmeath, Roscommon and Longford. In the latter county, Nicholas Dowdall was one of two tituladoes for Ballimulvee. This is the Ballymulvey that was later in the possesion of the Shuldhams.

There are most numerous references to Dowdalls in the *Irish Fiants of the Tudor Sovereigns*, from Stephen Dowdall of Athboy, merchant in 1559, up to Richard Dowdall, Losleive, Co. Monaghan in 1603. Merchant Patrick Dowdall of Drogheda was charged in 1572 for discharging '26 tuns of Juberaltare wines without paid the duties'. One of the more notable bearers of the surname was James Dowdall, second justice 'of the Chief Place' from 1565 until he was made chief justice in 1584.

Current telephone directories show around twenty each Dowdall entries in the North, and in the South.

The Irish for Dowdallshill in the Co. Louth parish of Dundalk is Mullach an Dúdálaigh.

BALLYNAHATTIN

The diameter of the greater stone circle of England's dramatic Stonehenge is 97 feet, with the inner circle measuring 76 feet. Three upright stones, being from 16 feet to 30 high, are sunk 4.5 to 8 feet below ground level. Fifty-six white patches, called Aubrey Holes after their 1666 discoverer, are found on the outer diameter of 284 feet. The early writers on Stonehenge in some cases attributed it to Merlin the Wizard, and the earliest known drawing of it, from a 14th century manuscript, is inscribed: 'This year [483] Merlin brought the Giant's Dance by art not by force from Ireland to Stonehenge'.

It is now generally accepted that the chief purpose of Stonehenge was to celebrate some great festival at the winter solstice. A trilithon is a prehistoric structure or monument consisting of three stones, two upright and one resting upon them as a lintel, and five of these form the central court of Stonehenge, dominating the whole monument. These can be compared with, and closely resemble the forecourts of the neolithic horned cairns in Ulster. However, the one which most resembled it no longer exists! In 1758 Thomas Wright writing in *Louthiania*, a survey of castles, antiquities and ancient remains in Co. Louth, described the 'ruinous remains of a temple or theatre on the planes [*sic*] of Ballynahatne, near Dundalk, enclosed on the one side with a rampart and ditch, and seems to have been a great work, of the same kind with that at Stonehenge in England, being open to the East.' His drawing of this monument, republished along with an article by Victor Buckley in *Archaeology Ireland* (Summer 1988), shows a massive circle of stones outside an earthwork, with a double ring of smaller stones in the interior. Henry Morris, writing in 1907 in *Louth Archaeological Journal* proclaimed that the site was Gone! Cleared away! Had Wright being dreaming? Morris' most extensive enquiries failed to locate any vestige of the site. It was, however, still there in 1837 when Lewis' *Topographical Dictionary of Ireland* appeared. Herein we read: 'On the plains of Ballynahatna are the remains of a Druidical Temple partly enclosed by a curving rampart on the outside of which is part of a circle of upright stones; and on a rising ground near this place is a circular fort surrounded by a double fosse and rampart, supposed to have been thrown up by the earliest inhabitants of the country.'

A surface field survey by the Office of Public Works in 1960 proved no more successful. However, an aerial photograph taken in 1970 shows the massive outline of an enclosure in Cairn Beg, the neighbouring townland to Ballynahattin, it being roughly 520 feet in diameter, with two smaller concentric circles in the interior.

Ballynahattin, in the Co. Louth parish of Dundalk, is from Baile na hAitinne, the townland of the furze.

GREENORE

Once named Snámh Ech, 'the swimming-ford of the horses', Carlingford, Co. Louth, is now Cairlinn in Irish. The 'ford' in its English form is from the northern word 'fiord', a sea-inlet, this name being one of a dozen that are wholly or partly Danish found in Ireland. Here is a 15th-century town tower-house, said to have been the site of a mint which was set up in 1467. Three storeys high and fieplaceless, it is remarkable in having mullioned windows which are decorated in pre-Norman Celtic motifs, such as interlacing, as well as a horse and a human head. Down by the quay is King John's Castle, allegedly founded by King John, who stayed there for three days in 1210, but it is likely that Hugh de Lacy may have founded it some years previously. Lord Inchiquin took possession of the castle in 1642, but it was delivered to Sir Charles Coote the following year. In 1689 it was fired upon by the retreating Jacobite forces, and General Schomberg later used it as hospital. Access nowadays to this castle is 'Over a railway bridge and grass'. This is one of thirteen bridges over the now dismantled railway that ran from Ferry Hill, some five miles down river from Newry to Greenore, crossing the Ryland River, Two Mile River, St Patrick River, the Golden River and some unnamed streams. Ferry Hill would appear to have been the site of a ferry crossing. Royal assent for the building of this railway was received in 1863, but it was not until 1873 that a 13-mile line from Dundalk to Greenore was opened for traffic, and sailing from Dundalk to Holyhead commenced. Three years later the 13½ mile section between Newry and Greenore was opened, enabling regular boat trains to run from Belfast to Greenore. This line was finally closed down in December 1951. The 'ore' in Greenore, as in Carnsore (Point), Co. Wexford, is the old Scandinavian name for the sandy point of a promontory, according to P.W. Joyce in *Names of Places*. Today's official Irish name is An Grianfort.

Meath

Concern with the environment might be thought to be a modern 'fad', but in 1574, when Mr John Bath of Dromconragh was granted a 21-year lease 'upon Clonturk', not only was he required to find the priest and repair the church, but he should 'plant one hondred ashes abowte the same meares within thre years next ensuing ... and shall preserve the said ashes (as above) ther growing at the end of the said terme ...' The 1654 *Civil Survey*, describing Clonturk 80 years later, informed: 'There is upon ye premisses One Castle wth a Stone house slated One Barne & a Gate house slated Three thatcht houses valued by ye Jury at 500£. Also an orchard & some few ash trees sett for Ornamt.' The Bath family, Irish papists, had 83 acres in the parish of Garrettstown, while the James Bath of Drumcondra, had over a thousand acres in Drumcondra, Ballybough, Drishoge, Clonmel, Ballgriffin, and 'at His farme in Glassnevine'.

Bath(e) is an English toponymic, originally de Bath(e), meaning 'of Bath(e)'. This family was mainly associated with the province of Leinster in medieval times, but it is claimed that the first of the name was Simon Bathe who had lands in Co. Limerick at the start 14th century. However, *Archbishop Alen's Register* lists Alan de Bathe in relation to a quit-claim regarding lands of Villa Walens, Ballyloman and Corbali in 1258. In 1327 Matthew de Bathe was a confidential subject of King Edward II and of his successor Edward III, and in 1333 the latter granted Matthew 'the manor of Rathfay in the County of Meath'. Now rendered Rathfeigh, it derives from Ráth Faiche, 'the fort of the open space/green'. In 1355 John de Bathe was a witness to a hearing regarding the port of Rogershaven in the manor of Swords.

At Tipperary in 1313 Maurice de Bathe, James de Valle, Thomas de Nangle, Maurice McBaghely and Gilbert son of Thomas Nolan, were charged that they by force of arms waylaid Alicia Walour on the highway between the town of Artmayl and Cassell, and against her will led her to Kilmc Clegh, and that Maurice de Bathe there raped her. And though courts at that time were quick to pronounce 'Therefore let him be hanged', and 'Therefore let her be hanged' for much lesser crimes, Maurice and pals got off with a fine.

The Irish Fiants of the Tudor Sovereigns (1521–1603) list the name Bathe *c.*120 times, wherein persons so named were given as principal solicitor, chancellor of exchequer, chief chamberlain of exchequer, clerk of castle chambers, chief serjeant of Kildare, sheriff of Meath, recorder of Drogheda, mayor of Drogheda, and second judge of common bench. Bathe lands were then at Ardmulchen, Dullardstown and Athcarne, Co. Meath, and at Drumcondra, Co. Dublin.

At a time when the oppression of Catholics in Ireland in the early 17th century was leading to learning being 'extinguished', those who travelled abroad often attained 'singular perfection and reputation in sundry sciences…' Among eight such persons noted was David Bathe.

The 1659 *Census* lists but two of the name – George Bath, Dixistown, and Peter Bath, Great Waterside, both places in the parish of Rathfeigh. The 1814 *Directory* list, Neville Bath, Esq., Mounthovel, in the Co. Cork parish of Carrigaline.

The frequency of this surname in our usual sources decreases down to our times, and in the combined telephone directories of this island there are but four entries for Bathe – one in Co. Kildare and three in Dublin; there are three for Bath – one in Kildare and two in Dublin, and a single de Bath is in Co. Wexford. We return to 1876 and *Owners of and* wherein there are two entries of the name. The Reps. of Joseph Bath had 25 acres in Co. Mayo, and Mrs Mary Bath, Oranmore, had a single Co. Galway acre. Might these have been descendants of Patrick Bath, Rathfeigh, Co. Meath, and Robert Bath, Culpin, in the same county, transplanted to Co. Roscommon some time between 1654 and 1658? Patrick received 150 acres at Ardcarne in the barony of Boyle, Co. Roscommon, and Robert was granted 118 acres in Lissonuffy in the barony of Roscommon in the same county.

BEGGSTOWN

'Nicknames', additional to a person's first-name and surname found in 16th- and 17th-century documents, mostly refer to hair colour, or to facial or physical characteristics. A man bearing the same first-name as his father had *óg, anglice* oge, added to his name, but *beag* (small), however, rarely features.

Irish surnames are mainly formed by placing Mac (son of) or Ó (descendant of) before a personal name. Beag was a personal name, and of course, existed before surnames came into use. Beag, son of Conla, lord of Teathbha (parts of Co. Westmeath and Co. Longford), died in 766; Beag was the name of the king of Ulster who died in 934. A chief of Teathbha who died in 949, had his name rendered Bec in the Annals of the Four Masters. Around the same time lived St Bec, son of Gairbhith, lord of Derlass (part of Co. Down).

Seán de Bhulbh's *Sloinnte na hÉireann/Irish Surnames* published in 1997, concurs with MacLysaght's *Surnames* that the surname Begg(s) comes from the Irish *beag*, little. The name is Scottish in Ulster, but elsewhere the Normans adopted the epithet beag. *Surnames* says that this is rendered Bueg in Co. Cork, but does not definitively state how the surname should be rendered in Irish. De Bhulbh gives it as Beag (? Nóra Bheag), and Revd Patrick Woulfe's *Sloinnte Gaedheal* is Gall as Beag and Ó Beig.

One of the six listed witnesses to a document of 19 July 1259 at Clondolchane (Clondalkin, Co. Dublin), was Richard Beg. This man was provost to Archbishop Luke. Henry Bege was among those questioned about tenancy in the same area around the same time. Dean Alyn's will of 12 December 1505 mentions a David Begge of Dyveleke (Duleek, Co. Meath). To the poor he left the houses he had begun to build for them. 'The poor to be received and preferred in the said house are not any poor whatever, but faithful Catholics of good repute, honest life and English nation; especially of the nation of the Alynes, Barretes, Beggs, Hillis, Dillones and Rodiers in the dioceses of Meath and Dublin'.

The Justiciary Rolls for the years 1308 to 1313 list ten persons of this surname, variously rendered Beg, Bege and Begs, mainly as jurors, in the counties of Dublin, Meath, Louth, Kildare, and Limerick. *The Calendar of Inquisitions* for Co. Dublin lists persons of this name from 1517 up to 1660. A juror of 1527 was Robert Begg of Mydnyghteston (? Midnightstown – we have not located it). Others were from Newcastle Lyons, Tassagard (Teach Sagard, now Saggart), Henrieston, Painestown (Co. Meath), Freyselston (Fletcherstown, Co. Meath), Moyashyr (Moyagher, Magh Fhiachra, Co. Meath), and Boranstown/ Baronstown. This latter was rendered Bairanstown (Baranstown, Co. Dublin) in *Transplantation to Connaught 1654–58*, as the place of origin of Matthew Begg who received 297 acres at Deran & Kilbride (now Kilbride) in Co. Roscommon. Then also George Begg of Flesherstown (the above Fletcherstown), had been granted 150 acres at Aughrim, Co. Roscommon.

The Co. Meath volume of the Civil Survey 1654–8, shows John Begg of Athboy with a share in 850 acres at Moyagher (Magh Fhiachra), and Robert Begg of Navan and 'Begg of ffletcherstowne' with a share in 147 acres in the parish of Teltown. Beggs are listed as tituladoes in the Civil Survey of 1659 for Cos. Westmeath, Roscommon, Tipperary, Clare, and Antrim, as well as being among the principal Irish names in the Co. Antrim barony of Belfast.

The largest Beggs holdings in 1876 were the 1,075 acres at Bellview, Coolbawn, Co. Tipperary, and the 1,117 acres in Co. Limerick.

Telephone dirctories in the Republic list over 25 each of Beggs and Biggs, mainly in Dublin. In the North there are *c.*234 Beggs listed, and a single Biggs. Its not possible to say how many of these bear the English surname Bigg (big, strong), as these names interchanged, a fact borne out by the presence of both Beggstown and Bigstown in Co. Meath.

LAGORE

If it appears that the first element of a place-name is *loch*, where a lake no longer exists, then perforce, it must be assumed that the lake has long since dried up. It is generally taken that the first element of the original Irish for Lagore, the name of a Co. Meath townland is *loch*. P.W. Joyce in his *Names of Places*, gives the Irish as Loch Gabhra 'lake of the horse', adding that the lake has been long dried up. (*Gabhar*, now taken to mean a goat, in early times also meant a horse). The Annals of the Four Masters say that in Anno Mundi 3581 nine lakes erupted in Ireland, one of which was Loch Gobhar. In the year 848 AD the island of Loch Gobhar was plundered. So not only did a lake exist, but had an island therein! John O'Donovan's 1851 translation of the Annals adds a footnote: 'This island was explored some years since, and several curious antiques were found there. The lake has now entirely dried up'. The name is now written Loch Gabhair (Lake of the goats).

William Petty's *Hiberniae Delineatio* – his Atlas of Ireland, published in 1685 – hows two lakes – a small and a large lake, Little Lagore and Big Lagore. The first was the source of the river now named Broadmeadow Water, and the latter somewhat to the south of the river, was connected by a short tributary. The Co. Meath book of the 1654 Civil Survey renders these placenames Biglagoore and Littlelagoore, and gives 'the Gower water' as the northern boundary of the townland of Raystown. In 1640 a large portion of the parish of Dunshaughlin wherein Big- and Littlelagore was owned by Joseph Plunkett, Irish papist.

In 1814 Lagore is listed as the residence of Patrick Thunder, Esquire, and *Owners of Land* (1876) lists Michael Thunder as holding 548 acres in Co. Dublin; 77 acres in Co. Westmeath, and 1,065 acres at Lagore. There were also Thunder holdings of 374 and 1,713 acres in Co. Wexford. MacLysaght's *Surnames* says that Thunder is a name of Norse origin found in Cos. Louth and Dublin from medieval times. Though MacLysaght does not subscribe to it, Ó Tórna is used as the Irish of Thunder. He gives (O) Torney as the only anglicized form of Ó Tórna.

The above Plunketts later acquired three peerages, one of which was the earldom of Fingall. Daisy Burke of Galway who married Lord Fingall in 1883 wrote *Seventy Years Young: Memories of Elizabeth, Countess of Fingall*, an account of 'that twilit world of Catholic Ascendancy Ireland, a world in transition from viceregal, country-house Ireland of Dublin drawing rooms and Meath hunting fields . . .' She relates an incident from those hunting fields. 'In another ditch a Meath gentleman fell one day at the head of the hunt and lay, while thirty others or more went over him. Patrick Thunder of Lagore was his magnificent sounding name and address. Every time he lifted his head, "Duck Pat"! called another rider, high in the air. "Duck Pat"! cried another, coming after him. Thirty times Pat Thunder of Lagore ducked his head and lived to tell the tale.'

The Thunders had been in north Leinster for hundreds of years before that. There was an Alex Thunder at Huntstown, Co. Kildare, in 1445; an inventory of all the goods of Thomas Fynglas and his wife Rose Fitz Eustace, dated 22 September 1475 indicates that Patrick Thonder was owed 3*s*. 8*d*.; Alex Thonder was at Newcastle in 1529; Elizabeth Thonder was listed at the Knocks in the parish of Dunshaughlin, Co. Meath in 1558. Elizabeth Thonder was left the lands of the Knock and the Maw in her husband's will, signed in 1550. This was again mentioned in 1609. Geoffrey and Reygnagh Thundyr were among the jurors at a hearing at Knocktopher on 14 October 1428, regarding the ownership of a field called 'le Skardagh', in the tenement of Robinstown.

There are 20 Thunder telephone entries for the whole island, one of which is in Co. Galway, the remainder being in the Dublin 01 area. Ó Tórna has three entries, again all in the 01 area.

ASHBOURNE

Gasitéar na hÉireann / Gazetteer of Ireland, along with the six booklets published by Brainse Logainmneacha na Suirbhéireachta Ordanáis on the placenames of Cos. Kilkenny, Limerick, Louth, Monaghan, Offaly, and Waterford, under the general title *Liostaí Logainmneacha*, as well as *Logainmneacha na hÉireann: Contae Luimnigh*, and the six volumes published by the Northern Ireland Placename Project, four for Co. Down and one each for Cos. Antrim and Derry, all helpfully provide indexes to both the Irish and English versions of placenames. This is also true of Canon Power's *The Place-Names of Decies*. Most other sources, however, only provide an index of the English forms. In Aindrias Ó Múineacháin's *Dócha agus Duainéis* we find the placename Cnoc Bhaile Uí Mheachair, Co. Tipperary. For the purpose of locating this place it was necessary to know its English form. Was it Ballymeagher Hill? Ballymaher Hill? Or Meagherstown Hill etc.? Or Knockballymeagher etc.? None of these is to be found in the *Index of Townlands, Parishes and Baronies* (1851). This place, Ó Múineacháin informs us, was the birthplace of Edward Gibson, attorney, father of one William Gibson. Edward Gibson (1837–1913) given in *A Dictionary of Irish History* 1800–1980 as being born in Dublin, was a Unionist politician, and was elected MP for Trinity in 1875. In 1885 he was appointed lord chancellor of Ireland, and was also raised to the peerage. He adopted the title of Baron Ashbourne, after his then place of residence. William (1868–1992), who succeeded him as second Lord Ashbourne, was a scholar and active member of the Gaelic League. He was a generous – and anonymous – financial benefactor of the League, of which he was president for a time. Most notably he was the *first* to speak Irish in the House of Lords in London when on 27 June 1918 he started with 'Beidh sé i mo chumas gan ach Gaeilge a labhairt agus mise ag cur i gcéill daoibh ar an gceist seo. Tá Gaeilge againn in Éirinn . . .' Most strangely, when he decided to use his name in Irish, he called himself Liam Mac Giolla Bhríde.

Were the Gibsons of Cnoc Bhaile Uí Mheachair in any way connected with the Gibsons of Rockforest in the Co. Tipperary parish of Corbally, where Captain Gibson had 5,214 acres in 1876. Apart from the captain, one Daniel Gibson, Derrinsalla, Birr, had 32 Co. Tipperary acres. There were Gibson holdings in 6 Leinster counties; 4 in the province of Ulster, and a single holding in Co. Sligo. Most of these were of modest size, the larger ones being in Cos. Westmeath and Meath.

Edward MacLysaght's *Surnames* says that Gibson '. . . in Ireland usually a name of Scottish origin, which like Gibb, is a branch of the Clan Buchanan. Gibson is very numerous in the Belfast area. Gibson and Gibney have been occasionally assumed instead of Giblin'.

Three were plain Misters, two were reverend gentleman, and three were esquires. The 1659 Census lists a titulado each in Dunmuskye (Dunmucky), Clonshogh (Clonshagh), and Baldongan, all in Co. Dublin. Francis Gibson was a Co. Westmeath commissioner for the 1660 poll-money ordinance, and Richard of Clonsaugh was a Co. Cavan comissioner for 1660 and 1661.

Ashbourne is in the Co. Meath parish of Killegland. This parish name was earlier spelled Killeglan, a closer anglicised form of the now official Irish name, Cill Dhéagláin.

ATHBOY

The fact that he was nearly fifty before he got married would not necessarily mean that the 3rd earl of Darnley was in any way mentally deficient, though he did suffer from delusions. Many persons of less ennobled status suffered delusions of far greater grandeur than that of the earl – the poor man believed that he was a teapot. In 1766, when he had held the family title and estates for nearly twenty years, he unexpectedly got married. His bride was an adjacdent heiress named Stoyte, whose inheritance was well situated to form an adjunct to his own Meath/ Westmeath estate. In spite of his initial alarm that his spout would come off in the night, he fathered at least seven children between 1766 and 1781.

On 29 June 1725 John Bligh, with addresses in Kent and London in England, and at Clifton Lodge, Co. Meath, was created earl of Darnley, Viscount Darnley and Baron Clifton (Baron Clifton in England). *The Penguin Dictionary of*

Surnames says that Bligh(e) is a variant of Blyth(e), meaning 'cheerful, gentle', though possibly with references to 'gentle/pleasant streams', a name which the author Basil Cottle considers strange for 'the uncompromising Captain' – he of *Mutiny on the Bounty*. Edward MacLysaght's *Surnames* gives this surname as Ó Blighe, adding that in Connaught it is derived from a Norse personal name. Elsewhere it is a synonym of Blythe, which is of dual origin; from the adjective Blithe and the place Blyth: as such the form used in Irish is de Blagdh.

In the 1659 Census Major and William Bligh were tituladoes of Damaske Street in Dublin; and John and William Blith were Co. Meath commissioners for the poll-money ordinance of 1660 and 1661, both also being commissioners for the town of Athboy. Taylor and Skinner's *Maps* (1783) shows 'Blighe Esq.' at Brittas, Co. Meath, and the 1814 *Directory* shows Thomas Blighe at Brittas. The only other of the name listed in that directory was Samuel Blighe Esq. of Daisy Hill, Durrow, Co. Laois. The Blighs were still scarce in 1876, and *Owners of Land* lists but Major F.C. Bligh of 40 Lower Dominick Street, Dublin, owner of 491 acres in Co. Meath, and the earl of Darnley, Clifton Lodge, Athboy, who had a whopping 21,858 acres in the same county. John, 4th earl of Darnley, an absentee, normally resident in England, had returned two relatives to Parliament for the manor borough of Athboy, though both were absent from the divisions of 1799, and the earl's attitude to the proposed Act of Union remained uncertain. When he visited Ireland he pressed Marquess Cornwallis, British master-general of the ordnance, to grant the vacancy of storekeeper at Chatham to one of his clients. As Darnley as been particularly abusive when he had been previously refused, the viceroy at first turned down the request, though concerned that this would make Darnley Anti-Unionist. Cornwallis reflected that it was 'a sad thing to be forced to manage knaves, but it is ten times worse to deal with fools'.

Athboy situated on a river of the same name, is the anglicised form of Baile Átha Buí, 'the town of the yellow ford'. Clifton Lodge is marked on the Ordnance Survey map, as is the nearby Co. Meath Gaeltacht of Ráth Cairn. Spelled Bligh and Blyth (occasionally with a terminal 'e'), the name is listed 46 times in Southern telephone directories and apart from the Dublin area it is numerous in the Cork area, in the 09 area of Mayo and Galway. There are 20 listed in Northern *Phone Book*.

AGHER

Presumably all those whose ancestors bore the Irish name Mac Giolla Gheimhridh, anglicised Mac Alivery, now bear the surname Winter (*geimhreadh*, winter), as there is not a single entry of Mac Alivery in any of the country's telephone directories. The first to be named Winter was in England and was because of birth in a hard winter, or because 'of white hair, or lugubriousness', with Winters meaning 'son of Winter'. *The Phone Book* of Northern Ireland has no entry of either forms, while in the Dublin area it is Winters 65, Winter 52, and in the remainder of the country Winters 50, Winter 10. An early note-worthy bearer of the name was Admiral Sir William Winter, who was instructed in 1580 to search the Irish coast for Spanish ships. This led to the discovery of the Spanish-Italian force at Dún an Óir at Smerwick, Co. Kerry, and the massacre of the 600 troops there. Three captives had their legs broken at a forge, and were hanged, drawn and quartered the next day.

After a night spent in his cabin suffering from the effects of sea sickness, Lord Henry Cromwell arrived at the Bay of Dublin on 9 July 1655, and 'was met on the sands by the Lord Deputy and Council, and most of the officers and gentry of Ireland, nigh 500 horses, with ten coaches and four horses apiece, and a very magnificent entertainment, more than could be expected from so poor and ruined country', reported the journal *Perfect Proceedings*. Cromwell was inaugurated lord chancellor of Trinity College, where Samuel Winter was the newly-established provost. Winter took a practical interest in converting Catholics, and among the books he carried with him on his tour of Ulster was a catechism in Irish. However, he liked indulgent living, and had a love of good horses. He had shipped thoroughbreds from England, and caused a furore when one of them was stolen while he was on his Ulster tour. In a footnote in his *An Epoch in Irish History* (1903), John P. Mahaffy writes: 'There is a peculiar breed of very large horses still kept at Mr Winter's place, Agher, in Westmeath. It would be interesting to know whether they are derived from the Provost's importation.' His will shows that he acquired considerable estates in Ireland- one in Co. Offaly of 1,000 acres, and a still larger one at Agher, Westmeath. These must have been grants of confiscated lands from the commissioners to make up for the loss of his comfortable living in England. In 1731 several houses of the Revd Sankey Winter, dean of Kildare, were set on fire and burned.

Taylor and Skinner's *Maps* (1783) shows 'Winter Esq.' at Agher, on the road between Kilcock and Summerhill, and the 1814 *Directory* shows John P. Winter at Agher, Co. Meath. There were also Winters at Palmira, Co. Cavan; Killinan, Co. Westmeath, and Duighira, Co. Sligo. In 1836 John Pratt Winter, esq., Agher, was listed as a magistrate for Cos. Kildare and Meath. *Owners of Land* (1876) lists the Reps. of Francis Winters with 436 acres in Co. Kilkenny; George Winter, Fiji Islands, with 773 acres in Co. Offaly, and Samuel Winter, Clondriss, Killucan, with 839 Co. Cavan acres. The then resident at Agher was John Winter, who, besides the 1,640 acres there, he additionally had 206 acres in Co. Kildare, 395 acres in Co. Kilkenny, and 940 acres in Co. Cavan.

We have found no Agher in Co. Westmeath, but there are two in Co. Meath-
one in the parish of Gallow, and the other in a parish of the same name. The
official Irish for this place, which was originally named Agherpallice, is Achair
(meaning uncertain).

FAGANSTOWN

The flexible and inventive way our ancestors shaped and used their native Irish
language may be appreciated by scanning down through the definition of the
word *crann* in Ua Duinnin's *Focloir Gaedhilge agus Bearla*. From its common
definition 'a tree', it widens out to mean 'a bole; mast, shaft, a handle, a bolt, a
bar, a beam, a stave, a timber, and figuratively, a beam of light'. Combined with
other words it has many additional and wide-ranging meanings. *Crann saingeal*,
sanctuary railing; *crann trasna*, a transom; *crann teallaigh*, a fire-poker; *crann
reidhtigh*, a peacemaker; *crann solais*, a chandelier, but figuratively a noble person;
cranmn snaimh, a canoe, particularly a dug-out; a bedstead. And more and more!
But not included here, and we cannot recall where we came across it is *crann clis*
(*cleas*, a play, a game, sport; a feat, device, trick; craft; art, science). This was used
to denote the penis, and whether this was used out of playfulness or tricking
with words, or as a code, we cannot say. The same kind of naming continued
down to the days of our Kerry youth, two samples which we recall – 'John
Thomas', giving the member not only a personal name and a surname; and
'Fagan', a plain surname, addressing the member by surname only, in the
manner of the ruling classes.

The surname Fagan is usually of Norman origin in Cos. Dublin and Meath,
is not Irish in spite of its Irish appearance (-gán is one of the most common
termination of Irish surnames). Nor is it English but derives from the Latin
word *paganus*. Ó Faodhagáin, the name of an Oriel sept, was sometimes
anglicised Fagan, and usually Fegan in Co. Louth. 'As early as 1200 one William
Fagan was the owner of extensive property in the city of Dublin, and 50 years
later we find the family firmly established in the neighbouring counties with
a seat, acquired a little later, at Feltrim, Co. Dublin' (MacLysaght, *Irish Families*).
The name is not really numerous here, numbering an estimated 2,000, mainly
in Leinster, with 50 per cent of those in Dublin.

Christopher Fagane was mayor of Dublin in 1574, when at a meeting of the
Dublin Assembly on the fourth Friday after Easter, the second item dealt with
read as follows: 'Where(as) it is thought that this cittie is exceedinglie infected
with the horrible vice of whoredome, and the preachers of Goddes worde do
contynuallie pronounce Goddes vengeaunce to be at hande yf the same be not

speedylie remedyed; it is therefore ordeyned and established by auctoritie of this assemblie that whatsoever maide from hensforth shall defile her bodie with fylthie fornicacion within the cittie or suburbis, being duelie convicted thereof, by testimonye of her neighbours or otherwise, shall forthwith be comytted to pryson, and there remayne in irons or stocks during xxi daies, and then to be brought forthe to the market place and pilloried two market daies, and soo be banysshed the cittie for ever, unless after she be maryed to sum honest man, and then upon her amendment to be restored and receyved as an inhabitant, and that the partie whiche commytted fornycacion with her shall lykewise be commytted to prison and pilloried as is aforesaid ...' Oh, what 'Fagan' has to answer for!

The fiants of the Tudor sovereigns (1521–1603) list the first Fagan in 1559 when Christopher Fagan, yeoman, was pardoned. In 1568 George Fagan was granted a small messauge in the Dublin parish of St Werburg. In 1573 James Fagan, yeoman, of Waterford was pardoned, and the same year Christophre Fagane, merchant of Dublin, was granted a licence in regard the tithes of the parish of Martrie, Co. Meath. Three years later William Faggan of Clonmel, was granted a two-year licence to make and sell aqua vitae in the towns of 'Carrige, Casshell and Clonmell'. In 1599 John Poolie was granted the wardship of and marriage of Elionar Fagan, daughter and heir of Thomas, son and heir of Christopher Fagan late of Dublin, alderman, and custody of the lands during minority. There were a number of Fagan pardons down the years in Cos. Dublin, Westmeath and Waterford. Among those pardoned in a fiant of 1602 were Edmond ban Fagan of Ballentolcho, Co. Waterford; Teige m'Cahell Fagan of same; Tomultagh Fagan of Killmore; Thomas m'Mullaghen and Cahell duff Fagan of Carlanstown; Manus oge and Cormuck Fagan of Foyran; William ruo Fagan of Baullane, and Gillpatrick m'Conor Fagan of Ballecunnoill.

Faganstown (Baile Fágáin) is a townland name in the Co. Meath parish of Gernonstown.

DRUMBARAGH

Was Richard Woodward, bishop of Cloyne, the Revd R. Woodward, who on 1 June 1803 forwarded through Mr Knox, the tidy sum of £100 to the Revd Thomas Barry, parish priest of Mallow? We know not what service the parish priest had performed to earn this money, but one has to be somewhat suspicious as the payment was made through the Secret Service Money for Ireland as revealed in Gilbert's *Documents Relating to Ireland, 1795–1804*. In 1787

Woodward published *The Present State of the Church of Ireland*, containing a 'Description of its Precarious Situation and the Consequence Danger to the Public, an alarmist pamphlet in reaction to the Munster Rightboys' demand that tithes should be abolished, or at least abated. This was clearly more than a narrow defence of the tithes system, and Woodward linked the survival of the Established Church to the survival of the social order for which it stood.

The surname Woodward is an occupational name from 'wood-keeper, forester'. It is not listed in MacLysaght's *Surnames*, though the name has been in Ireland since at least the early 14th century. On 14 March 1326 William Woodward along with nineteen others examined the extent of the manor of St Sepulchre, and on oath swore that at St Sepulchre's there 'are a stone hall badly roofed with shingles and unsafe, a chamber annexed, a kitchen and a chapel badly roofed; of no value, because nothing could be got from them, and they need great repair; there was a prison there, now broken and thrown down'.

Among the 'Adventurers for Land in Ireland 1642–46' was Hezekiah Woodward, who got a grant of 222 acres in the barony of Clanwilliam. The appropriate map in Prendergast's *Cromwellian Settlement of Ireland* does not give the exact location of this land, but it appears to be in the Golden – New Inn area. It was at Cloghprior, further to the north in Co. Tipperary that William Woodward was listed, along with Edward Card as tituladoes in the 1659 Census. Benjamin Woodward was titulado of Kells, Co. Kilkenny; Lyonell Woodward was titulado of New Ross, Co. Wexford, and in the same county Captain Richard Woodward, gent., was titulado of Ballenaparke.

Taylor and Skinner's 1778 *Maps* lists 'Rd. Dr Woodward Esq.' at Drumbarra (Droim Bearach) in the Co. Meath parish of Kells, and the 1814 *Directory* gives this as the residence of H. Woodward, Esq. The *Directory* also gives Revd H. Woodward at Woodly, Fethard, Co. Tipperary. On 4 February 1847 both the *Packet* and the *Tipperary Vindicator* published a letter from the Revd Woodward, rector of Fethard, regarding a visit he made to Co. Mayo. A poor man who joined him on the road spoke of the prevailing famine, saying that he would rather die in the ditch 'than do anything out of the way'. Praising this patient sufferer, Woodward added: 'The country is full of such instances of meek submission to the will of a chastising Providence ...'

Owners of Land (1876) lists the Revd Thomas Woodward, Downpatrick, Co. Down, with one acre in Co. Dublin, and 1,222 acres in Co. Longford; the 60 Co. Armagh acres of the Revd Charles Woodward, England, were in the hands of his Reps; Charles Woodward (no address supplied) had 147 Co. Cavan acres, and Fanny L. Woodward, London, had 85 Co. Clare acres. Current telephone directories list 14 Woodwards in Cos. Down, Antrim and Derry, with two in Co. Cork and one in Co. Kerry.

DOOLYSTOWN

Of the surname Dooley/Dooly/Dowly MacLysaght's *Irish Families* says: 'The sept has produced no outstanding personality in Ireland.' Outside of Ireland, however, there was the fictitious Mr Dooley, a Chicago saloonkeeper in Finlay Peter Dunn's novels. And what of Tom Dooley, he who was admonished to 'hang down his head and cry', the subject of a 1960s (?) ballad? And wasn't there a noted musical group called The Dooleys? And indeed the hurling heroes of Offaly! Mainly anglicised Dooley and Dooly, Ó Dubblaoich (*dubh*, black; *laoch*, hero or warrior), this Westmeath sept was described in the Annals of the Four Masters as lords of Fertullagh (Fir Tullach, 'the men of the hills'). The Annals note the killing of Ó Dubblaoich, lord of Feara Tulach, by his own people in 1140, and the killing of Toirealbbach Ua Conchobbair, heir apparent to the monarch of Ireland, at Bealach Muine na Siride in 1144 by Ua Dubblaich, lord of Feara Tulach. They were driven from Fir Tulach by the O'Melaghlins and the Tyrrells and migrated to the Ely O'Carroll country where they acquired a footing on the western slopes of Slieve Bloom.

In 1513 Hewe O Dowly received a gift of a hackney from Gerald Fitz Gerald, earl of Kildare, and was among those given a horse in 1517. Patrick O Dowley was among a Wexford group pardoned in 1553, and William and Robert Dowly, butchers of Irishtown, Kilkenny, were among those pardoned in 1557. Among those of Upper Ossory pardoned in 1591 was Dermot O Dooly. Though none of the name was listed a titulado in the 1659 Census, Dooley/ Dowley/Duley was among the principal Irish names in a barony each of Cos. Tipperary, Offaly and Kilkenny, and in five baronies of Laois.

None of this name appeared to have had sufficient wealth to have a residence shown on Taylor and Skinner's 1778 *Maps* though Daniel Dooly was of sufficient substance to have been a witness to a Frankford, Co. Offaly, will of 1795. In 1799 David Thompson, Banagher, in the same county, left an annuity to his wife, Elinor Thompson otherwise Dooly. Peter Dooly, Maree, Co. Galway, was a witness to a Lahardaun, Co. Galway, will of 1818, while William Dooly, Elingrove, Co. Offaly was witness to a will of 1831. This latter place is rendered Ellen Grove in *Owners of Land* (1876) where Mrs Elizabeth Dooly lived on 19 acres. She also had 79 acres in Co. Tipperary. The largest Dooley holding in the country was the 1,002 acres of Samuel Dooley, Mountbriscoe, Birr, Co. Offaly. (This was the residence of Nugent Briscoe in 1814.) There were two other smallish Dooley holdings in Co. Offaly; modest holdings in Cos. Laois and Westmeath, and small holdings in Cos. Kilkenny, and Wexford.

In 1819 the magistrates and principal inhabitants of Parsonstown, believing that 'the lower classes had entered into a Conspiracy against the Laws and Constitution of their country', founded 'The Parsonstown Loyal Association' at a meeting held in Dooley's Ball Room, Birr. Henry Dooley was Master of the Masonic Lodge in 1889 and two of his daughters had been matrons of the Workhouse from 1871 until 1887.

Conversion to Protestantism in Ireland in times gone by was betimes from conviction, though frequently for advantage and advancement. Nor were the Dool(e)ys any different. Is it likely that John Dooley, who was high constable of Dublin, was a Catholic? In 1823 he prayed to be continued in his position in a submission to Dublin Corporation. (He was to continue so for at least another ten years.) That same year the corporation sent a petition to the House of Commons regarding a bill in favour of the Roman Catholics of Ireland. It begged the House not to exempt the Catholics from 'those disabilities which the wisdom and prudence of our forefathers considered indespensible to the safety of the Protestant Establishment', claiming that the tenets of the Protestant Church had been 'vitally attacked by sacrilegious and blasphemous incendiaries'.

Rendered Doolystown in the Civil Survey of 1654, it is Baile Dúlaoich in Irish.

MAPERATH

Those of us who learned 'compulsory' Latin at school (and we recall studying it in our final year at primary school under the now much maligned Irish Christian Brothers), will remember the first lesson 'Amo, amas, amat', 'I love, you love, she or he loves'. This Latin verb gave rise to the personal name of Amabel, 'lovable', of which Mabel was a diminutive form. Mabel in turn had its own diminutive form, Mabb, which became a surname. This English surname, also spelled Mapp, Mape and Mappe, was among the principal Irish families in Ireland down to the end of the reign of Henry VIII, and towards the end of the 16th, and beginning of the 17th century. It gave name to Mabestown in the Co. Dublin parish of Kinsaley; to Mapestown in the Co. Waterford parish of Kilrush; to Mabestown in the Co. Westmeath parish of Castletowndelvin; to Mabestown in the Co. Meath parish of Kilbride, and to Maperath in the Co. Meath parish of Loughan (or Castlekeeran).

The Description of Ireland in anno 1598 lists Map of Mapston, and Map of Maprath among the chief gentlemen of Co. Meath. The parish of Dewleene (now Dulane), in the barony of Kells is given in the 1654 Civil Survey as being bounded on the east with the parish of Kells, on the west with the parish of Loghan, on the north with the parish of Moynalty and on the south with the Blackwater. Here in 1640, at Maperath, was Gerrald Mape, Irish papist, on 430 acres. He possessed a further 418 acres at The Mote (now Moat, parish of

Kilbeg), Cornesauce (now Cornasaus, parish of Dulane), Curragh (parish of Dulane) & Clonfanan.

Ringforts, variously called lios, rath, cathair, caiseal and dún in Irish, developed in the Early Bronze Age, and it is estimated that the number in Ireland runs into tens of thousands. The latest date for which excavation has produced clear evidence of occupation is the 11th century, though historical data suggest that the forts were occupied at even a later date. It is almost certain that the fort to which the Mape family gave its name, had an older name. *Onomasticon Goedelicum* lists over five hundred placenames with ráith as the first element, and of those in Co. Meath whose more precise location is unknown, one may be what later became known as Maperath; its Irish is Rath an Mhábaigh.

The surname Mape appears not to have survived in Ireland, nor do we know when they departed Co. Meath, but Taylor and Skinner's 1778 *Maps* shows Maprath as the residence of 'Rowley, Esquire', and in 1814 Thomas Rowley Esq. was living here. This is an English surname, meaning 'roughwood/clearing', being in Ireland as far back as the Ulster Plantation. This was adopted by the Connaught family Ó Rothláin as one of its anglicised forms, with Rolan(d) and Rowland being somewhat better representations of the original Irish.

In 1876 Henry Rowley, Maperath, Kells, had 584 Co. Meath acres; the Hon. H.L. Rowley, Carlton Club, London, had 1,472 acres; the Hon. Richard Rowley (no address supplied) had 1,142 acres; Standish G. Rowley, Sylvan Park, Crossakeel, had 1,165 acres, and the Hon. Hercules Rowley, Marley House, Rathfarnham, had 1,231 Co. Dublin acres. Today the Rolands are few, outnumbered by the Rowlands and Rowleys, who are now mainly in Co. Mayo, particularly the latter name.

DUNSHAUGHLIN

Heads are not shrunk to fit hats; hands are not trimmed to slip into gloves, nor are feet pared to wiggle into shoes – if such were so then there would have been a different ending to the story of Cinderella. There is a perception abroad that the authorities at times shorten the original Irish of placenames to more readily fit on road-signs and on the stamp cancelling franking mark on letters. If such a perception is correct, then the same solution might be applied in all cases: increase the size of the hats, gloves, shoes, road-signs and the circular franking marks. We cannot say if such accommodations were the reasons for the official An Gort, An Chathair etc, but the loss felt by some residents of Dunshaughlin, at the accepted Irish for that place, Dún Seachlainn instead of

Domhnach Seachlainn, cannot be blamed on the authorities. Dunshaughlin has been the anglicised form of this placename, long predating road-signs and the postal service. The Ordnance Survey, advised by An Coimisiún Logainmeacha, in deciding the Irish form of a placename, sometimes choose the version that has had common acceptance though it might be known to be inaccurate. But apart from some difficulties with road-signs and franking marks, would there have been any great disturbance in replacing the incorrect Dún Seachlainn, 'the fort of Seachlann' with the attested Domhnach Seachlainn, 'the church of Seachlann'?

Domhnach, a church, especially one founded by St Patrick, was founded by Sechnall (St Secundinus), who was sent with Auxilius and Iserninus in 439 to help St Patrick in Ireland. Gaelicized Sechnall, Seachnall and Seachlann it gave rise to the personal name Mael Seachnaill or Mael Seachlainn, 'devotee of St Seachnall'. This in turn gave rise to the surname Ó Maoilsheachlainn, anglicised (O) Melaghlin, the name of one of the royal houses of Ireland. This family were the descendants of Maoilsheaclainn, better known as Malachy II king of Ireland from 980 to 1002. After the Anglo-Norman invasion the O'Melaghlins, like all the Gaelic princes and chiefs of Meath and central Ireland, were greatly reduced in power. They continued to decline until they disappeared altogether as O Melaghlin in 1691. The remnant of the sept remaining in their ancestral territory were thereafter known as Mac Loughlin. Mac Giolla Seachloinn is listed by the late 14th-century poet Seán Mór Ó Dubbagáin in *Topographical Poems*, as chief of Southern Brega. This area appears to have stretched from Castlekieran to the sea, and from the Boyne to Annagassan. Mac Giolla Seachloinn does not seem to have survived as a surname, though we mention McGillaghen which is listed in the 1659 Census as being among the principal Irish names of the Co. Sligo barony of Tireragh.

The 1654 Civil Survey of Co. Meath, spelling this parish name Donshaghlin, lists among the landowners there in 1640, Robert Bath of Bonestown. It is surmised that a family named Bowen had given its name to Bonestown before ever the Anglo-Norman family of Bathe arrived in Co. Meath. The Bath family was prominent in Leinster in medieval times. In 1814 Neville Bath was listed as living at Mount-hovel in the vicinity of Cork city; in 1836 Joseph Bath Esq. attorney', was living at 6 Mecklenburgh Street, Dublin, and *Owners of Land* (1876) shows Reps. of Joseph Bath in possession of 25 Co. Mayo acres, and Mrs Mary Bath, Oranmore, with one acre in Galway city. The combined telephone directories of Ireland list but three entries of the name Bath, all being in the city of Dublin.

Offaly

Among the Co. Offaly 'Families of 16th century' noted in *The Description of Ireland* (1598) was Briscoe, one of whom had married Eleanor Kearney of Scraghe, near Tullamore. This information was gleaned in 1878 when the *Description* was published, from an inscription over the door of the ruins of the 1588 castle of Scraghe. The 'Representatives in the 19th century' were the Briscoes of Riversdale. Lewis' *Topographical Dictionary of Ireland* (1837) informs us that Shrahikerne castle was built, as appears from an inscription on its ruins, in 1588 by John Briscoe, an officer in Queen Elizabeth's army: its name signifies 'Kearney of the Shragh', 'the remains of whose family house, previously to the building of the castle, are also to be seen'. It appears that the name had already been abbreviated to Srah. This appears to be the Srah in the parish of Kilbride. Kilbride was an earlier name for the Co. Offaly parish of Tullamore. Srah names townlands in Cos. Galway (4), Offaly (2), Mayo (4), Laois (2), Roscommon (2). Spelled SRAGH it names townlands in Cos. Carlow, Clare, Kilkenny, Sligo and Tipperary (3). Srah in Co. Mayo is rendered in *Gasaitéar na hEireann/Gazetteer of Ireland* as 'An tSraith', meaning 'river valley, low-lying land along the river, strath'. This was spelled Strahe in an Elizabethan fiant of 1601 when, among others, Andrew. Briskoe received a pardon. Simington's *Transportation to Connaght, 1654–58* notes that John Briscoe of Sraigh, Co. Kilkenny, was to transport to 200 acres in the Co. Mayo parish of Ballyhean. In 1658 the English adventurer Thomas Briscoe was granted 222 Irish acres (539 English) in the Co. Tipperary barony of Clanwilliam, which we estimate was somewhere around Donohill.

    Gabriell Briscoe was one of two tituladoes in 'Killeninge or Killenenny', in the Co. Dublin barony of Newcastle and Uppercross, while Edward Bryscoe, merchant, was among the tituladoes of St Patrick's Close. Taylor and Skinner's *Maps* (1778) shows 'Briscoe Esq.' at Scraggin (now Screggan), Co. Offaly, southwest of Tullamore; 'Briscow Esq.' at Ganarea, east of Carrick-on-Suir, and at Tinvoan, both in Co. Tipperary. The 1814 *Directory* renders the latter two 'Garrynarca' and 'Tenvane'. Other Briscoes in this *Directory* are at Ross in the Co. Offaly parish of Lynelly, and Mountbriscoe in the same county, and at Willmount, Co. Kilkenny. Both Willmount and Tenvane are in the vicinity of

Carrick-on-Suir. *Owners of Land* (1876) lists John F. Briscoe, Grangemore, Killucan, with 379 Co. Westmeath acres, and Robert Briscoe, Fermoy, with 394 acres. To the present time there is a Briscoe Terrace in the town of Fermoy. The Revd Francis Briscoe, Kilmessan Glebe, had 56 Co. Tipperary acres; Richard Briscoe, Thurles, had 105 acres, and Henry W. Briscoe, Tinvane, had 127 Co. Tipperary acres and a further 105 in Co. Waterford. The largest holding, however, was the 2,836 Co. Offaly acres of Edward T. Briscoe, Riversdale, in the Co. Westmeath parish of Killucan. Co. Kilkenny, however, had the greatest number of holdings, though two of those were non resident. Abraham Briscoe, Bellisle House, Dalkey, had 484 acres, and Richard Briscoe, Australia, had 103 acres. There were two at Harristown, Pilltown – Edward W. Briscoe, with 186 acres, and Rivers Briscoe, with 115 acres.

Edward T. Briscoe of the above 2,836 Co. Westmeath acres was a JP in 1837 and was listed among the King's County Grand Jury, while among the then magistrates of Co. Kilkenny was Henry Harrison Briscoe, Esq., Clonconey, in the parish of Clonmore. In that same parish is Graiguevine which had William Frispe, gent., as titulado according to the 1659 Census. Robert Fryspe, gent., was titulado of Fiddown. We wonder if this is the rare name, now rendered Fripps, and found in the Mullinavat area of south Kilkenny and in Co. Waterford. Indeed it was this surname that led us – willy-nilly – to investigate the Briscoes. The current telephone directory covering the North has but two Briscoe entries, with nineteen in the Dublin area, one of whom has the gaelicised form Brioscú. Outside Dublin there are 47 Briscoes in Cos. Donegal, Louth, Westmeath, Kilkenny, Galway, Waterford, Cork, Tipperary and Kerry.

The most eminent of the name was probably Dublin-born Robert Briscoe (1894–1969) who took the Republican side during the 1922–4 Irish Civil War, and was a founder member of Fianna Fáil. A Zionist, he passed on his guerrilla war experience to Jabotinsky, who came to Ireland to see him and pioneered the so-called 'coffin ship' operation to bring Jews to Palestine after Second World War. It is said that his father, on landing in Ireland, sought a similar, but more acceptable-sounding surname than his own. He saw, it is claimed, the name Briscoe over a business premises, which he was satisfied fitted his bill.

CLONMACNOIS

'Big fleas have small fleas upon their backs to bite them, small fleas have lesser fleas and so *ad infinitum*', and if anyone has fault with that, we can only plead that this is the Tipperary version. Clement Charleton of Newbliss, Co. Monaghan, was one of those who received a contract in 1881 for the maintenance of the roads in that county. He was almost certainly a Protestant, and probably a 'small flea'; the 'lesser fleas' whom he employed in the labouring were almost certainly Roman Catholics. The surname Charleton, sometimes Charlton, though it has a Cromwellian connection with Co. Sligo, had been in Ireland since the 14th century. It became established in Cos. Tyrone and Fermanagh early in the 17th century. The only one of the name listed in the 1659 *Census* was George Charlton, a titulado for Bull Lane in the city of Dublin. There was but one Charleton Esq. 'seated' on Taylor & Skinner's *Maps* (1778), the unnamed 'seat' being north-west of Randelstown Co. Antrim. The 1814 *Directory* lists but one of the name – Capt. Charleton, at Curraghtown, Navan, Co. Meath. Four of the six Charletons listed in *Owners of Land* (1876) were in Co. Monaghan, on 64, 64 and 127 acres at Tully, Emyvale; the fourth, on 50 acres, was from Belfast. William Charlton, Philipstown, Dundalk, had 37 acres in Co. Louth, but the best-off was William Charlton, Clonmacnois, Shannonbridge Co. Offaly, with 344 in that county. Of the 22 listed in telephone directories of the Republic, the majority are in Connaught and Co. Donegal. The *Phone Book* of Northern Ireland contains 24 Charlton entries.

Annála Ríoghtachta Éireann/Annals of the Four Masters give the original Irish as Cluain Mac Nois mic Fidaigh. It is situated on the Esker Riada, the meeting point on the Shannon of Leath Mogha and Leath Cuinn, Conn and Mogh Nuadhad's halves of Ireland. Brendan Lehane's *Companion Guide to Ireland* (1973) informs that the Tourist Board had 'planted an information caravan beside the site, where notes of the individual ruins are available'. The precursor, no doubt, of the Interpretative Centre, albeit small and mobile. Here in 545 St Ciaráin built a monastery which became the chief monastery in what was then Connaught. In 884 Mrs Turgesius recited pagan oracles from the high altar while her husband burned the place, but neither the oracles nor the burning appear to have put a halt to its progress, for by the times of the Normans there were twelve churches here. It was burned and plundered many times after, but it never recovered from the 1552 invasion of the English garrison from Athlone, of whose visit it was said that 'not a bell, large or small, or an image, or an altar, or a book, or a gem, or even glass in a window, was left which was not carried away'.

Nearly half a mile from the monastic settlement was the Nuns' Church, the first record of which was in 1026. Among the events noted for that year by was the paved way from 'Garrdha in Bhainbh co hIlaidh na ttri ccros' *Annála Ríoghtachta Éireann*. This was first translated as from 'the Garden of the Sucking Pig to the monument or penitential station of the Three Crosses', though a footnote informs that Mageoghegan explained the first placename as if written 'Garrdha a bhanabbaidh', that is, the 'Abbess her gardaine'. The paved way (an clochán) must have been exceptional in some manner to rate mention among the plunderings, battles, depredations, hostings and successions of the year 1026.

Today Clonmacnois is rendered Cluain Mhic Nóis.

KILCOLGAN

Cochall, the suggested root of the surname Mac Cochláin, means 'hood, hooded garment', and cochallach, 'hooded, cowled' also means "hot-tempered, bushy'. Initally anglicised Mac Co(u)ghlan, this name, like O Co(u)ghlan, is now rendered Co(u)ghlan – bereft of Mac and O. Ó Cochláin was the name of the well-known Munster sept of Barrymore, but our interest today is in *Mac Cochláin*. Their ancient territory was in the Banagher-Clonmacnois area of Co. Offaly, formerly known as Delvin Mac Coughlan. Listed 41 times in the Annals of the Four Masters, the earliest being the recorded death of Aedh Mac Cochláin, lord of Dealbhna-Eathra in 1134. The last entry was for 1602, when it was recorded that Seán Óg Mac Cochláin was among the Irish who harassed Ó Súilleabháin Béara on his famous retreat northwards from West Cork. 'Upon their arrival there, the inhabitants of the lands and tribes in their vicinity collected behind and before them, and shouted in every direction around them'. About 1249 Conor McCoughlan of the Castles was described as 'a great destroyer of the English'.

'But women are always hard to deal with in cases of ejectment …', wrote John P. Prendergast in his *Cromwellian Settlement*. In 1657, Gregory Clements, an adventurer whose lot had fallen in the barony of Garrycastle, formerly Delvin Mac Coughlan, complained that he had been kept out of possession for two years by Mrs Coughlan of Kilcolgan, Cill Cholgan. Instead of being ordered to instantly vacate, she was given a six months' dispensation, the better to provide a settlement for herself and family in Connaught. She and her son Francis were given a total of 4,421 acres in Ahascragh, Fohanagh, Killosolan, Abbeygormacan, and Kiltullagh in Co. Galway; in Killasser and Toomore in Co. Mayo, and in Moore in Co. Roscommon. John Coughlan of Cloonleny/Cloonkenny was decreed 150 acres at Kiltullagh, and John Coughlan of Kincorr was granted 44 acres in Creeve and Kilmacumsy, these being in Co. Roscommon.

Lewis's *Topographical Dictionary* says that the last male representative of this family was Thomas Coughlan MP who died in 1790. His estate went to Denis Bowes O'Daly Esq., MP, the Dalys being descended maternally from the MacCoughlans. In a footnote in *Cambrensis Eversus* the editor Matthew Kelly informs that the last head of the MacCoghlans was locally known as The Maw. An Mhagh?, 'the plain', but we could not discover any place so-named in Co. Offaly. Was it then An Mádh? This means 'a trump at cards; fortune, fate', but figuratively 'a chief or prince, the Pretender'. This is now rendered Mámh.

The dispossessed Colonel Coughlan headed a band in Leinster in 1660, being the equivalent of Ulster's Redmond O Hanlon. Another military member of the family was Colonel Coghlan who was to cause Lord Dunraven considerable anxiety. In 1816 the widower Dunraven had, in his 64th year married a twice married widow Margaret Mary Coughlan, sister of the colonel. Not content with the £150 annual alimony, the colonel sought to extract a further £150 from the lord by 'purile and unjustifiable menaces'. *Owners of Land* (1876) shows not a single Coughlan landowner in Co. Offaly. The majority of those listed in the Southern telephone directories, outside of the Dublin area, are spelled Coughlan and are to be found in Co. Cork. Four have repossessed the original Mac Cochláin – all in Dublin, and two have resumed Ó Cochláin.

MONASTERORIS

The 101 entries in telephone directories south of the Border of the surname Manley, are mainly found in Co. Cork, where, according to MacLysaght's *Surnames* it is often pronounced Mauly. One cannot but wonder whence this strange change of pronunciation. MacLysaght gives the original Irish as Ó Máinle, though he offers neither explanation nor translation. Manley is sometimes used as the anglicised form of Ó Maonghaile (*maon*, wealth, *gal*, valour), the name of a Mayo sept, though this is more usually Monnelly, Munnelly or Monley. Indeed, 16th-century records render this O'Monilla and Monylla.

Manley, however, is an English surname meaning 'brave, manly, independent, upright', and it is almost certain that both William Manley, listed in the 1659 Census as a titulado of Rabucke and Owenstowne in Co. Dublin, and James Manley, co-titulado of Castle Fleming, in the Co. Laois barony of Ossory, bore the English surname. In 1814 Captain Manley was at Auburn Cottage, Sligo, and H. Manley, Esq., was at Ringing's Point, Belfast, Co. Antrim. Apart from Henry C. Manley, Whitehouse, Co. Antrim, who had a single acre (without an extra rood or perch!), the remainder of the Manley landowners of 1876 were in the province of Leinster. Joseph Manley, Martello Terrace, Bray, Co. Wicklow, had 538 acres in Co. Westmeath; Miss Manley, 15 Eccles Street, had three acres in the city of Dublin, and Jos. Manley (a minor), Castleknock, had 127 Co. Dublin acres. Joshua Manley, Monasteroris, Edenderry, Co. Offaly, was by far the largest landowner of the family. Besides the 1,995 acres at Monasteroris, he had 183 acres in Co. Kildare. The Annals of the Four Masters give this as Mainistir Fheorais. It is possible that Joshua was a descendant of James Manley, the 1659 titulado in neighbouring Co. Laois.

Judging by Breandán Ó Conchúir's *Scríobhaithe Chorcaí 1700–1850*, no Ó Máinle took to the pen, but across the water a Mrs Manley is listed in B.G. MacCarthy's *Women Writers, 1621–1744*: 'Women in Shakespeare's time did not write plays, because the blank-verse form called for a technique in language which they did not possess, but with the Restoration period came a spate of women-dramatists, most notably Aphra Behn, Mrs Centlivre, Mrs Manley, Mrs Pix and Mrs Trotter. It was said of Mrs Manley that she endeavoured to achieve by 'slanderous salacity' what she could not achieve by literary ability. Her later work was disguised autobiography, where she veiled her facts under the appearance of fiction … If a woman had written the life of Mrs Manley, thoroughly authenticating every fact, suitably deploring her immmoral adventures and drawing elevated lessons from every lapse from grace, she really might have managed to escape severe popular censure; at any rate, she would have a much better chance of doing so than if she enlivened her subject by giving it, as Mrs Manley did, the form of a novel'.

PHILIPSTOWN

The Greek name Phllip meaning 'horse-lover', extremely popular in medieval England, was brought to Ireland by Anglo-Norman settlers, where it was hibernicized as Pilib. We cannot say why the owl, now officially *ulchabhán* or *cailleach oíche* (night witch), was known as Pilib an chleite, nor can we say why Tibb's Eve came to be called 'the owl's day', Lá Philib an Chleite. Pilibín, the diminutive of this personal name, is defined as 'little Philip, anything very small, an egg, a barnacle, a lapwing or plover; a thatching tool used for drawing the straw together; *pilib eitre*, a grasshopper, also daddy-long-legs; *pilib míogach*, a variety of coast or hunting plover, a black or ringed plover …', but in rural Ireland the plover continues to be called the pilibeen. The surname Phillips is English, but has to some extent taken the place of (Mac)Philbin, the name of one of the hibernicized branches of the Connaught Burkes which formed a sept of the Irish type. Ballyphilibeen in the Co. Cork parish of Kilbrin, is baile Mic Philibín, according to P.W. Joyce in *Names of Places*. Ballyphilip names townlands in Cos. Cork, Down, Kilkenny, Offaly, Limerick (2), Tipperary (4), Waterford, Wexford and Wicklow, with Ballyphillips in Cos. Waterford and Tipperary. It is not possible in most cases to say if Philip represents a personal name or a surname in the above, as would also be the case with Philipstown, in Cos. Kildare, Louth (3), and Meath. However, Philipstown of Co. Offaly, now officially Daingean (a fort), when in 1557 'by the Act of Philip And Mary, King's and Queen's Counties were being formed, a place called Dangan was renamed Philipstown'. Charles Phillips, was rated 'the most distinguished man the town of Sligo has produced in modern times' by T.O Rorke in *The History of Sligo* (1889), but we do not if he was a transformed (Mac)Philbin or of the English Phillips. He did however deliver speeches in favour of Catholic Emancipation at Sligo, Dublin, Cork, Liverpool, and on Dinas Island in the lakes of Killarney.

Born in 1725, he attended Trinity College where he was awarded the medal for oratory, being later called to both the Irish and English Bars. He became a friend of John Philpot Curran, and later his biographer. His style of oratory was praised by some, but criticised in the main, and one wonders how many present day politicans would withstand the barrage aimed at Charles Phillips Esq. B.A. His speeches abounded with 'sesquipedalian diction, broken metaphors, mixed metaphors, endless alliteration, jingling antitheses, bombast and a hundred other deformities or blemishes, which people with a tenth of his talent manage generally to avoid'.

LEAP

'The Thing was about the size of a sheep, thin, gaunt and shadowy in parts. Its face was human, or to be more accurate, inhuman, in its vileness, with large holes of blackness for eyes, loose slobbery lips, and a thick saliva-dripping jaw, sloping back suddenly into its neck. Nose it had none …'. This is but the beginning of the description by Mrs Jonathan Darby in the early part of the century, of the 'horrifying elemental figure' seen in Leap Castle on several occasions by different people. This castle, in the townland of Leap in the Co. Offaly parish of Aghnacon, was built, along with a number of other castles, sometime during the two century period subsequent to 1350, when the O Carrolls regained possession of Éile Uí Cearuill. This massive structure, built on the site of an earlier fortification, was, according to the Four Masters, 'a castle better fortified and defended' than any other, until its capture and demolition by Gearóid Óg, ninth earl of Kildare, in 1516. Its replacement was destroyed in 1922, with thirty bombs and twenty cases of petrol, 'one of the most depressingly senseless acts of the civil war', according to John Feehan in *The Landscape of Slieve Bloom*, but welcoming its restoration then (1978) in hand. The Leap estate and castle passed into the Darby family through marriage, and during the Darby tenure, 'the servants had a dread of approaching the upper dungeons at night, for prisoners, it was said, were thrown to their death from the top of the castle in the days of the O Carrolls, and there is still a well-documented tradition of a ghost in the castle down to the present day'. Darby is the name of a well-known English family who came to Laois in the 16th century, but the native Irish MacDiarmada, anglicised as (O)Darmody and Dermody, found in Co. Tipperary and the adjacent Leinster counties, was sometimes changed to Darby. The Irish name for Léim Uí Bhánáin, 'the leap of (O)Bannon', was anglicised as Lemavanon as far back as the 15th century, and in a 1581 pardon of John O Carroll for his 'alienation and intrusions', it was spelled Lem Ivanan. The most important of several septs of (O) Bannon Banare was that of the barony of Lower Ormond in Co. Tipperary. It was used sometimes as a synonym of White through the erroneous presumption that the name derived from *bán*, white. The surname Banim, believed to be corrupt form of Bannon, named the 19th-century brother novelists Michael and John Banim. In 1878 'Banon, E.J., Reps. of', of Broughall Castle, Frankford had 3,896 acres in Co. Offaly, and William H. Darby of Leap Castle, Roscrea, had 4,367 acres in the same county.

HOPESTOWN

The spa at Castleconnell, Co. Limerick, whose waters had proved 'very efficacious in scorbutic affections, bilious complaints, obstructions in the liver, jaundice and worms', resembled those of Spa, Germany, according to Lewis' *Topographical Dictionary* (1837), and the spa at Ballincar in the Co. Offaly parish of Drumcullen, wherein 'water of a yellow hue', was said by the same authority to be the same nature as that of Castleconnell. There was a second spa in this parish at Clonbela, about two and a half miles from Birr. This townland name is spelled Clonbeale (More and Beg) in *The Index of Townlands* (1851), and is 'Clonbella' when it names the residence of J. Bomford Molloy Esq. in 1814, and was Clonebela(beg) on Sir William Petty's map of 1685. John Bomford Molloy JP is listed among the 'Families of the King's County' in John Wright's *The King's County Directory* (1888). All of these families had close connections with England, either having other residences there, or through marriage, and practically all the males had served or were serving in the British Army. J. Bomford was Ensign in 69th Regt., having been educated at Marlborough College. Bernard Charles Molloy, a descendent of the O'Molloys of Fearcall, was elected MP for the Birr division of King's County in 1886, being the youngest son of Kedo of 'Charlstown House', Clara. This gentleman, however, is not listed among the 'families', and one wonders if being a Roman Catholic had any bearing on this. In 1867 he volunteered for the pontifical army then engaged against Garibaldi, and entered the French service in 1870. He was nominated by Pope Pius IX a Cameriere Segreto di Cappa e Spado. He was a member of Parnell's 'Irish Party', and of his politics Wright states that they 'stretched to the extent of a mild form of Home Rule'. Nor are 'Dillon and Dagg' listed among the gentry, these being the gentlemen who 'tried their hand, in a modest way', at the manufacture of mineral waters in the mill at Springfield, previously making oil cake. This is also in the parish of Drumcullen, though we know not its proximity to Clonbeale or Ballincar, or, indeed, if their 'waters' were used in the manufacture of the mineral waters. Springfield names townlands in Cos. Clare (2), Cork (3), Donegal, Galway (2), Leitrim, Limerick, Mayo, Laois, Sligo, Tipperary (7), Waterford (2), Wickow (2), and the town of Springfield in Co. Antrim. It is listed in *Ainmneacha Gaeilge na mBailte Poist* for Co. Fermanagh as Achadh an Fhuaráin, 'the field of the spring/well while that of Dublin is Achadh an Tobair. There are eight Springfields in the USA, the best known to people from Corca Dhuibhne in Co. Kerry being Springfield Mass. Springfield of Co. Offaly is Páirc an Tobair.

GEASHILL

Had Bord Fáilte its Tidy Towns Competition going in 1890, Geashill in Co. Offaly would undoubtedly have featured high on the award-winning list, as indeed it has since its 'commendation' in 1973 and its 'special award' in 1974. Lord Migby, who died in 1899, 'had converted the village into what it is now, one of the neatest, cleanest, and best kept in Ireland'. Digby, who then owned the greater part of the parish, with 43,630 acres, was the descendant of Sir Robert Digby, who acquired the land in 1620 through his marriage to one of the Fitzpatricks. They in turn 'acquired' it from the O Dempseys, ancient owners of the district, and the remains of whose castle were still to be seen in 1837, according to Lewis' *Topographical Dictionary*. It is unlilkely that the O'Dempseys peacefully yielded up their estates, as might be clear from mention of members of that clan found in a fragment of an Irish Chronicle from 1392 to 1407. In 1134 Aodh Ó Díomasaigh, an excellent son of an under-king, was killed by Galls on a day he had taken prey from them. In 1394 Tomhaltach Ó Díomasaigh was killed by the Galls and his head brought to Duhlin to the king, and in 1404 Cathaoir Ó Díomasaigh, a man renowned for his hospitality and prowess, was killed by the Galls of Leinster. The 'O' of this name is rarely, if ever, used with the anglicised form Dempsey, the surname deriving from Ó Díomasaigh (*díomasach*, proud). Ó Diomasaigh was one of the very few Irish chieftains to have defeated Strongbow in a military engagement. According to the Census of 1659 there were 139 Protestants and 591 Catholics in the barony of Geashill, the second most populous of the Irish heing the Dempseys. Rarely pipping them was the puzzling name of Quime. It was at Geashill that the two sons of Milesius, Eireamon and Heber battled, resulting in the death of Heber, and Eireamon becoming the first Milesian monarch of Ireland. It was during the reign of his son Irial Fáidh, 'the prophet', that the woods in this locality were cleared. *Onomasticon Goedelicum* gives the Irish of this name as written 'Géisill, g. Géisille' in 1362, this being the offical form today. *Géis* is a now rarely-used word for swan, the generally-used one being *eala*, but Adrian Room in *A*

Dictionary of Irish Place-Names, an indiscriminate compilation mainly drawn from two sources, does not specify the source of his contention that Géisill means 'a place of swans'.

RUSSAGH

'To Brene O King at Portlester the 16 day of May anno 17 H.VIII (1525) £4 3s. 4d. which was the last some of 30 kyne that he and his brethirn had upon Ballanorghyr in Glannevaddog. A cartron in pledg of 12 kine which Padyn O Hurke paid Feraile Duff of Nyr and an othir cartron which Moylaghlyn mc Heu did yeve unto the said Geralde and his ayrys for evyr. Witnis Padyn O Hurke & others': this is an item from *Crown Surveys of Lands, 1540–41*. Portlester is in the Co. Meath parish of Killaconnigan, while Ballanorgher, later shortened to Ardnurcher, halved between Cos. Offaly and Westmeath is the anglicised form of Baile Átha an Urchair, with Horseleap as an alternative 'English' name. Two of the surnames herein are O King and O Hurke, this latter being variously rendered O Hurgy, O Hurge, and O Hurgha elsewhere in the *Surveys*.

Of the surname King, MacLysaght's *Surnames* says: 'Usually an English name, but it is also widely used as an anglicised form of several names by pseudo-translation (*rí*-king); viz. Conry, Conroy, Cunree, Mac Aree and MacKeary in Oriel, and even sometimes of Gilroy and MacKinn. There is also a rare name Ó Cionga, now King, which belongs to Lough Ree'. *Annals of the Four Masters* note the death of Ó Ciongadh, lector of Dearmhach in 1103, and of Tomás Ó Cinga in 1342, apparently within the Co. Sligo barony of Leyny. From 1578 to 1603 persons bearing the surname O Kinge/O Kinga are listed among the 'pardoned' in 18 of the *Irish Fiants of the Tudor Sovereigns*. They are mostly in Cos. Offaly and Westmeath, but some also in Cos. Galway and Meath. In 1573 in Co. Westmeath were listed Tirlagh, Leysagh, Sollo and Brian O Kinge. In 1581 it was Carbery, Cormok, William, and Sowell O Kynge of Rouskough in Co. Offaly, and in 1602 it was Murtho, Connor, William, and Toll O Kinge, all 'of Foxes country'.

MacLysaght's *Irish Families* informs us that 'Tadhg Ó Catharnaigh (anglice O Catharny, mod. Carney or Kearney), chief of Teffia, Co. Meath (d.1084) was called sionnach, that is, The Fox, and in due course this branch acquired the name Fox as a distinct surname'. We take it that the above Rouskough is today's Russagh in the Co. Offaly parish of Ardnurcher/Horseleap, derived from the Irish Rúscach. 'The inhabitants of this part of Westmeath have lost the Irish language and forgotten the old traditions. I was never in any part of Ireland where the people knew less in this way, observed John O'Donovan

(1809–1861), antiquary and scholar. *Owners of Land* of (1876) shows Kings with land in 28 of the 32 counties of Ireland.

Apart from the above mention of O Hurke/O Hurge/O Hurgha we found a Manus O Hurkoy, Ballynekarry, among the pardoned of 1592. Is this the same surname? And is this place Ballynacarrow in the Co. Sligo parish of Kilvarnet? O Horchoy is listed in the 1659 *Census* among the principal Irish names in the Co. Sligo barony of Corran. We trawled MacLysaght looking for some variant form of this surname, assuming that it started with a vowel. This led us to the surname Argue: 'This Co. Cavan name is not of English origin, but, if Irish, the Gaelic form of it has not been determined with certainty. In Co. Leitrim, not far from Co. Cavan, there is a place called Killargue, which O'Donovan says is Cill Fhearga, that is, the church of St. Fearga. Killargue is also called Kilarga. It is probable therefore that the surname is Mac Giolla Fhearga. I think the family tradition that it is of Huguenot origin may be discounted. However, *An Sloinnteoir Gaeilge & an tAinmneoir* (Ó Droighneáin & Ó Murchú: 1991) lists Ó hEarga as the Irish from which Argue derives. Might this be our O Hurgha? The above *Owners* lists but one of this surname, that being Thomas Argue, Conaghcoo in the Co. Cavan parish of Annagh, having 22 acres there.

Telephone directories in the North list 11 Argues, mainly in Belfast and Portadown. There are 26 in the South, 14 of which are in Co. Cavan.

Westmeath

Creach, in the sense of a raid, has been variously translated into English as: depredation, foray, preying expedition, preying party, predatory excursion and predatory expedition. This was the taking of cattle, an activity that had continued over many centuries of the historic period, and, perhaps, over a long span of prehistory as well, and whether as beneficiaries or losers, the people were accustomed to regard the *creach* as an ordinary event of life. This was the theme of the great prose epic, *An Táin Bó Chailgne* or 'Cattle Raid of Cooley', as well as that of lesser tales associated with it: *Táin Bó Dartada, Táin Bó Regamain* and *Táin Bó Flidias*. Certain of these raids were taken for granted as part of the natural order of things, but others, called *creach fill (feall*, deceit, treachery), were regarded as unethical. One such is recorded as having taken place in Westmeath in 1402. On 14 October 1906 a proposal was made that would be regarded more as a creach fill than a creach. The man that had been called 'that pestilent ass', Laurence Ginnell, MP for north Roscommon, speaking of the grazing system at a meeting at The Downs, Co. Westmeath, advocated a policy of 'cattle-driving' which became known as the 'Downs policy'. Ginnell advocated 'cattle-driving', involving the ranchers' cattle being illegally removed from the grazier's land at night and then brought to a secret market, placed on the land of neighbouring farmers, or more simply left to wander along country roads. Augustine Birrell, the chief secretary of Ireland wrote that Ginnell was 'a solitary unpopular fellow, a very bad speaker, of no personal influence, hated by his own party, but a clever writer …' Birrell claimed that Ginnell wanted to be prosecuted, and longed to be sent to prison, but the Chief Secretary added: 'Still, if I can avoid making him a hero I am anxious to do so …'

In June 1916, subsequent to the 1916 Rising, Frongoch internment camp in North Wales was opened to 1,800 Irishmen, and a great champion of the men there was Larry Ginnell, who often visited them, as did his wife, Alice. He wore a frock coat with deep pockets in the tails, and when surrounded by prisoners in the yard, he whispered now and then, 'post office is open behind, lads, post office open behind'. This was the signal to dive into the pockets and extract letters and place new ones in. He was eventually prohibited from visiting the prison, because of breaking prison regulations. 'He still outwitted the authorities by getting in, using his Irish name. He had signed himself as Labhrás Mac Fingal' (Séan O Mahony, *Frongoch: University of Revolution*).

Edward MacLysaght's *Surnames* gives the name Ginnell as Mac Fhionnghail (*fionn ghail*, fair valour), a branch of the Mac Ginleys of Donegal who settled in Co. Westmeath. It was written Mac Ginnelly in the 1659 Census when it was listed among the principal Irish names in the Co. Donegal barony of Kilmacrennan. Only one of the name was listed as owning land in *Owners of Land*, that being Michael Mac Ginley who had a mere three acres in Co. Tyrone. Of the eight listed in the telephone directory, four are in Co. Westmeath. Four Ginnellys are also listed.

Downs names townlands in Cos. Limerick, Monaghan, Tyrone, Wicklow Armagh, Laois, and Westmeath. Sometimes rendered The Downs, this is the anglicised form of Na Dúnta, 'the forts', having an English plural.

PARISTOWN

'The illiterate -sh' which is responsible for the pronunciation of liqourice as liqourish, is the same as caused the surname Paris to be mispronounced Parish, according to Basil Cottle in his *Penguin Dictionary of Surnames*. This surname derives from the tribe Parisii, from whence Paris, France. Giving the alternative spelling of Parris, MacLysaght's *Surnames* says that this English name, rare in Ireland, is associated with Youghal, Co. Cork from the early 14th century and was later to be found in Leinster. Pharis, however, is not a synonym of Parris but of Farris.

In his attempted 'final settlement of the Scottish problem' in 1303, Edward I assembled a fleet of 173 ships to take an assisting Irish army to Scotland, and Peter de Paris was the 'Admirallus flote Hibernie', the first ever Irish admiral. Further confirmation of the surname's derivation from the city name is found in a report of a court case of 1340 when James and Isabella de Parys and David and Agnes de Offington were in dispute regarding 30 acres in Balykenan and 'the third part of two parts of a watermill in the same vill and forty acres in Lethtyoke and ten shillings of the revenues in the said vills'. The first of these places is in the Co. Laois parish of Kilmanman and now spelled Ballykenneen, and the second is Loughteogue in the Co. Laois parish of Dysartenos. In a 1564 list of rentals of 'all messuages, lands, and tenements of the Chapel of Holy Trinity, Callan', Edward Parishe is mentioned as owning land in 'le este Bowton'. We have not located this place, but we wonder if it is Bolton in the parish of Callan. Owen O'Kelly's *The Place-Names of County Kilkenny* says that this is from Buailtín, 'a small paddock'.

Henry Parris, a Co. Tipperary commissioner for the poll-money ordinances of 1660 and 1661, was listed as titulado in the townland of Ardmayle in the same county. In 1640 the 1,764 acres here, whereon 'a good Castle & a faire Manchon house with severall other small Cabbins, an oarchard & Garden with many quicksetts 7 other Impvments' were the property of Theobald Butler of Ardmayle, Irish papist. Henry Paris was one of the commissioners of the Revenue within the precinct of Clonmel for the enactment of the Cromwellian Settlement, and he reported that the transplantation had been so effectually carried on in the county of Tipperary, and especially in the barony of Eliogarty, that 'no inhabitant of the Irish nation that knows the country is left in that barony, which may be a great prejudice to the Commonwealth, for want of information of the bounds of the respective territories and lands therein upon admeasurement; it is therefore ordered, that it be referred to the Commissioners at Loughrea, to consider of four fitt and knowing persons of the Irish nation lately removed out of that barony into Connaught, and to return them with their families to reside in or near their old habitations, for the due information of the surveyors ...' We wonder who they were and did they get to stay.

Of the name Parish there are two in the *Phone Book* of Northern Ireland, one in the Dublin area, and one in Co. Kerry; of the name Parris there is one in the Dublin area, and there is one Paris in Northern Ireland and one in Dublin. Paristown in the Co. Westmeath parish of Killua, was rendered 'Parrytown' on Petty's 1685 map, and it clearly would be easy to visualise Parrystown changing into Paristown; its Irish form is Baile Phairis.

GAYBROOK

To get off 'scot-free' is a term still in use, and means to escape without penalty or punishment. Our dictionary defines 'scot' as 'a payment', contribution, 'reckoning'; especially payment for entertainment, and 'scot free' means free from payment of 'scot', tavern score, fine, etc.; exempt from injury, punishment, etc.; scatheless. The phrase 'scot and lot' (earlier 'lot and scot') was a tax levied by a municipal corporation in proportionate shares upon its members for the defraying of municipal expenses. To pay (a person off) lot and scot (fig.) was to pay out thoroughly, to settle with. In a Dublin will of 1693 a legacy of £20 was to be distributed among 20 widows of the parish of St Bride's 'that have been inhabiters therein and payed scott and lott'. This was the will of John Gay of Dublin. His youngest son William of Coleingstown (? Collinstown), Co.

Kildare, and another son John were each to get £20 per annum out of his lands at Redmondstown, Co. Westmeath. Redmondstown was the ancient name of Gaybrook according to Paul Walsh's *Placenames of Westmeath*, and today Baile Réamainn is its Irish name. 'John Gay was sheriff in 1663 and obtained in 1666 by certificate the lands of Redmondstown which he named Gaybrook, part of the forfeited estate of Edmond Darcy ... Irish, Baile Réamuinn. The 1814 *Directory* lists Ralph Smyth, esq. as resident at Gaybrook, and *Owners of Land* (1876) has Robert Smyth on its 6,287 acres. The 1982 combined 'rural' telephone directory shows two Gayes in Co. Westmeath, one being in Gaybrook. There are four Gay entries in Co. Cork; the *Phone Book* of Northern Ireland lists three in Co. Down, and the Dublin directory has three Gays and two Gayes.

The surname Gay usually means 'gay, cheerful', and this English surname is not listed by MacLysaght in his *Surnames*. The 1659 Census lists Charles Gay, gent., as one of the tituladoes of the North Liberties of Cork City, and John Gay, gent., a titulado of Dublin's St Werburgh's Street. And though Nicholas Gay, esq. was among the Co. Westmeath subscribers to Taylor & Skinner's 1783 *Maps*, he is not therein placed. By 1876, when *Owners of Land* was published, there was but a single person of this name owning land. This was William Gay of Lisburn Co. Antrim, who barely made the 'cut-off' point with 1 acre and 35 perches.

John Gay (1685–1732), English poet, who became one of the circle of Swift, Pope and Arbuthnot, was described as 'a loveable though irresponsible man'. In a letter to Swift dated 8 December 1713, Pope wrote of 'one Mr Gay, an unhappy Youth that writes Pastorals during Divine Service ...' In *Letters from Georgian Ireland*, the correspondence of Mary Delany, we learn that whereas Handel was much admired and performed in Dublin, John Gay's satirical opera, *The Beggars' Opera*, first performed in 1728, was a perennial favourite.

One of the many persons in government service who assisted Michael Collins in his struggle with Dublin Castle after 1916 was a Sinn Fein sympathiser names Thomas Gay. He was the Dublin Corporation librarian in Capel Street, and it was to this place that Joe Kavanagh, one of the Castle detectives who gave significant help to Collins, came and passed on a message to Gay corroborating a warning concerning what became known as the 'German Plot'. Indeed, it was in Gay's house in Clontarf that Collins used meet Kavanagh and another detective named James MacNamara.

BETHLEHEM

Of the Stanleys in Ireland listed in *The Irish Fiants of the Tudor Sovereigns* one was a marshal at Drogheda (1551); one a marshal of the army (1560); Sir William

Stanley, knight, was chief justice of the province of Munster in 1584 to 'treat with rebels and traitors'; Captain Sir William Stanley was commissioned to execute marshal law throughout Ireland (1561); there was Richard Stanley, undergaoler of the Castle of Trym and there was Patrick Stanley formerly of London, 'custardmonger', who received a pardon in 1548 during the reign of Edward VI. And there were Stanley merchants. In 1594 Gyles Stanley, gent., was granted the office of one of the pursuivants at arms, and in 1603 Sir George Stanley, knight, was commissioned to appoint the bounds and limits of the King's and Queen's counties. (Custermonger, first recorded in 1514, was one who sold fish, fruit etc. from a barrow.)

In 1558 George Stanley, knight, was granted the halfmanor of Castleknock; in 1561 he leased the lands of Lorgyn, Killenwryche and Killenshoneken, in the lordship of Killrowe in Kerkell; and in 1563 the same gent was granted the lease of the rectories of the Blessed Virgin Mary of Trym and Kildalkey, together with some of the abbey of Clonard, Co. Meath. In 1588 Henry Stanley of Cross Hall, England, was granted the lease of these same lands. In 1589 William Stanley 'absented himself in foreign parts and has been outlawed for treason'. A fiant of 1595 reads: 'Livery to Agnes Salsbury alias Stanley, one of the sisters and coheirs of Henry Stanley, late of Crosshall, owner of land at Glaskearne, Co. Westmeath.' A fiant of 1565 reads: 'Pardon to Bart Gernone for the homicide in self-defence of Walter Stanley of Newtown of Tarmonfeghen.'

According to the *Penguin Dictionary of Surnames* the English surname, Stanley (rarely Stanly), derives from 'stony clearing/field', the names of places in twelve English counties, though it is chiefly a Glos.-Warwicks surname. It is the family name of the earls of Derby and barons Sheffield. It is on record in Ireland since the 13th century, mainly in Cos. Louth and Meath, but is now fairly numerous in both Leinster and Munster. None feature on Taylor and Skinner's 1778 *Maps* but the 1814 *Directory* lists three – at Cookstown, Bray, Co. Wicklow; at Flean, Shanagolden, Co. Limerick, and at Bethlehem, Athlone, Co. Westmeath. William Stanley of England had the largest Stanley holding listed in *Owners of Land* (1876) with 1,050 Co. Monaghan acres. There were modest Stanley holdings in Cos. Cork, Kerry and Tipperary, while those in Armagh, and Tyrone were somewhat larger. Those of Cos. Dublin, Kildare, Westmeath were also modest, and four of the five in Co. Laois were at Evrill. One of the Stanleys of Westmeath had an English address, while the other – Rebecca – had 168 acres at Bethlehem.

The 1659 Census gives Cornet Stanley and James Stanley as 1660 commissioners of the poll-money ordinance for Cos. Roscommon and Wicklow. Michael Stanley was titulado of the parish of Athleague and Robert Stanley of the townland of Ballinturley. Both are in Co. Roscommon. Quartermaster Stanley was titulado of the Dublin City parish of St Werburgh's, while the only one to bear the surname without the 'e' was Sir Thomas Stanly, knight, titulado of the Co. Waterford parish of Dysert.

With the current discussions on education in Ireland and the new proposals for the management of its schools, it is interesting to hark back to Edward George Stanley, 14th earl of Derby (1799–1869), three times prime minister. His most outstanding achievement in Ireland while chief secterary, was the creation of a system of National Education in 1831. He sought a system, he said, 'from which would be banished forever the suspicion of proselytism and which, admitting children of all religious persuasions, should not interfere with the peculiar tenets of any'. However, John Stanley, the deputy of the king of England who arrived in Ireland in 1414, did nothing to endear himself to the Irish. According to the Four Masters he was 'a man who gave neither mercy nor protection to clergy, laity, or men of science, but subjected as many of them as he came upon to cold, hardship and famine'.

Entries in the islands telephone directories are exclusively spelled Stanley, there being around 100 each in Northern Ireland's *Phone Book*, the 1982 combined 'rural' directory, and the 01 Dublin district area directory.

Bethlehem (Bethil) in the Co. Westmeath parish of Kilkenny West, close by Lough Reagh, formerly a convent of the Poor Clares, was plundered and burned by some English soldiers in 1642.

HOPESTOWN

There are thirty-two townlands named Springfield in Ireland, that in Co. Dublin being Achadh an Tobair, that of Fermanagh deriving from Achadh an Fhuaráin, and that of Co. Limerick being Gort na Tiobraide. Springfield in Co. Westmeath has the alias Spitlefield, and of this Paul Walsh in his *Placenames of Westmeath* writes: 'Discard the bogus "Springfield" which is considered respectable. Really it is not half so respectable as "Spittlefield" which means "hospital field" or land which provided maintenance for the sick. There is no reason why any person, unless ignorant, should prefer "Springfield" except that the latter is bald "anglo-saxon".' No doubt Paul Walsh would have some *lasca teangan* for those responsible for the naming of 'top-of-the-market' housing – in Dublin particularly – in 'bald anglo-saxon' names.

'Thomas Hopp of Mullingare is seised in fee farme of the site of the late dissolved house of Friars Preachers in the town of Mulingare, and of 18 acres of land called Killineteggard and Spittlefield' (Inq. Jac 1, No. 6). And an entry for 19 February 1776 from the diary of Sir Richard Levinge of Levington Park, Co. Westmeath, close by Lough Owel reads: 'Mr Thomas Hope dined with me; and, after dinner, he married my carpenter, George Kane, to my housemaid, Honora Burke, in the Flagg Parlour'. This Thomas Hope, who died in 1777, was a

Dominican priest from the Dominican Friary in Mullingar, and Taghmon parish had been his responsibility for years.

The surname Hope derives from the Old-English hop, 'a small enclosed valley', and from the 14th to the 19th century was associated with Co. Westmeath. Apart from Alexander Hope who was listed as a titulado in the townland of Ballyfeeny in the Co. Roscommon parish of Kilglass, the Hopes were among the principal Irish names in the Co. Westmeath barony of Moyashel and Magheradernon according to the 1659 Census. The same source lists Oliver Hope as a titulado for Churchtown in the barony of Rathconrath, and Alexander and Richard, father and son, gents, as tituladoes in the parish of Templeoran, all in Co. Westmeath.

Hopestown in the Co. Westmeath parish of Mullingar is given by Walsh as Baile Hop, and while one is tempted to suspect a connection with the surname Hope in Habsborough in the same parish, Walsh writes: 'A fancy name which originated with the Widman family of Hanstown. The older name was Taylorstown'. Habestown now called Habsborough 'Lyons, Grand Juries, Historical Appendix 326'.

The family was still in Co. Westmeath in 1876 where 487 acres were in possession of the Reps. of Michael Hope, Gartlandstown in the parish of Faughalstown. The 11,770 acre Monaghan estate of Anne Adile Hope had been purchased by her deceased husband, Henry Thomas Hope, Deepdene, Surrey, England in 1853, and the even larger 13,995 acre Hope estate in Co. Tyrone was the property of Thomas Arthur Hope, Wavertree, Lancs., England. The only other Hope possessor of land in the province of Ulster was that of the Reps. of George Hope, Millfield, Co. Antrim, with a most modest, though highly valued, two acres. Jimmy Hope, the linen weaver, United Irishman of Brown Square, Belfast, who fought at Ballinahinch in 1798, and endeavoured with Thomas Russell to effect another 'Rising Out' in 1803, was born in Templepatrick, Co. Antrim.

RATHWIRE

Perhaps there is no significance in the ratio of Darcy against D'Arcy as indicated by the entries in telephone directories, nor indeed in their location. The name is found in all four provinces under both spellings, though not so numerous in Ulster. Darcy is the more common spelling, with the greatest numbers in Cos. Tipperary, Clare, Cork, and Limerick in Munster; and in Cos. Carlow, Wexford, Meath and Kilkenny in Leinster. Those spelling the name D'Arcy are in the largest number in Cos. Galway and Wexford, though also numerous in

Cos. Cork, Meath, Kildare, Tipperary, Clare and Westmeath. Of this surname MacLysaght's *Surnames* says: 'Darcy, Ó Dorchaidhe (dorcha, dark). One of the "Tribes of Galway", also anglicised Dorcey, it is the name of two septs, one in Mayo and Galway, the other in Co. Wexford. Most Darcy families in Leinster are usually of Norman origin viz. D'Arci'. Contrary to what one might suppose, it has been proven that the Darcys of the Galway 'Tribes' were of true Irish stock, being descended from the Dorceys of Partry, Co. Mayo.

The Census of 1659 shows Darcy as titulado in Co. Clare in Munster; one barony each in Cos. Kildare and Offaly; two in Co. Meath, but it was in Co. Westmeath that they were in greatest numbers. Apart from being among the pincipal Irish names in the baronies of Fertullagh and Clononan, they were tituladoes in seven of the county's baronies. Taylor and Skinners *Maps* (1778) shows Darcy/D'Arcy, Esquires at Newforest, Corbally, Lynches Folly, Kiltolla (Co. Galway); at Knockaderry, Co. Limerick; and Corbetstown, Co. Westmeath. The 1814 *Directory* seats fifteen of the name, the majority being in Co. Galway. At that time at Newforest was Richard D'Arcy, Esq; at Kiltolla was John Darcy, Esq., while in Co. Mayo, at Houndswood, was Martin D'Arcy, Esq. At Corbelstown in Co. Westmeath was Francis D'Arcy, Esq. (Edmund Darcy was a titulado here in 1659). Also in Co. Westmeath, at Hydepark, was John Darcy, Esq.

One of the six Darcys listed in *Owners of Land* (1876) as possessing land in Co. Galway, was Hyacinth D'Arcy at Newforest on 4,434 acres, with an additional 3,817 acres in Co. Mayo, and in Mayo, we find Dominick D'Arcy, Doo Castle, Ballymoat, with 1,091 acres. In Co. Roscommon was Major John T. D'Arcy, Castlepark, Ballinasloe, with 1,961 acres. Francis D'Arcy, Castle Irvine, Co. Fermanagh had 1,108 acres there, and a further 1,669 acres in Co. Tyrone. The Darcys were in three Munster counties, and in Cos. Wicklow, Wexford, Meath, Westmeath, Louth, Carlow, and Dublin county and city. In the city was John D'Arcy & Son, Anchor Brewery, 18–26 Bridgefoot Street, on four acres.

The Annals of Connacht record the death of Darcy of Rathwire at the beginning of winter 1415. In 1419 Tomas Bacach, son of the earl of Ormond, went to England to help the king thereof against the king of France, but a dangerous sickness came upon the Irishmen in the strange land and killed many of them. 'And a blue fly entered Wiliam Darcy's mouth, and afterwards his whole body swelled and he died thereof' (co ndeachaid cuil gorm i mbeol Uilliam darsighe). Ratwire in the Co. Westmeath parish of Killucan, derives from Ráth Ghuaire (the rath/enclosure of Guaire). Recalling the manner of anglicisation of Irish surnames we wondered that it had never been rendered 'Dark'. We merely mention that there is one such name in the Dublin area directory.

WINDMILL

Tradition has it, according to Hart's *Pedigrees of Ireland*, that Waltero de Aliton, a Frenchman, travelled to Ireland with his wife, to avoid the displeasure of his royal father-in-law, thereby becoming the eponymous founder of the Dalton family. Giving 'de Dalatúin' as the Irish, MacLysaght's *Surnames* says that this toponymic was formerly D'Alton, an Anglo-Norman family who became completely hibernicised. Hart says that Waltero, through his valour and good conduct soon advanced 'to considerable offices and employments', acquiring 'great estates and possessions' in Co. Westmeath. Listing the pedigree of the family, he notes the Daltons of Empher, the Daltons of Nochavall, the Daltons of Ballynacarrow, those of Dungolman, of Dundonell, of Molinmelchan, of Milltown, Rolanstown, Skeabegg and Ballymore. No mention however of the Daltons of Baile na Cloiche. *Onomasticon Goedelicum* writes of this: 'Baile na Cloiche. Caisleán Bhaile na Chloiche do dénamh la mac mhic Lucais Daltuini.' This had become Stonestown by translation on Sir William Petty's map of 1685, and since has become Windwill or Blackislands, being in the parish of Enniscofffey, Co. Westmeath. We do not know what topographical features gave rise to Blackislands, but one supposes that nothing but a 'windmill' would result in a place being called Windmill, even in the uncertain field of placenames. Windmill also names townlands in the Co. Kildare parish of Kilmore, the Co. Louth parishes of Dunleer and Dysart, and the Co. Tipperary parish of St Patrick's Rock. Derby Ryan, Irish papist of Cashel, is noted in the Civil Survey of 1654–6 as having 181 acres here at Windmill in 1640. There is Windmill Hill and Windmill Lands in the Co. Dublin parishes of Newcastle and Swords; Windmill Hill is in the Co. Fermanagh parish of Rossory, and Windmillpark alias Chanterland in the Co. Roscommon parish of Elphin. We have not located the pre-1649 townland name of Carnemullenge in the parish of Ogulla in the *Index of Townlands* (1851), but spelled Cornemulling on Sir William Petty's map of 1685, it may derive from *cor* (round hill/pit), or *carn* (cairn, pile, heap) *an mhuilinn* (of the mill). The Irish name for Windmill is Baile na g Cloch (the town of the stones).

YORKFIELD

The hen, noted neither for elegance, song, nor exceptional athletic ability, would not be a favoured first-name, as for instance was *cú*, a hound. *Cearc*, normally meaning a hen, is given in MacLysaght's *Surnames* as the final element in the now obsolete surname Mac Conchearca. It appears however that it is not the hen that is in question here. MacLysaght gives 'son of the hound of Cearc' as the meaning of this name. And recalling the many ways by which Irish surnames were 'englished' – translation, half-translation, mistranslation, equation, and a mix of all betimes, one wonders how the surname York(e) became the modern form of Mac Conchearca. This had previously been anglicised Mac Engarky and Mac Ingarke. Might it be because of a similarity of sound between cearc and 'york'? The English surname York(e) is believed to have been originally from the British *eburac*, 'a yew-tree', which was latinized, then mistakenly turned by the Anglo-Saxons into Eoforwic (as if to mean 'wild boar Wick'), and eventually scandinavianized by the Vikings into York.

Spelled York and Yorke, this name, not very numerous in Ireland, has nine of the first spelling, of which three are in Co. Waterford, and 20 of the latter, largely in Cos. Longford and Westmeath. In 1836 Bretham Yorke, esq., lived at 17 Montpelier Hill, Dublin, and Anne Yorke, staymaker, was at 60 Stephen Street. Patt Yorke, 23 Cross Kevin Street, was the only bearer of that surname in the 1850 Dublin city directory. Only three of the name had land in Ireland in 1876, according to *Owners of Land* – David, Henry and James York, Edan, Portglenone, Co. Antrim, having respectively, 41, 42 and 26 acres. This may have been a larger farm that had been divided between the three.

Edan names townlands in Cos. Leitrim, Donegal, Antrim, Mayo, Roscommon, Tyrone, with a further three in Co. Derry. This comes from Éadan indicatina 'hill-brow'. Portglenone is from Port Chluain Eoghain, 'the port of the meadow of Eoghan'. *Port* means 'a bank, earthwork or platform, a shore, a port, a harbour, a ferry; a raised ridge or way; a passage; a fort, a house, a monastery or place'. Yorkfield, in the Co. Westmeath parish of Dysart, probably has the surname York as its first element, but Paul Walsh's *Placenames of Westmeath* gives no information on this townland name, simply stating 'No Irish'.

If today one were to advertise a lecture to take place in Ireland entitled 'The Turning of the Tide', concerning the importance of the Irish language and the connection between it and Irish nationalism, one certainly need not book any of the larger halls. This might be from indifference, or more likely the fact that this connection is known and accepted. However, when Fr Christopher Yorke spoke on this subject in the Ancient Concert Rooms in Dublin on 6 September 1899, there was an attendance of 1,200. Regarded by Dr Douglas Hyde as the finest speaker he had ever heard, Yorke derided the culture of the 'clane pleat', and damned the newspapers as promoters of anglicisation. Yorke (1864–1925) was born at Long Walk, Galway, the son of a sea-captain and Bridget Kelly of Inishmore, Co. Mayo. He boarded in St Jarlath's College and then went to Maynooth where his class mates included Owen O'Growney. He was ordained in San Francisco, and for a time he was considered bishop material. However, his outspokedness and alignment with the Irish Catholics there, soon put an end to that. His biography, written by J. Busher, and published in 1971, was suitably named *Consecrated Thunderbolt*.

TORE

Though the excessive consumption of alcohol is betimes blamed for some misdemeanours, one suspects that rather than being the cause, it simply releases what is already inside. And while accepting that the supposed advent of Meniere's disease was the cause of Dean Swift's apparent insanity, one similarly wonders if the meanness and boorishness he often then displayed, could be attributed to his nature rather than to the disease. When he misplaced his golden bottle-screw he accused one of his guests of having stolen it, and he was not in the least apologetic when he located it where he himself had left it. He explained that the very good reason he had picked on this particular individual was that he was the poorest. This was a Mr Pilkington, a penniless Irish parson, who with his wife, Letitia, was among the visitors at the Deanery. This young couple had been befriended by Swift, who had found the clergyman a job in England. Together with Stella and Vanessa, Letitia was among the more prominent of the many women friends of the Dean. But when the friendship went sour after seven years, Swift savagely commented that 'he (Pilkington) has proved the falsest rogue and she the most profligate whore in either kingdom'. When Mr Pilkington later divorced Letitia, she, accompanied by her son, returned to Dublin destitute. To save herself having to pay for transport from Dunleary to Ringsend she decided to stay on board until the ship docked at Ringsend. That night a storm blew up and the ship was thrown onto the North Bull, a notorious place for ship wrecks, where the local inhabitants made good pickings salvaging goods from wrecked vessels. Mrs Pilkington's boat was washed up on the sand, and she and her son were able to step off 'so that without expense or difficulties', she wrote in her *Memoirs of Letitia Pilkington* 'we walked to Ringsend'.

Pilkington, an English surname, derived from a Lancs. place-name meaning 'farm of the followers of an Anglo-Saxon named Pileca', first appeared in Co. Louth early in the 15th century. Later in the Cromwellian period, it was in Cos. Kildare and Meath. According to MacLysaght's *Surnames* it was fairly common in Co. Clare in the 19th century. Thomas Pilkington, listed as a titulado of the West Ward of Wexford town and its Liberties in the 1659 Census, was the only one of the name therein. In neighbouring Waterford city in 1674 a question arose regarding the behaviour of one Ralph Pilkington and the soldiers at Passage, and though the matter was investigated it appears to have finally been dropped.

'Pilkington Esq.' is shown at Tore ('Tore' is the anglicised form of *tuar*, 'an animal enclosure, a bleaching green) near Tyrrellspass on Taylor and Skinner's *Maps* (1778), and the 1814 *Directory* has a Mrs Pilkington, there. In Co. Westmeath, *Owners of Land* (1876) lists William Pilkington, Kilbride, Rochfortbridge, with 376 acres; Henry M. Pilkington, Tore, with 1,683 acres there, together with 89 acres in Co. Offaly, and Frederick Pilkington, Carbury, Enfield, had 588 Co. Kildare acres, and 41 in Co. Louth. There were two Pilkington holdings in Co. Kilkenny, and the two Pilkington landowners in Co. Laois were associated with the Carrick Mills at Ballacolla. There were three small holdings in Co. Clare, and three more in Co. Galway.

Apart from the Pilkingtons who have featured with distinction in Co. Offaly hurling in recent years, the best known of the name associated with national affairs was Liam Pilkington, Commander of the 3rd Western Division of the IRA. After the death of Liam Lynch in 1923 he was appointed to the Army Council.

POTTIAGHAN

There is but one entry of the English surname Monday in current telephone directories of this island, that being in Co. Derry. The name means 'a person born on a Monday', or possibly 'holder of Mondayland' (you worked for your lord on Mondays). It is also possible that this is the Irish surname, MacGiolla Eoin, 'devotee of Saint John', a surname that mainly belonged to Cos. Tyrone and Donegal. This has variously been anglicised as MacGlone, MacAloon, Gloon, 'including one which is a particularly unfortunate mistranslation-Monday (from Dé Luain!)'. MacGloin, the more common 'English' form of this name is sometimes used for (Mac)Glynn, as are (Mac) Glennan and Glenn. This latter has two distinct origins – (1) the English surname Glen(n), 'glen' Keltic, (2) the Irish Ó Ghleanna (i.e., of the glen), one of the few residential Gaelic surnames. (Others are Ardagh, Athy, Bray, Corbally, Finglas, Galbally, Sutton, Rath, Santry, Slane and Trim.) This has been anglicised Glenny and Glanny. All these, as we remarked, have been used as variants of (Mac) Glynn. This is Mag Fhlainn (*flann*, ruddy). The initial G of Glynn and Mac Glynn comes from the G at the end of Mag. Mag is a variant of Mac often used with names beginning with vowels or aspirated F.

In the Annals of Connaght we read that Florint (Flann) Mac Flainn was elected archbishop of Tuam in 1250. He crossed over to England in 1255 to interview the king of England, returning to Ireland the same year having obtained all his petitions. He died in Bristol the following year. The main septs of this family originated in the Westmeath/Roscommon area, whence they spread west of the Shannon, and even as far north as Donegal. M'Lyne is mentioned in a number of Elizabethan fiants of the latter half of the 16th century. That of 1570 listed James M'Lyne of Rahinmore, Co. Westmeath, among the pardoned. Ráithín Mór, 'the big little fort', though ráithín may also mean 'a row, sods of turf built up to dry, a clamp'.

It is interesting then to note that *Owners of Land* (1876) lists but one Glynn holding in Co. Westmeath. This was a single acre and two roods at Pottiaghan, in the parish of Killare. Paul Walsh's *Placenames of Westmeath* gives this as deriving from Poiteachán, 'wet ground'. He adds a late 16th-century comment: 'These commons are in the possession of a lawless set of people who pay no rent, tithe or county cess.' Other 'owners' were John M'Glynn, Derrintony, Drumshanbo, with 15 Co. Leitrim acres; James Glynn, Murlough, with 35 Co. Donegal acres; three Glynn holdings of 83, 155 and 22 acres, at Cappahard, at Tullycommon, Corrofin, and at Alragah or Corgrigg, Kilmihil – all in Co. Clare. In Co. Down, there was a good number of Glennys, and in Cos. Derry and Tyrone a number of Glenns. We do not know if John M'Gloin, Foxford, with 1,078 Co. Mayo acres, was a genuine Mac Giolla Eoin, or a Mac Fhlainn under a different guise.

Between 1623 and 1635 David mcGlynne had taken mortgages on Derrycoaly, and on Bolybeg and Taghkin in Carrowkeele Cloydrumnehagh, all in Co. Mayo's barony of Kilmaine.

Sean Mag Fhlainn (1843–1915), born in Móinín an Cumair, Béal Átha Glúinín, Co. Galway, was a journalist and newspaper editor. He also was a collector of stories, songs, folklore, and these together with his correspondence are now deposited in the National Library. Of him it was said: 'Mr Glynn is one of the finest Irish scholars of the day and he is certainly among the ablest in editing Irish-Gaelic.'

Wexford

'Once when Sir Richard Sinnott summoned the Grand Jury, every one of them was a Sinnott, which prompted the Lord Justice to humorously remark, 'To judge by their considerable estates and good living they must have obtained their fair lands by name, "Sin–nott"' (Hilary Murphy: *Families of Co. Wexford*). This naive understanding of the origin of this surname apparently was responsible for the ancient Sinnott motto 'Without Sin'. Awareness of earlier renditions of the name in Wexford records, viz., Sinath, Sinad, Synagh, Sinagh, Sinod, Synot, might have saved them from this error. It is now generally believed that the name is from Old English *sigenoo*, meaning victory, bold. An account from *c.*1680 says that the Sinnotts were men remarkable for school learning and persons endowed with heroic spirits and martially disposed minds, vigorously active in their constant loyal affection to the crown of England.

The first Sinnott to land in Wexford with the Normans is believed to be of Flemish descent in Pembrokeshire. They became the most prolific of all Anglo-Norman families in this county, and still maintain their numerical strength. Fiants of 1549 to 1552 show them at Farrellstown, Ballyladge, Ballyharan, Clylon, Killyeran (Killurin), Malrancane (Mulrankin), Mollestown and Wisestown. It appears that a number of these placenames are no longer extant, but did Farrellstown, Ballyharan, Mollestown and Wisestown contain the names of previous owners? Wyse in the latter placename is another Anglo-Norman surname.

The Co. Wexford book of the Civil Survey of 1654 shows Sinnotts in six baronies – Ballaghkeen with a total of 3123 acres; Shelmaliere 3020 acres; Bargy 420 acres; Shelburne 127 acres; Scarawalsh 1190 acres, and Forth 1,083 acres. The 1659 Censor lists the Sinnotts amony the principal Irish names in five of Wexford's baronies, and in the towns of Enniscorthy and Wexford. This Census also names the townland of Synottsbalsee in the parish of Kilsceran (now Kilscoran), and the parish of Synottsland in the barony of Forth.

In 1876 (over 200 years later) when *Owners of Land* was published, every one of Ireland's 15 Sinnott holdings was in Co. Wexford. The largest was the 984 acres at The Abbey, Enniscorthy. Others were 204 acres, 159 acres and nine in single figures – at Commons, Murrinstown; Commons, Bridgetown; Commons, Killurin; and Orristown, Killurin.

A Sinnott holding of 920 acres in 1654 was that of Arthur Synnott, Irish papist, whereon 'A Castle & Baune'. This was in the parish of Ballylolan (modern parish of Ballylannan). This was rendered Ballinlonan in a fiant of 1602, being the address of Donogh O Kie, listed among hundreds of pardoned persons. (There was but one other of this surname in the entire fiants 1521–1603, that being Richard O Key of Vintray (Ventry, Ceann Tra) in Co. Kerry). This surname appears to be a Gaelic surname, but which? The Ormond Deeds inform of a grant given at Kilsyllan on 28 October 1345. Robert Oky had his portion in 'Gortynywr in tenemento de Kylinkatyn, and that of Ysabelle Oke was tenemento et tres acras in Cappagh, and that of Thomas Oky being in tenemento de Balymagan'. Also listed in this document was Lochinilack.

The noted Sinnott loyalty to the crown of England had changed when it came to the fight for Irish independence, though not the 'heroic spirits' and 'martially disposed minds'. T.D. Sinnott was a central figure in the literary and revolutionary movement in Enniscorthy until 1916, and Seán Sinnott played a leading part in the War of Independence in South Wexford. The Irish for Sinnottsmill is Muileánn an tSionoídigh.

BALLYSOP

The Irish word *sop*, 'wisp, small bundle (of straw etc.)', is still in regular use in Ireland, as in 'a sop of straw ', 'a sop of hay' etc. The English word 'sop', a piece of bread or the like dipped or steeped in water, wine etc., also means 'a thing of little worth', and both might possibly be traced to a common Norwegian ancestor. *Sop in ionad na scuaibe* means 'a wisp in place of a brush, a substitute', and *sop i mbéal dorais* was a pad of straw at the door on which tailors and other craftsmen used to sit to avoid a window tax.

Ballysop (Baile Sop, townland of the wisps) is a townland name in the Co. Wexford parish of Ballybrazil. Here Nicholas Gifford had 1,891 acres in 1876 as recorded in *Owners of Land*. Also in this county were the 206 acres of Edward Gifford, Lime House, London. Louis Gifford (no address) had 797 acres in Co. Offaly and 206 in Co. Meath. The 1814 *Directory* has 'Nicholas Gifford, Esq.' at Ballysop, and the 1837 Lewis' *Topographical Dictionary* informs that after the battle of New Ross, during the 1798 disturbances, the insurgent army took possession of Ballysop, 'now the seat of Rev. William Gifford'. During those same 'disturbances', 17-year old Lieutenant William Gifford was found by the rebels in the mail coach from Limerick, and piked to death.

Documents Relating to Ireland 1795–1804, which includes the 'Accounts of Secret Service Money, Ireland, 1803', lists Mr Giffard as advancing £11. 7s. 6d. to Mr Owens of Co. Wexford on 30 April 1803; £22. 15s. 0d. 'for informers' on 10 August, and a further sum of the same amount 'per receipt', on 31 August. The most notorious bearer of this surname was John Giffard (1745–1819), of Dromartin Castle, near Dublin, but born in Co. Wexford. Son of Englishman John Giffard and Dorcas Murphy of Oulartleigh, Co. Wexford, he was 'not only a sinecurist but a particularly unsavoury one', 'an ascendancy activist depending on Castle patronage for his livelihood. He constantly protested that he was a patriot first and foremost, and that he would never do anything but for the good of the country. In other words he was announcing that he was for sale, and the Government bought him with the job as Director of the City Watch' (John O'Donovan, *Life by the Liffey*). During the 1803 election Henry Grattan said of him to his face: 'In the city a firebrand – in the court a liar – in the streets a bully – in the field a coward. And so obnoxious is he to the very party he wishes to espouse, that he is only supportable by doing those dirty acts the less vile refuse to execute.'

Around 1170 Strongbow granted the south Co. Carlow barony of St Mullins and its half cantred to Peter Giffard. Gifford's Grove, 'a little grove of underwood' in Dublin's Kilmainham is recorded in a document of 1574; in 1596 Captain Richard Gifford was granted a marriage settlement of Ballymaggarrett, Co. Roscommon, and persons of this name were listed in the *Census* of 1659 among the tituladoes and commissioners in counties Cork, Kildare, Meath, and Offaly. De Bhulbh's *Sloinnte na hÉireann/Irish Surnames* says that this is a Scottish surname of a Norman origin, meaning 'bloated, puffy-cheeked'.

Probably the best known person bearing this name was artist Grace Gifford, who married 1916 Proclamation signatory Joseph Mary Plunkett hours before he was executed for his part in the 1916 Rising. Muriel, one of her three sisters, married Thomas MacDonagh, another signatory of the Proclamation. Converts to Catholicism, all sisters took an active part in the Republican movement. The two other sisters were Nellie (later to call herself Eibhlín) and Sydney, who wrote under the name 'John Brennan'. Sydney wrote *The Years Flew By*, but high-up or low-down we have been unable to lay hands on a copy, and we wonder if they were connected with Charles F. Gifford, 5 Foster Place, and Turkey Lodge, Fairview, Clontarf, Dublin, in 1850.

There are 13 entries of Gifford in the *Phone Book* of Northern Ireland, mostly in Belfast and Lisburn, and all 10 entries south of the Border are in the Dublin 01 area.

GOREY

In 1837 the Co. Wexford town of Gorey was described as having one long street
neatly and uniformly built, the whole town containing 548 houses. In the last
quarter of the 18th century the main street was mainly inhabited by planter
families living in substantial houses, wherein we are informed 'the bigger
landlords' spent the season in the town. Among these was the Lett family. A
hundred years later, however they would hardly be enumerated among the
'bigger landlords', going by the 1876 *Owners of Land*. In that year Co. Wexford
had 125 landlords with a 1,000 acres or more, the largest being the 17,830 acres
of Right Hon. Lord Carew, Castleboro; the largest Lett holding was the 517
acres of Benjamin Lett, Ballyvergin, Adamstown. Apart from the 12 acres of the
Revd Charles Lett, Finvoy, Co. Antrim, all other Lett holdings at that time were
in Co. Wexford. There was 388 acres at Millpark, Enniscorthy; 190 acres at
Bridgetown; 57 at Hollyfort, Enniscorthy; 16 at Tomgarrow, and 14 at
Tinnacross. Two Letts resident in Dublin had 208 and 205 Co. Wexford acres.

'The founder of the principal Wexford family of the name was the
Cromwellian Captain Thomas Lett who came from Warwickshire and probably
received a grant of land in the county,' according to Hilary Murphy's *Families of
Co. Wexford*. Thomas had three sons, Charles, William and Thomas, who lived,
respectively, at Milehouse, near Enniscorthy, at Ballyvergin, and at Newcastle,
Kilmannon. The same source says that the Letts are believed to have originally
come from the shores of the Baltic Sea. 'Some authorities say they first settled
in Lithuania where they formed a separate and distinct people and spoke a
language called Lettish.' However, Edward MacLysaght in his *Surnames* quotes
Reaney as saying that this surname derived from the Latin, *laetitia*, joy, being pet
form of the firstname Lettice. He adds that it is worth considering the Norman
de Lette, observing that the justicary Rolls mention a John de Leyt, and that the
listing of Adam Lyth as a juror in a Co. Carlow inquisition of 1307 might also
be relevant.

Taylor and Skinner's *Maps* (1778) shows 'Lett Esq.' at Newcastle, south-west
of the town of Wexford, and the 1814 *Directory* lists Letts at Boolabawn, at
Greenville, at Kilgibbon and at Sunfield.

Most of the Letts were zealous Protestant loyalists at the time of the 1798
Insurrection, and two of the children of William Lett of Kilgibbon, high
constable of Shelmalier West, were among others incarcerated in the infamous
Scullabogue Barn. However, they were rescued before the barn was set alight
and its 37 Protestants massacred. Their rescue was effected at the request of two
Catholic neighbours, Thomas Murphy of Park, and a man named Brien. The
latter's son was later given a house and five acres freehold at Ballymorris. (The
price of two lives?) On the other hand, Joshua Lett, who possessed extensive

lands near Enniscorthy, gave the hospitality of his home to the wounded rebel leader Thomas Cloney. At Cloney's court-martial members of the Lett family gave evidence of the humanity he had shown to loyalists during the Insurrection. Indeed, thirteen-year old Jemmy Moore-Lett of Newcastle joined the rebel side, and his four sisters, known as the 'rebel angels' embroidered banners for the insurgents.

Lewis's *Topographical Dictionary* (1837) giving Newborrough as an alias for Gorey, says that 'its modern appellation has never grown into general use'. Gorey derived from Guaire, the original Irish name. *Guaire* is defined as 'a sand bank above high watermark'. It also meant 'rough hair, a bristle'; *guaire toirc anoir on Pholainn* was hog-bristle imported from Poland (for use in shoemaking).

The *Phone Book* of Northern Ireland lists not a single Lett, and of the 25 telephone entries, in the South, apart from the nine emigrants in the Dublin 01 area, 13 are in Co. Wexford, and one each in Cos. Kildare and Wicklow.

BEGERY ISLAND

There is no island indicated in Wexford Harbour on the current Ordnance Survey ½"=1 mile map, though there is a sandbank seated north of its mouth. Lewis in his *Topographical Dictionary* (1837) says of the northern shore of Wexford Harbour that 'inside the sand hills is an extensive cockle bed, and westward of this is a small island called Breast'. The Meets and Bounds (delineation) of the parish of St Margaret's, in the Co. Wexford barony of Shelmaliere, as outlined in the Civil Survey (1654) for Co. Wexford, begin: 'The said Parish beginneth at the Sea east to the Bar of Wexford and from thence to the little Island called the Brest ...'. William Petty's 1685 map of Co. Wexford has, in the southern part of the harbour, what appears to be either Beaule or Beavle Iland; further north is Great Iland, more or less where the sand bank is indicated today; and just off the northern shore is Begory. Not, it will be noted, Begory Iland, just Begory, and in a footnote to his edition of the *Annals of the Four Masters* in 1851, John O'Donovan writes 'Beg-Eire that is, Little Ireland, now Begery, a small island close to the land in Wexford Haven. This is translated Parva Hibernia in the Lives of St Ibar and St Abban ... According to O'Clery's Irish Calendar, St Ibhar, who died in the year 500, erected a church on this island, where his festival was kept on the 23rd of April. Begery is destined to lose its insular character in the improvements of Wexford Haven which are now in progress.' This, apparently, accounts for the islandless harbour today. Interestingly, the *Index of Townlands* of that same year of 1851 lists Begerin Island, 21 acres, in the parish of St Margaret's; Begerin (Lloyd) and Begerin (Loftus), are quite some distance away in the parish of Oldross, some four miles east of New Ross. Today Begerin Island is shown on the map as being about a mile inland, with the semicircular Curracloe Channel hitting the coast at positions about two miles apart, and enclosing a couple of hundred acres.

Titulado for Curracloe, also in the parish of St Margaret's, according to the Census of 1659 was William Trevill, Gent. We have not come across this surname elsewhere, but considering the absence of standardised spelling, and the interchanging of 'v' and 'u' in the 17th century, we wondered if the surname Truell might not be the same. This is the name of a landed gentry family in Co. Wicklow since the early 17th century. Taylor and Skinner's 1778 *Maps* shows 'Rd. Mr Truel' at Clonmanin (now Clonmannan), and in 1814 the Revd Robert Truel resided at the same address. And to the present day this name, though scarce, is still to be found in Co. Wicklow.

For the year AD 819 the Four Masters record, 'The plundering of Edar by the foreigners, who carried off a great prey of women. The plundering of Beg-Eire and Dairinis-Caemhain by them also', and in the year 884 'Crunnmhael, Abbot of Beg-Eire and lector of Tamhlacht, was drowned at Tochar-Eachdhach'. In Irish Begerin is Beigéirinn (? *beag* + *Éirinn*?).

BROADWAY

The Graces, the FitzMaurices and the Redmonds of Loftus Hall, Co. Wexford, whose supposed eponymous ancestor is Raymond le Gros (though it was reported by Giraldus Cambrensis that he had no legitimate children), may take comfort from the belief that Raymond appeared not to have taken part in an act of extreme brutality in 1170 when seventy of the principal citizens of Waterford were captured. Though large sums of money were offered for their ransom, their legs were broken and they were hurled over a precipice into the sea. The surname Redmond, gaelicised as Réamonn, is an Anglo-Norman family of importance throughout Irish history, and associated almost entirely with south County Wexford. Indeed by 1659 when the Census was taken, the Redmonds were among the principal Irish names in practically every Co. Wexford barony, though the only Redmond to be named a titulado was Robert, for the townland of Kariskillowe, in the Co. Roscommon parish of Aghrinn (Aughrim).

The 1654 Civil Survey lists Owen McCahir Redmond as owning 100 acres; Oliver McGerrott Redmond, 60 acres; John Redmond with over 300 acres; Alexander Redmond with nearly 500 acres, and Art McQuine Redmond with 52 acres. All the above were Irish papists, and all the holdings were in the parish of Ardamaine, Co. Wexford. Indeed so important was this family that they gave their name to Redmondstown in the parish of Ballynaslaney; Redmondstown in the parish of Rathpatrick, both in Co. Wexford; to Redmondstown in the Co. Tipperary parish of Kilgrant, and to Redmondstown in the Co. Westmeath parish of Churchtown. Taylor and Skinner's *Maps* (1778) shows 'Newtown' and 'Killygown' in Co. Wexford as the residences of 'Redmonds Esqrs.', and the 1814 *Directory* lists the 'seats' of seven Redmonds, five of which were in Co. Wexford – at Betty-ville, Clonjordan, Knockduff, Somerton and Ballytrent, with Broadway given as the Post-town of the latter. In Co. Wexford thirteen of the name feature in *Owners of Land* (1876), ranging from one acre up to John P. Redmond, Raglan Road, Dublin, with 2,026 acres. The second largest proprietor was P.W. Redmond, Ballytrent, with 1,483 acres. We have not located any suggested Irish for this, and while this might appear to be 'Trent's town', we have no evidence that such is so, nor have we discovered such a surname in any list. Broadway, in the parish of St Iberius, is given in *Gasitéar na hÉireann / Gazetteer of Ireland* as Gráinseach Iúir, 'the grange of the yew tree'. We cannot say when the old Irish name took on its American appearance, and while there was a Grange in this parish in 1654, it appears not be be an abbreviated version of Gráinseach Iúir, as both the names Grange and Broadway are still extant. This village is situated on the northern extremity of Lady's Island lake, and had a population of 160 in 1837, according to Lewis' *Topographical Dictionary*.

John Edward Redmond (1856–1918), MP for Wexford, was an ardent supporter of Charles S. Parnell, even to the extent of going to gaol in 1888. He went on to lead the Parnellite wing after the split in the party, pinning his hopes on the British allowing Home Rule, with Ireland still part of the United Kingdom. This was conceded in 1914, though he had to accept the idea of partition due to Unionist opposition, and the postponement of Home Rule due to the start of the First World War. The Rising of 1916 ruined him both personally and politically, and two years later he was dead and his policy rejected by the majority of the Irish people.

KILLEGNY

'It is ordered, that no person or persons shall dare insult, abuse, injure, or hurt the reverend Mr Francis, his family, domesticks, mansion-houses &c. All who disobey these orders, shall be taken by a guard, brought into camp, to be tried by court-martial, and punished according to their sentence. ROCHE, Commander in chief of the united army of the county of Wexford.' And though the above is printed in Sir Richard Musgrave's *The Irish Rebellion*, the story of the rebellion of 1798, he describes Philip Roche, author of the above Protection order, as 'an inhuman savage', who inculcated 'the extirpation of hereticks', and was present, and presided at 'many massacres on Vinegar Hill'. Fr Roche was hanged on the bridge of Wexford, 'for various crimes'. But however stirred Musgrave was by Fr Roche, his real spleen was directed against the Revd Mr James Gordon, the clergyman who succeeded the above-mentioned Revd Francis as rector in the parish of Killegny. Gordon wrote the *History of the Rebellion in 1798*, which was published in Dublin in 1801. Because it did not accord with Musgrave's views, Musgrave attributed Gordon's dissenting account, not to any concern about the truth, but 'knowing the set of savages he had to deal with, has, with more regard to policy than accuracy, written a history of the rebellion, for the obvious purpose of conciliating the priests and the popish multitude, to secure the punctual payment of his tythes;and for that purpose he abuses the magistrates, the military, and the yeomen, and he imputes many of the atrocities committed during the rebellion to local provocation ...' Gordon defended Fr Roche against Musgrave's charges, and Musgrave's response was: 'Good God! that a protestant clergyman should become the encomiast of a monster who was the instrument of so much human misery...'

Killegny is a parish in the Co. Wexford barony of Bantry, on the eastern side of the county bordering Co. Kilkenny. The name comes from Cill Eanga (the church of Eanag/Eannac, possibly a saint's name.)

Mr Francis, 'a gentleman venerable for his age, his piety, and learning', according to Musgrave, moved with his family to Dublin in the winter of 1798. 'He was in rapid decline, from a spitting of blood, occasioned by rude and brutal treatment from the rebels; and he died in the beginning of the year 1799, leaving his family in the utmost distress.' During his captivity, according to Musgrave, 'a ruffian' named Gormachan demanded at sword-point to know if the reverend was a Christian and if he could bless himself, and later he was marched to mass at the point of a horse-pistol held by 'one of the missionaries, a ferocious savage, by name Drohan'.

The 1814 *Directory* of Dublin lists Mrs Elija Francis, 32 Queen Street, and John Francis, watch case maker, 65½ Bride Street. The surname Francis has no Gaelic background, being Norman le Franceis, 'the French person', though it was quite numerous as Proinseis in the Irish speaking area near Galway city. *Owners of Land* 1876) lists two of the name in Co. Down, at Ballygowan and Strandtown, owning 7 and 38 acres; one in Warrenpoint, Co. Armagh, with 26 acres, and Thomas Francis, Ballybogan, Castlebridge, with 100 acres in Co. Wexford. The Northern Ireland *Phone Book* lists more that fifty of the name Francis, with Southern directories showing roughly the same number, divided between the Dublin area and the remainder of the country. Of the latter, Co. Galway had the greatest concentration.

BALLYKEEROGE

In the *Irish Fiants of the Tutor Sovereigns (1521–1603)* the Sutton men were variously described as 'Gentlemen' and 'Horsemen', and as 'Idlemen' (1550). *The Shorter Oxford English Dictionary* defines 'Idleman' as: '1. One who has no occupation; formerly in Ireland, a gentleman. 2. One employed to do odd jobs 1845'. MacLysaght's *Surnames* says that the surname Sutton is possibly a toponymic from the Irish placename (though Dublin's Sutton is from Cill Fhionntáin, 'Fionntan's church'), giving de Sutún as its gaelicised form. The English surname Sutton, is a locative meaning 'southern/south facing farm' or 'to the south of the farm/village', naming places in almost every county in England. Among the Irish Suttons we find Henry Sutton alias genkaghe (?*geancech*, snub-nosed), Richard oge (*og*, young) Sutton, and William Sutton, alias Da begg. If this man's, name was not William we would have speculated that Da begg was Daithí beag, 'small David'. The Suttons had been prominent in Co. Wexford since the 13th century, the earliest being Roger de Sutton, mentioned in a charter of 1231–4. He was then the tenant of Tellarought, the parish north-west of Ballybrazil (which includes the townland of Ballykerogue),' according to Hilary Murphy's *Families of Co. Wexford*. The same source refers to the Suttons as a Norman family. The above Ballykerogue is rendered Ballykeeroge in the *Index of Townlands*, and P.W. Joyce in his *Names of Places* says that the second element of this place-name is more likely to be Ciaróg, a man's name, rather than *ciaróg*, 'a cock-roach, a black chafer, an earwig', being the diminutive of *ciar*, black, dark'. *Irish Personal Names* (by Ó Corráin and Maguire) lists Ciarán and its female equivalent Ciarnat/Ciarnait 'dark lady', and Ciarmhac, 'dark son'. But no Ciaróg. There is no dispute that the Irish is Baile Ciaróg, but does *ciaróg* mean 'beetle'.

The Suttons had castles and lands in Co. Wexford at Oldcourt, Priesthaggard, Fethard, Aclare, Clonmines, Ballyverney, Ballysop, Aclamon, and Great Clonard, but their principal stronghold, until they were dispossessed in the Cromwellian confiscation of the 1650s was Ballykeeroge Castle, near Campile. 'We are told that when Cromwell's soldiers attacked Ballykerogue Castle they were strongly resisted. They eventually set fire to the castle and twenty-three of the twenty-five Suttons perished. One who escaped was killed at the place still known as Sutton's Cross. It is interesting to find Suttons still living in the vicinity' (*Families of Co. Wexford*).

The Suttons are mentioned in around 150 of the Tudor fiants (1521–1603), the vast majority in those of Elizabeth. Among the transplanters to the Barony of Boyle, Co. Roscommon, from Kildare, Meath and Dublin in 1655, was Garret Sutton, Richardstown, who received 100 acres in the parish of Tumna. Remarkably there was but one of the name on Taylor and Skinner's *Maps*

(1778), that being at Longgraigue in the Co. Wexford parish of Clongeen, a branch of the family that became Protestants. The branch which settled at Wheelagower, near Kiltealy, remained there for several generations 'It is said that in penal times one member of this family was obliged to put in an appearance at the Protestant church once or twice a year so as to keep up the pretence of having conformed to the Protestant religion, which enabled the family to hold on to their property' (*Families of Co. Wexford*). In 1876 according to *Owners of Land* the only Sutton holdings in the country were the 48 acres of Ellen Sutton, Wheelagower, and Michael Sutton's 176 acres at Ryane, Oylegate. Not mighty holdings, but the Suttons had tenaciously remained in that locality for almost 700 years. And today's telephone directories, more than a hundred years later, show the Suttons to be still numerous in Co. Wexford, and in Co. Cork. In lesser numbers they are in Cos. Kilkenny, Waterford, Tipperary, Clare and Limerick. There are *c.*110 in the Dublin area directory, with 17 in the *Phone Book* of Northern Ireland.

There were both Catholic and Protestant clergymen among the Suttons, as there was a rebel and a footballer. Matthew Sutton was among the political prisoners transported to Botany Bay after the rebellion of 1798, and Michael J. Sutton won an All-Ireland as a substitute with the Wexford team of 1917. He captained the New Ross O'Hanrahan's team which won the senior county football championship in 1920, and was a member of the IRA during the War of Independence.

COURTOWN

There is but a single Stopford listed in the Census of 1659, that being James Stopford, titulado in Saint Michael's parish in Dublin city. Current telephone directories of our island list five of the name – two in the Dublin area, two in Co. Antrim and one in Co. Galway.

Stopford/Stoppard/Stopforth is an English surname derived from Old English *stoc* + *port*, market at a hamlet; place (Stockport) in Cheshire. None of this name was among the landowners in Co. Wexford in 1640, a county where they later settled. In 1876 they were listed as owning 1,426 acres in the parish of Ardamaine. An early member of this family was H. Stopford, who was a judge in the high court set up at Clonmel, Co. Tipperary in 1642, to compile evidence relating to the insurrection of 1640, and to try the accused of involvement therein. In the year of the insurrection the landowners in Ardamaine parish were Peirce Synnott, Edward mcJames Kenshalagh, Owen mcCahir Redmond, Oliver mcGerrott Redmond and John Redmond, all Irish papists.

This family were to become Lords Stopford, earls of Courtown, and Arthur Young in his *Tour in Ireland, 1776–79* tells of a visit to Courtown: 'Got to Lord Courtown's, who, with an attention highly flattering, took every means to have me well informed. His seat at Courtown is a very agreeable place ... Lord Courtown is a very good farmer. The first field of turneps I saw in Ireland was here, and he was thinning and weeding them with boys, in order to hoe them with more effect, the land in order, well dunged, and the plants forward and flourishing.' Later he writes: 'July 14, Sunday – to church, and was surprised to find a large congregation: this is not often the case in Ireland out of a mass-house – Gallop on the strand; it is a fine firm beautiful sand for miles. The paddies were swimming their horses in the sea to cure the mange, or keep them in health'.

'Few classes of men have had so much abuse heaped on them as Irish landlords, and with justification,' writes Cecil Woodham-Smith in *The Great Hunger*, the story of the Famine of 1846, but adding that Lord Stopford, later 5th earl of Courtown, had built Courtown Harbour in the 1820s to develop the local fishing industry; the large sums it cost had an adverse effect on the family finances, but unfortunately it was not a success, owing to silting. In 1847 Lord Courtown had a new pier built and a fish-curing establishment set up. He contributed £1,500 to the Gorey Relief Committee, and in addition to employing about 100 men on his estate gave work to numbers of the Gorey and Riverchapel poor during the winter of 1846–7, raised two sums of £8,000 and £6,000 for drainage and finally employed every labourer on his property. Both he and Lord Stopford were active on relief committees, Boards of Guardians, fever committees and the magistrates' bench, attending almost daily, sometimes twice daily, and working in discouraging circumstances'. Indeed, there were occasions when Lord Stopford and his father were the only members of a committee who bothered to attend.

Courtown is Baile na Cúirte.

RAMSFORT

Two of the fourteen listed by 'Abel Ram Esq.' as having dispossessed him of his lands (worth £1,200 per annum) in 1641, were, according to Ram, Shane Sarragh, Carrybeg, gentleman, and Donagh Shaneballagh, the priest, two surnames that are not to be found in MacLysaght's *Surnames*. He named a further three who had been seen among other rebels in Limerick, one whom he names as Morrison Vadagh, of Ballantlea, gentleman. This surname might be a variant of Vady, an abbreviated form of MacAvaddy, Mac an Mhadaidh, of which MacLysaght says, 'The derivation from madadh, dog, is not fully accepted, though it seems probable'. Found in the Civil Survey of 1654, which gives details of ownership of land in 1641, is the surname Vadock/ Vadicke/ Wadocke, and one wonders if there is any connection. Abel Ram, lived at Ramsfort, in the parish of Killmakilloge, Co. Wexford, but this had become Ramsfortpark (or Ballowen) before the publication of the *Index of Townlands* (1851). Sir Richard Musgrave's *Rebellion in Ireland* writes: 'The county of Wexford was desolated in the year 1641; and the houses of the bishop of Ferns and Mr Ram of Ramsford, were destroyed as well in the rebellion of that period as in the late one …', the late one being 1798. Of the surname Ram, MacLysaght writes: 'this English name of obvious derivation, prominent in Co. Wexford in the seventeenth and eighteenth centuries, is now almost obsolete,' and while there was a Revd Abel J. Ram, Rolleston, with 1,813 acres in Co. Wexford in 1876, there is not a single entry of the name in the current telephone directory. And remarkably, though Ramsgrange named a townland in the parish of Dunbrody (later St James and Dunbrody), as found in the Civil Survey 1654, indicating that the Ram family had been in the county sufficiently long to have a place named for them, not a single member of the family is listed therein as owning a single acre in 1641. The total acreage of the parish of Dunbrody is given in the Survey as 2,880 acres, all of which then belonged to John Etchingham, English Protestant. But like the Normans who became níos Gaelaí ná na Gaeil, 'more Irish than the Irish', likewise the Etchinghams, Seán Etchingham was one of the Enniscorthy leaders sentenced to death after the Easter Rising of 1916, though the sentence was later commuted. 'He was a native of Ballintray and a journalist by profession. In 1919 he was appointed by Dáil Éireann as the Republic's first Minister for Fisheries, a post which he held until 1922. He was also the first Republican Chairman of the Wexford County Council and of the County Committee of Agriculture. He acted as chairman of the County Board of the GAA for many years. After a long illness, brought on by his sufferings in the cause of the country, he died at his home in Courtown in 1923. He was then 56. He is buried in the ancient graveyard of Ardamaine': (Richard Roche, *Here's to Their Memory*). The telephone directories show seven entries of this name in Dublin city. Persons of this name have been involved in Irish language and cultural activties.

The Irish for Ramsfort is Baile Eoghain.

PRIESTHAGGARD

The graveyard at Kilcrumper near Fermoy, Co. Cork, is probahly best known as the resting place of Liam Lynch, chief of staff of the Republican Army, killed in action in 1923. This placename is Cill Chruimhthir, 'the church of the priest or presbyter'. *Cruimhthir* is an obsolete word, long replaced by *sagart*, also in Clooncruffer, in the Co. Roscommon parish of Ardcarn. Sagart is common in local names, for example, Kylenasaggart, Coill na Sagart, 'the wood of the priests' in Co. Kilkenny, and Carrickataggart, Carraig an tSagairt, 'the rock of the priest' in Co. Donegal. The word 'priest' forms part of thirteen townland names and, while we do not know if any of these are translations from an original Irish names, *Gasitéar na hÉireann / Gazetteer of Ireland* gives Priestland as Fearann an tSagairt. Priesthaggard in the Co. Wexford parish of Kilmokea is spelled Pricahagard on William Petty's 1685 map of that county, and in the 1654 Civil Survey (a source not noted for its consistency in spelling) it is rendered Price Haggard four times.

The surname Price derives from the Welsh Ap Rhys, and is in Ireland since the 14th century, though not specially associated with any particular locality. It is to found in but one townland name, Price's Lot in the Co. Tipperary parish of St John Baptist. Telephone directories show a fairly wide spread of the name, though there is a predominance in area of Cos. Kildare, Meath, Westmeath, Wicklow and Wexford, and also Sligo and Donegal.

Listed in *Owners of Land* (1876) at Fruit Hill, Priesthaggard, Co. Wexford, with 148 acres, was Julia Glascott, with J.H. Glascott, M'Murroughs, New Ross on 114 acres, and W. M. Glascott, Alderton, Priesthaggard, with 2,821 acres. There was a 'Glascott Esq.' at Fruit-hill in 1814, and a 'Glascott Esq.' is shown at Alderton on Taylor and Skinner's *Maps* (1778).

William Glascott is listed as titulado in the Census of 1659 for the Co. Cork parish of Kilbrogan, though none of the name is to be found in the Co. Wexford book of the 1654 Civil Survey.

Dorothea Herbert in her most interesting *Retrospections 1770–1806* writes of 1779: 'We had now Childrens Balls breakfasts. Suppers &c where Mr Kelly the famous dancing Master presided, And No drawing Room or Levee ever displayed half the State, form, dress, and fuss that was seen in those Parties – Our Chief Heroines were Lady Catherine Nugent – Miss Glascott – and Grace Cuffe…'. Current telephone directories list no Glascotts in Co. Wexford; of the nine listed, six are in Carrick-on-Suir, Co. Tipperary.

Neither MacLysaght's *Surnames*, nor Basil Cottle's *Dictionary of Surnames* makes any mention of the Glascotts, but William Glascott must have been in Cork long enough prior to 1659, to have established the status that made him a titulado; and the family, Protestant and later also Catholic, have been in Ireland since, moving from Cork to Wexford and eventually to Co. Tipperary.

Wicklow

Owner of 411 acres in Co. Wicklow as listed in *Owners of Land* (1876) was Charles Hume, Polworth, Scotland. It was from Polworth that the first persons of the surname Hume came to Ireland. Patrick Hume of Polworth was controller of Scotland in 1499, and two of his great-great grandsons were granted estates in Fermanagh during the Plantation of 1609. None of the name however, is listed as still having land in Fermanagh in 1876. They were numerous in Co. Offaly where nine of the name had holdings, six of which were at Clonbulloge, Rathangan. There were three holdings of 21, 27 and 28 acres at Ballytoley, Ballynure, Co. Antrim; a two-acre holding at Letterkenny, Co. Donegal; one of 46 acres in Co. Down, and three holdings in Co. Wicklow – 115, 411 and 1,203 acres. The 1,203 acres belonged to William Hume, Humewood, Kilteagan, it being the largest Hume holding in the country. Liam Price in his *The Place-names of Co. Wicklow* does not give any Irish name for Humewood, but informs that this place had been previously named Butlerswood. In 1708 Butlerswood and the adjacent lands were granted to William Hume of Hacketstown. It was still called Butlerswood in 1741, but in 1764 the owner was named George Hume of Humeswood, so the name was changed *c.*1750. The name Butlerswood dates from the 13th century.

The surname Hume is of dual derivation, that of Scotland from the barony of Home, and that of England deriving from the Old Danish *hulm*. The Humes of Humewood were described as 'middling gentry'. There was a Protestant loyalist belief that Hume's yeomanry units were United Irishmen, and loyalist impatience with his liberal outlook knew no bounds; the complaint was made 'I wish Mr Hume of Humewood was properly cautioned for screening the disaffected of his own neighbourhood.' At the end of the 1798 insurrection William Hume of Humewood, member of Parliament for Wicklow, magistrate and captain of the Lower Talbotstown cavalry, was killed near his home in a skirmish with rebels, though it was generally conceded that Hume himself had not been a hate-figure of the rebels.

The Humes of Polworth stock, John and Alexander, had received estates at Carrynroe and Drumcose, Co. Fermanagh. John had received 2,000 acres, and later bought out his brother, as well as the estate of Moyglasse. This made him the biggest landowner in Fermanagh, with an annual income of £30,000 in the last century.

And if the Humes of Humewood were designated 'middling gentry', it was said of the (rare) Antrim Humes that the name was 'a low name'. Most remarkable, however, was that Hume was then said to have been pronounced Wham ('as our Scottish patois hath it'). Johnny Wham, the bellman of Ballymena, was described as the 'most respectable and worthy of note' of that family. On 7 June 1798, and on days following that, he perched himself in the market-house steeple above his bell, and as each contingent of United Irishmen appeared, he called out 'More friends fur Clough, Cullybackey or elsewhere'. Samuel Hume, son or nephew of Johnny Wham, was said to have been doing his bit of pretended loyalty for his landlord. 'Partisan Magistrates kept such fellows as Hume to concoct stories after, and even before '98. On these lies, they burned houses, flogged, half-hanged, imprisoned and maltreated men, and especially women and girls, to goad the people into insurrection, unarmed and helpless ...' (Fitzpatrick, *The Sham Squire*).

There is a single entry of the name Wham (in Carrickfergus, Co. Antrim) in the Irish telephone directories. But whence the surname Whan (34 entries), almost exclusively north of the Border?

MULLINAVEIGUE

General Joseph Holt, the 1798 Co. Wicklow leader, clearly could write a fluent letter with all the flourishes and style common to his time, though his spelling was more 'flexible' than most. That spelling, however, gives an indication of his accent when he writes 'main' for 'mean', and 'plase' for 'please'. Those flourishes however cannot conceal the obsequiousness in his letter to Mrs Peter Lettuce née La Touche, subsequent to his surrender and sentencing to transportation. This was in seeking her assistance in his request that his 'dear wife and childer' be allowed to travel with him. No doubt that part of the reason for this leading 1798 rebel being unfairly ignored by later historians was the 'catholicing' by both sides, of the rebellion; but the suspicion that he may have given information concerning his accomplices as a possible contributing (if not the sole) factor cannot be ignored. Though the information he gave on 16 November 1798 was not on oath, nor all of what he revealed was about robbers and robberies.

He was born of Protestant settler stock in Ballydonnell, Co. Wicklow, in 1759, and later lived at Mullinaveigue in the Co. Wicklow parish of Calary.

Mullinaveigue is from Muileann an mheidhg, which Liam Price in his *Place-names of Co. Wicklow* says means 'the whey mill', quoting O'Curry as saying that this is a nickname for 'an inefficient mill'.

Considering his record – the burning of twenty loyalists' homes above Roundwood from Derrybawn to Ballinastoe, among other things (his own house had been burned in 1798) – Holt was leniently treated: he was allowed to have his wife and one of his children travel with him when transported, and received preferential treatment on board ship. The suspicion of a conspiracy in 1806 to seize the military at Parramatta, New South Wales, led to the recommendation that the four principals receive 1000 lashes each. Holt and a Fr James Harold, both of whom had been arrested on suspicion of complicity, were compelled to witness several floggings of suspects. The flogging of one Maurice Fitzgerald was described by Holt: 'I never saw two trashers in a barn moove more handeyer than those two man killers did ...' Holt was allowed to return home in 1814.

The earliest reference to the surname Holt found by MacLysaght, as related in his *Surnames*, was for the year 1295. 'It appears several times in Co. Cork in the next century; later we find it in Ulster.' This English surname derives from the Old-English meaning 'wood'. De Bhulbh's book *Sloinnte na hÉireann/Irish Surnames* gives 'Hólt' as the Irish form. Marc Holte of the Carrickfergus area of Co. Antrim is mentioned in a fiant of 1571, and the 1659 *Census* lists Richard Holt as titulado in Drumcar in Co. Louth, and Thomas Hoult titulado in the parish of St Catherine in Dublin city. Samuel Holt was 'seated' at Sallins Lodge, Bodenstown, Co. Kildare in Lewis' 1837 *Topographical Dictionary,* and in 1876 there were two Holt holdings – 229 and 269 acres at Bodenstown, Co. Kildare. Zella Holt, London, had two Co. Louth acres.

Hart's *Irish Pedigrees* does not list Holt, but does have Houlte listed among the families in Ireland in the 17th century. The only other reference to this spelling – presuming that it is the same name – we have come across, was to Dublin-born writer Norah Hoult (1898–1984).

Most of the 53 telephone entries in *Eolaí Telefóin na hÉireann* are in Leinster, and the two Hoult entries are in Co. Mayo. In the *Phone Book* of Northern Ireland there is a single Hoult entry, that being in Co. Down, and the 12 Holts are in Cos. Down and Antrim.

ROCK BIG

MacLysaght in his *Surnames* (1969) informs us that Jackson is a most numerous English surname in Ireland, especially in Ulster, since mid-seventeenth century.

He gives no Irish version of the name and ignores Mac Siacais/Siacuis given as the Irish by Patrick Woulfe in his *Sloinnte Gaedheal is Gall/Irish Names and Surnames* (1923). Woulfe gives M'Sekays and M'Shekish as early Anglicised forms. The first we located in a fiant of 1579 when John M'Shekish was among the pardoned of Cos. Waterford/Wexford, and Teig M'Sekays of Ballibarre is among those pardoned in a 1585 Fiant. We have not located 'Ballibarre', but other placenames in this fiant indicate that it is/was in Co. Limerick.

Cromwellian Thomas Jackson was among the 'adventurers for land' in Ireland in 1653, and was granted such in the south Tipperary area of Cashel/Knocklofty/Carrick-on-Suir/Ballingarry. The Census of 1659 shows the Jackson as tituladoes and commissioners, but not among the principal Irish names, in Cos. Kilkenny, Cork, Waterford, Mayo, Louth and Kildare. Taylor and Skinner's *Maps* (1778) locates Jackson 'seats' in Cos. Antrim, Armagh, Derry, Monaghan, Cavan, Westmeath and Mayo.

The 1814 *Directory to the Market Towns, Villages, Gentlemen's Seats and other Noted Places in Ireland* lists 25 Jackson 'Seats' – 11 in Ulster, 7 in Munster (mainly in Tipperary and Waterford), 6 in Leinster, and one in Connaught. *Owners of Land* (1876) shows Jackson holdings in 26 of Ireland's 32 counties. They were in all of Ulster's 9 counties; in 8 Leinster counties; all 5 in Connaught, and in 4 of Munster's six. Ten of the holdings were in excess of 1,000 acres, the largest being the 3,491 Co. Cork acres of William O. Jackson, Ahanesk, Midleton. He had a further 1,052 Co. Waterford acres. Close behind was the 3,134 Co. Mayo acres of Oliver Vaughan Jackson, Carrowmore, Ballina. Henry Vincent Jackson, Inane, Co. Tipperary, had 1,088 acres in that county, and a further 1,765 Co. Kildare acres. The largest number of holdings in any one county was the 11 in Co. Kildare, followed by 10 in Co. Derry. Anne Jackson's 11 acres at Inishlounaght, Clonmel was the only one of Co. Tipperary's three holdings in the area where Thomas Jackson had been granted land in 1653.

Probably the best-known incident in the life of Wicklow girl Anne Devlin was her half-hanging by yeomanry in an unsuccessful effort to get her to betray Robert Emmet in 1803. Indeed, the erroneous impression was that this was a one-off portrayal of her steadfastness is scotched by Kieran Sheedy in his *The Tellicherry Five* (1997). He writes of the 'steely resolve' of the Wicklow women related to, and associated with Michael Dwyer. Following the 1798 Rebellion these women attended public executions of local men, shielding their bodies from mutilation by the yeomanry, and later Anne and two of Michael Dwyer's sisters even disinterred the bodies of Ulstermen Sam Mc Allister and Adam Magee at night, in order to transfer their remains to Kilranalagh Cemetery. Steely indeed! John Jackson, a yeoman, was sentenced to 500 lashes for harbouring Dwyer. A Protestant friend and neighbour of Dwyer's who was also suspected of sheltering him was named Billy the Rock Jackson. We wondered about this nickname and concluded that he was named for townlands in the

Co.Wicklow parish of Arklow, named Rock Big and Rock Little. These are two hills south of Arklow, 200 and 413 feet respectively, and now collectively known as Arklow Rock. However, Jacob Nevill's 1760 map of Co.Wicklow names them Big Rock and Little Rock. Liam Price's *The Place-names of Co.Wicklow* gives Carraig as the Irish. Today the names are An Charraig Mór and An Charraig Bheag.

No doubt there are many eminent persons named Jackson, but our favourite is the celebrated 18th-century Irish piper, Limerickman Walter 'Piper' Jackson, composer of many tunes including 'Jackson's Morning Brush' , 'Jackson's Bottle of Brandy' and 'Jackson's Cravat'. Telephone directories contain some 1,000 Jackson entries, roughly half-and-half to the north and to the south of the Border.

DELGANY

The most appropriate manner in which Ireland felt it might display its love and respect for the Revd Euseby Digby Cleaver of Delgany, Co.Wicklow, on his death in 1894, was by placing a sod of the soil of Gouganebarra, Co. Cork, a bunch of shamrock from Delgany, Co.Wicklow, and a medal of St Finnbarr in his coffin on the occasion of his burial in Dolgelly in Wales. Well, perhaps not 'Ireland', as much as those who then saw the importance of the languishing Irish language, being greatly saddened by the loss of this Church of England minister, who had spent his working life ministering at Oxford, Pimlico, Romford and Dolgelly. 'Dúirt Eoin MacNeill gur mhó a d'éirigh leis a dhéanamh ná suim iomlán, nó geall leis, na niarrachtaí a rinne daoine eile lena linn' (Eoin MacNeill said that he succeeded in achieving more than practically the entirety of the efforts of all the others working at that time) (Breathnach and Ni Mhurchu, *Beathaisnéis a hAon*). He was exceedingly generous in his financial assistance to every effort to arouse interest in the Irish language in the 19th century, and it is estimated that he spent thousands of pounds. He donated money to every Irish language organisation that existed at that time; he presented prizes to encourage the teaching of Irish in the Gaeltacht, distributing there 1000 copies of a Catholic Irish-language prayer-book. He financed the publication of Dr Douglas Hyde's *Leabhar Scéalaíochta*, and this is the Eubesy Digby Cleaver to whom An Craoibhinn Aoibhinn dedicated the book. He was one of the founders of the Ossianic Society in 1853, and in 1893 he was one of the vice-presidents of Connradh na Gaeilge. The third edition of his *Duanaire na Nuadh-Gaedhlige*, a mixture of newly-composed songs and translations, came out in 1891. It is not known where he learned his Irish, but it is presumed that it was in Co. Roscommon, where, he claimed, he spent some of his youth. In fact his father, the Revd William Cleaver, was the owner of an estate of 757 acres at Lissigallan, in the Co. Roscommon parish of Fuerty. His grandfather, also Euseby, born *c*.1770, was the Protestant archbishop of Dublin. This land came to the Cleaver family in the early part of the 19th century. The Revd William Cleaver of Cranbook, Kent, in England willed the place in 1861, and the Revd William Henry Cleaver of Oakfield, Oxfordshire, willed it 3 January 1909. Our Euseby had one son, born in the early 1890s, and there are now but two entries of that name in the telephone directories. Delgany is Deilgne in Irish, and Liam Price in *The Place-names of Co. Wicklow*, considering the two possible origins from the various anglicised forms from 800 AD onwards, writes, 'Deirgne may be from *dearg*, 'red', with the common suffix -ne, and Deilgne from *dealg*, 'thorn', with the same suffix.'

NEWTOWN MOUNT KENNEDY

We fancy it was the wry sense of humour of the Frenchman de Latocnaye, rather than a translating idiosyncrasy (whom his *Promenade d'un français dans l'Irelande* was being turned into *A Frenchman's Walk through Ireland 1786–97*) that led him to refer to Madame Latouche's holding of a school for twenty-four young girls, maintained at her own charge, and whom she married off to labourers 'of good character', as '… one of the most noble and most reasonable amusements of the rich that I have ever met with'. He was a guest at the Latouche's Bellevue, and it was while he was here that he heard the sad news of the death of Mr Burton Conyngham. Part of the regret was the embarrassment of presenting 'the letters of recommendation which Mr Burton Conyngham had given me', but he resolved to brazen it out, albeit 'the recipients might look upon them as messages from the other world'. On the Conyngham estate of Mount Kennedy he pays his respects 'to the oldest and biggest tree to be found, not only in Ireland, but I should say but in the mountains of Nice or of Provence'. 'The body of the tree is at least three feet in diameter, and wind and time having bent it to the ground, it took root in this situation, and has sent out branches of extraordinary size, so that in itself it is a little wood'. Twenty years earlier the Englishman Arthur Young, visiting General Cunninghame's 10,000 acre Mount Kennedy, was also sent to view the tree: 'In the middle of the lawn is one of the greatest natural curiosities in the kingdom; an immense arbutus tree unfortunatley blown down, but yet vegetating; one branch, which parts from the body near the ground, and afterwards divides into many large branches, is 6 feet 2 inches in circumference. The General buried part of the stem as it laid, and it is from several branches throwing out fine young shoots: it is a most venerable remnant. Killarney, the region of the arbutus, boasts of no such tree as this.' The 1814 *Directory to the Market Towns, Villages, Gentlemen's Seats, and Other Noted Places in Ireland* lists no Conyngham/Cunninghame in Co. Wicklow, but has 'George Gunn esq.' at Mount Kennedy. The La Touches were at 'Bellvue/Belview' in 1778 and in 1814, and in 1876 William Robert La Touche is listed with 1,798 acres there. John La Touche had 11,282 acres at Brannoxtown, Co. Kildare. That same year Robert A. Gun Cunninghame, 'Mount Kennedy', had 10,470 acres. We do not have any information, but it appears that a female Cunninghame who inherited the place, married a Gunn, whereby a 'Gunn esq' is given as owner in 1814, but we leave it to yourself to figure out how it came once again to be in the hands of the Cunninghams. This surname, of Scottish settlers, was widely adopted as the modern form of Irish names, and MacLysaght in his *Surnames* quotes Matheson's report on synonyms in birth registrations, that there was no less than 20 for Cunningham, Cunnegan, Kinnegan and even Coon. Both Mac Cuinneagáin, a Sligo sept of the Uí Fiachra, and Ó Cuinneagáin, a sept of ancient Uí Máine, comprising parts of Cos. Roscommon, Galway, Clare and Offaly, became Cunningham, with the earlier and more accurate anglicisations falling into disuse. The Irish for Newtown Mountkennedy is Baile an Chinnéidigh, 'Kennedy's town'.

BALLYARTHUR

The Penguin Dictionary of Surnames equates Sim, Simes, Simms, Symms, Symmes, with Simon, Simons, Simmons, Symon, Symons etc. A Census of Ireland 1659 lists James Sime and his son John, gents., as tituladoes of Magherareagh, in the Co. Donegal barony of Raphoe; John Syms titulado of Kishyquirke, in the Co. Limerick barony of Clanwilliam, and John Simes titulado of Kilkenny City. George Syms was one of the Co. Cork commissioners for the poll-money ordinances of 1660 and 1661, and John Syms held a similar post for Co. Limerick and Limerick City. Giving Simms as the sole spelling of this name, MacLysaght's *Surnames* says that it is well-known in Co. Antrim since the early 17th century, but that it also had a close association with Donegal.

Taylor and Skinner's *Maps* (1783) shows Symes Esq., at Ballyarthur, Baile Artúir, in the Co. Wicklow parish of Ballymacadam, the 1814 *Directory* lists the Revd J. Symmes as residing there. Also listed in Co. Wicklow were Revd Henry Symmes, Ballybeg; Mrs Symmes, Hillbrook, and S. Symmes Esq., Loggan. There were Symmes in Cos. Antrim, Galway, and Cork. *Owners of Land* (1876) shows three of the name Symes as having 592, 514 and 493 acres in Co. Wicklow, though none at Ballyarthur; one in Co. Dublin with 38 acres; one in Co. Kilkenny with 212 acres, and one in Co. Carlow with 514 acres. Anne Syms, Ardvally, had, 19 acres in Co. Cork; Alexander Syms had 705 acres in Co. Sligo, and Alexander Sim, Collooney, Co. Sligo, was the owner of 419 acres. However, the largest holder was N.P. Sim, Roigh, with 8,162 acres in Co. Mayo. We presume that this place is Raigh (*ráth*, a fort), in the Co. Mayo parish of Aghagower. This surname, in any of its variant spellings, is currently very rare north of the Border, but is found in Cos. Carlow, Wicklow, Cork, but especially in Cos. Donegal, Wexford and Waterford.

It is, we believe, reasonable to assume that there was a Symes resident at Ballyarthur when the Chevalier de Latocnaye visited there on his walk through Ireland in 1797–8. His book, entitled *A Frenchman's Walk through Ireland*, tells of his visit to that part of Co. Wicklow: 'On my way I came to a rather rapid river of several feet depth, which it was necessary to ford, or make a detour of four or five miles to find a bridge. The weather was warm, and I profited by the occasion to take a bath. A peasant, rather well-clothed, who had been talking to me about the gold mine, was much interested in this matter, and in order to have the pleasure of talking with me longer, he imitated my example, and was good enough to carry my clothes to the other side'. De Latocnaye tells that the peasants had been digging for gold at the foot of a rather high mountain, called Cruachan, from whence it would seem the gold had been washed down into the stream. 'This torrent is called in Irish 'The Golden Stream' and in English 'The Poor man's Stream', and from this it may be gathered that gold had been found long ago'. De Latocnaye says that he found the peasantry very curious as to the time of day: 'Every minute women and children would run from cabins by the wayside to ask the traveller what o'clock it was, perhaps for the pleasure of seeing a watch, or of having a chat.'

KEELOGES

The term 'rundale' was used to denote the intermixture of different farmers' plots in a single arable field, according to Arthur Young in *A Tour in Ireland 1776–79*, each farmer being required to share the various soil-types in his townland, leading to subdivision that 'could increase the degree of intermixture beyond all reason when every seperate plot was split as each change of tenure' (J.H. Andrews in *Plantation Acres*, 1985). This system was generally condemned because it impeded the amelioration of agriculture, the reclamation of hill pastures, but especially because it led to disputes among farmers. Landlords were anxious to change the system, and when opportunity arose, the first thing the surveyor did, according to a witness *c.*1825, was 'to throw it into squares'. However, 'squaring' was less common than 'striping'. Unlike the curved stripes attributed to the medieval ploughman, the stripe had straight sides, characteristic of the modern improver, but its form was narrowly rectangular, sometimes grotesquely so. On one estate, it was stated, the houses were built endways to fit onto their farms and where a man could avoid trespassing on his neighbour's land by jumping over it! Trespassing and 'right-of way' were, and continue to be, causes of contention among farmers. Caológ, the diminutive of *caol*, 'narrow', is given as meaning 'a narrow ridge' by Liam Price in *The Place-names of Co. Wicklow* and in referring to Keeloges (the anglicised form of Na Caológa, with an English plural), a townland in the parish of Kilcommon, he writes, 'A long narrow townland ... the name no doubt refers to long strips of ploughed land'. Ó Dónaill's *Focloir Gaelige agus Béarla* defines caológ as 'riverside field, meadow; small channel; sometimes branch of river', and perhaps any, or all of these various definitions may be variously applicable to the townlands of Keeloge in Cos.Galway, Kildare, Offaly 2, Leitrim, Longford, Laois, Westmeath and Wicklow; and to Keeloges in Cos.Donegal, Dublin, Galway (2), Kildare, Leitrim. Limerick (2), Longford, Mayo (2), Roscommon (2), Sligo, Wexford and Wicklow. We have heard the opinion expressed that *caológ* refers to hillside fields, where the division is like portions of an apple tart, each field narrowing to the top. Today's Keeloges in the Co. Mayo parish of Islandeady, spelled Elanedan in 1640, and owned by Lord Dillon, and the other Mayo townland of the same name, still in the parish of Burrishoole, then belonging to Lord Mayo, had the alias Carrownagellog, Ceathrú na gCaológ, 'the land-quarter of the stripes'. This name, no longer in Co. Mayo, continues in Co. Roscommen, anglicised as Carrownageeloge, this being in the parish of Oran.

KILRUDDERY

In an early ecumenical note, W.M. Thackeray, reporting on a post-Agricultural Show dinner at Naas, Co. Kildare, in his *The Irish Sketch Book* (1842), says that present were 'forty stout well-to-do farmers in the room, renters of fifty, seventy, a hundred acres of land. There were no clergymen present, though it would have been pleasant to have seen one of each persuasion, to say grace for the meeting and the meat.' At the conclusion of the meal, there were toasts and speeches, accompanied by punch, for those who preferred that beverage to wine. After 'the Queen', 'Prince Albert and the rest of the Royal Family', came 'the Lord Lieutenant', gettiing a cool reception, according to Thackeray's observation; then 'the Naas Society', 'the Sallymount Beagles' and 'the Kildare

Foxhounds'. That being finished an old farmer, in a grey coat, stood and, unrequested, sang. Thackeray gives these lines. 'At seven in the morning by most of the clocks/We rode to Kilruddery in search of a fox.' Padraig Breathnach in his *Songs of the Gael* (1921), in a footnote to 'Reynard the Fox', comments that he often heard it sung as a boy: 'the words always got a local colouring', and the above is clearly such. Kilruddery Demense and Kilruddery Deerpark, are townlands in the Co. Wicklow parishes of Bray and Delgany, and herein 'Kilruddery House', seat of the Earls of Meath. A later house here was designed by William Vitruvius Morrison, the third and last member of an architectural family, born 1794. He worked jointly with his father on Shelton Abbey, Ballyfin and Kilruddery, and Maurice Craig in his *The Architecture of Ireland* comments on the 'finicky pinnacled "Tudor" with which he tricked out such buildings as Ballygiblin'. From the twenty-nine different spellings of this placename in different documents dating from 1196 to 1760, Liam Price in *The Place-names of Co. Wicklow* surmises that the original may be Cill Rothaire or Cill Ruathaire, 'the church of the vagrants or wanderers', never considering the perhaps too obvious Cill Ridire, 'the church of the knight' as suggested by P.W. Joyce in *Names of Places*. He settles for 'knight' in Castleruddery in the parish of Donoghmore in the same county, but he had the support of *Leabhar Branach* as far back as the 16th century, this source giving it as Coislean an Riddire.

Bibliography

Surnames   Edward MacLysaght, *The Surnames of Ireland,* Dublin,
                     1985.
Census, 1659   A Census of Ireland, c. 1659, with supplementary material
                     from poll-money ordinances (1660–1).
Maps   Taylor and Skinner's *Maps of the Roads of Ireland,* 1778
Topographical Dictionary Lewis, Samuel, *A Topographical Dictionary of Ireland,* 1837.
Names of Places   P.W. Joyce, *Irish Names of Places,* Dublin, 1902
Owners of Land   *Return of Owners of Land of one acre and upwards,* HMSO,
                     1876

Bennett, George, *The History of Bandon,* Cork, 1973
Brady, A.M. & Cleeve, B., *A Biographical Dictionary of Irish Writers,* Gigginstown,
     1985
Brooks, Eric St John, *Knights' Fees in Counties Wexford, Carlow, and Kilkenny (13
     to 15th c.),* Dublin, 1950
Census of Ireland, *Alphabetical Index of Townlands Ireland,* Dublin, 1877
Census of Ireland, circa 1659, Dublin, 1939
Cottle, Basil, *The Penguin Dictionary of Surnames,* London, 1978
Curtis, Edmund (ed.), *Ormond Deeds,* 6 vols. Dublin, 1932–43
D'Alton, E.A., *History of Ireland,* Dublin, 1903
Davies, Sir John, *Discoverie of the True Causes why Ireland was never entirely subdued,*
     London, 1612
de Bhulbh, Sean, *Sloinnte na hEireann/Irish Surnames,* Limerick, 1997
de Breffny, Brian, *Irish Family Names,* Dublin, 1982
Dowling, Patrick John, *The Hedge Schools of Ireland,* Dublin, 1935
The Dublin Guild Merchants Roll, c.1190–1265, ed. P. Connolly and G. Martin,
     Dublin 1992.
Gerard, Frances A., *Picturesque Dublin, Old and New,* London, 1890
Gordon, James B., *History of the Rebellion in Ireland in the Year 1798,* Dublin, 1801
Griffith, Richard, *General Valuation of Ireland,* 3 vols., London, 1848
HMSO, *Calendar of State Papers relating to Ireland,* London, 1860
HMSO, *Return of Owners of Land of one acre and upwards,* Dublin, 1876
Hall, S.C. & Hall, A.M., *Handbook for Ireland,* 4 vols., London, 1853
Harbison, Peter, *Guide to National and Historic Monuments of Ireland,* Dublin, 1982
Hickey, D.J. & Doherty, J.E., *Irish History since 1800,* Dublin, 1980

Irish Fiants of the Tudor Sovereigns, 1521–1603, 3 vols., Dublin, 1994

Irish Manuscripts Comm., *The Calendar of Inquisitions ...* , Dublin, 1991

Joyce, P.W., *Irish Names of Places,* 3 vols., Dublin, n.d.

Lewis, Samuel, *A Topographical Dictionary of Ireland,* 2 vols. and atlas, London, 1837

Livingstone, Peadar, *The Fermanagh Story,* Enniskillen, 1969

Lodge, Edmund *Lodge's Peerage, Baronetage ... of the British Empire for 1912,* London, 1912

Macardle, Dorothy, *The Irish Republic,* London, 1937

MacLysaght, Edward, *Irish Families,* Dublin, 1972

MacLysaght, Edward, *Surnames of Ireland,* Dubin, 1985

Mac Niocaill, Gearóid (ed.), *Crown Surveys of Lands, 1540–4,* Dublin, 1992

Mountmorres, Lord, *The History of the Principal Transactions of the Irish Parliament, 1634–66,* London, 1792

Murphy, Hilary *Families of County Wexford,* Dublin 1986

Musgrave, Richard *The Irish Rebellion, Dublin, 1799*

Nolan, W. & Whelan, K., *Kilkenny. History and Society,* Dublin, 1990

Ó Corráin, D. & Maguire, F., *Gaelic Personal Names,* Dublin, 1981

O'Donovan, John (ed.), *The Topographical Poems of John O Dubhagain and Giolla na Naomh O Huidhrin,* Dublin, 1862

O'Donovan, John, *Life on the Liffey,* Dublin, 1986

O'Grady, H.A., *Strafford in Ireland,* 2 vols., Dublin 1923

O'Harte, John, *Irish Pedigrees,* London, 18878

O'Kelly, Owen, *Place-names of County Kilkenny,* Kilkenny, 1985

Ordnance Survey, *Gasaitear na hEireann/Gazetteer of Ireland,* Dublin, 1989

Ordnance Survey, *Liosta logeinmneacha contae Lu, county Louth,* Dublin, 1991

Ordnance Survey, *Liosta logeinmneachta contae Chill Chainnigh, county Kilkenny,* Dublin, 1993

Petty, Sir William, *Hiberniae Delineatio ...* , Dublin, 1685

Prendergast, J.P., *The Cromwellian Settlement of Ireland,* London, 1865

Price, Liam, *The Place-names of County Wicklow,* Dublin, 1967

Ridgeway, William, *State Trials in Ireland,* Dublin, 1795–1807

Roche, Richard, *Here's Their Memory,* Wexford, 1966

Simington, George, *The Civil Survey, 1654–56,* Dublin, 1931–61

Simington, George, *The Transplantation to Connaght, 1654–58,* Dublin, 1970

Stuart, James, *Historical Memoirs of the City of Armagh,* Newry, 1819

Taylor, G. & Skinner A., *Maps of the Roads of Ireland,* Dublin, 1778

Thackeray, W.M., *The Irish Sketch-book, London,* 1843

Walsh, Paul, *The Place-names of Westmeath,* Dublin, 1957

Westropp, T.J., *The Ancient Forts of Ireland,* Dublin, 1902

Woulfe, Patrick, *Sloinnte Gaedheal is Gall,* Dublin, 1923

Young, Arthur, *A Tour in Ireland,* 2 vols., London, 1780